DEEP LEARNING AND NEURAL NETWORKS

DEEP LEARNING AND NEURAL NETWORKS

Dr. Munesh Chandra Trivedi
Dr. Nandita Goyal

KHANNA BOOK PUBLISHING CO. (P) LTD.

Publisher of Engineering and Computer Books

4C/4344, Ansari Road, Darya Ganj, New Delhi-110002
Phone : 011-23244447-48 **Mobile:** +91-99109 09320
E-mail : contact@khannabooks.com
Website : www.khannabooks.com

Dear Readers,

To prevent the piracy, this book is secured with HIGH SECURITY HOLOGRAM on the front title cover. In case you don't find the hologram on the front cover title, please write us to at contact@khannabooks.com or whatsapp us at +91-99109 09320 and avail special gift voucher for yourself.

Specimen of Hologram on front Cover title:

Moreover, there is a SPECIAL DISCOUNT COUPON for you with EVERY HOLOGRAM.

How to avail this SPECIAL DISCOUNT:

Step 1: Scratch the hologram
Step 2: Under the scratch area, your "coupon code" is available
Step 3: Logon to www.khannabooks.com
Step 4: Use your "coupon code" in the shopping cart and get your copy at a special discount
Step 5: Enjoy your reading!

Thanks,
Khanna Publishing House

Price: ₹ 298.00

ISBN: 978-93-5538-398-3

Deep Learning and Neural Networks
by Dr. Munesh Chandra Trivedi,
Dr. Nandita Goyal

First Edition: 2025
Reprint: 2026

To view complete list of books, please scan the QR Code:

Published by:
Khanna Book Publishing Co. (P) Ltd.
CIN: U22110DL1998PTC095547

Visit us at: www.khannabooks.com
Write us at: contact@khannabooks.com

Printed in Bharat.

Preface

Neural networks are at the very core of deep learning. They are versatile, powerful, and scalable, making them ideal to tackle large and highly complex Machine Learning tasks. Neural networks and deep learning currently provide the best solutions to many problems in image recognition, speech recognition, and natural language processing. Understanding the behaviour of systems that learn to solve information processing problems (like pattern recognition and prediction) is crucial for the design of effective systems. In recent years, ideas and techniques in computational learning theory have matured to the point where theoretical advances are now contributing to machine learning applications, both through increased understanding and through the development of new practical algorithms.

This book introduces artificial neural networks, starting with a quick tour of the very first ANN architectures, then covering topics such as training neural nets, recurrent neural networks, and reinforcement learning. It will clarify what neural networks are and why you may want to use them.

This book begins with Machine Learning Basics, covers the mathematical and conceptual topics relevant to Deep Learning.

After that, this book covers Modern Deep Learning Algorithms and Techniques. In that section, this book covers deep feedforward networks, regularization, optimization algorithms, convolutional networks, sequence modelling, and practical methodology.

This Book also describes applications of Deep Learning. Such as natural language processing, speech recognition, computer vision, online recommendation systems, bioinformatics, and videogames.

This practical book shows you how even programmers who know close to nothing about this technology can use simple, efficient tools to implement programs capable of learning from data. In the end, this Deep Learning book describes the current research trends.

By the end, you will be familiar with the significant technological trends driving the rise of deep learning; build, train, and apply fully connected deep neural networks; implement efficient (vectorized) neural networks; identify key parameters in a neural network's architecture; and apply deep learning to your own applications.

Think of **"Deep Learning and Neural Networks"** as your companion on the path to becoming a proficient data scientist or analyst. Whether you are starting fresh or aiming to elevate your expertise, this book provides the practical guidance and hands-on experience you need to thrive in the rapidly evolving world of deep learning. Let us embark on this journey together and unlock the endless possibilities that data has to offer.

Contents

1

Information Flow in a Neural Network, Understanding Basic Structure and ANN.

1.1 BRIEF ABOUT ARTIFICIAL INTELLIGENCE

The most intricate organ in the human body is the brain. It facilitates our ability to reason, comprehend, and decide. A neuron is the key to its power.

Since the 1950s, researchers have been working to create robots that are smarter and better by mimicking how neurons function. Humans ultimately succeeded in building a computer that could recognise human voice after much trial and error. Only after the year 2000 were people able to achieve deep learning, a branch of artificial intelligence that can recognise and differentiate between different images and movie.

1.1.1 How Does AI Work?

As the hype around AI has accelerated, vendors have been scrambling to promote how their products and services use it. Often, what they refer to as AI is simply a component of the technology, such as machine learning. AI requires a foundation of specialized hardware and software for writing and training machine learning algorithms. No single programming language is synonymous with AI, but Python, R, Java, C++ and Julia have features popular with AI developers.

In general, AI systems work by ingesting large amounts of labelled training data, analysing the data for correlations and patterns, and using these patterns to make predictions about future states. In this way, a chatbot that is fed examples of text can learn to generate lifelike exchanges with people, or an image recognition tool can learn to identify and describe objects in images by reviewing millions of examples. New, rapidly improving generative AI techniques can create realistic text, images, music and other media.

AI programming focuses on cognitive skills that include the following:

Learning: This aspect of AI programming focuses on acquiring data and creating rules for how to turn it into actionable information. The rules, which are called algorithms, provide computing devices with step-by-step instructions for how to complete a specific task.

Reasoning: This aspect of AI programming focuses on choosing the right algorithm to reach a desired outcome.

Self-correction: This aspect of AI programming is designed to continually fine-tune algorithms and ensure they provide the most accurate results possible.

Creativity: This aspect of AI uses neural networks, rules-based systems, statistical methods and other AI techniques to generate new images, new text, new music and new ideas.

1.1.2 Why is Artificial Intelligence Important?

AI is important for its potential to change how we live, work and play. It has been effectively used in business to automate tasks done by humans, including customer service work, lead generation, fraud detection and quality control. In a number of areas, AI can perform tasks much better than humans. Particularly when it comes to repetitive, detail-oriented tasks, such as analysing large numbers of legal documents to ensure relevant fields are filled in properly, AI tools often complete jobs quickly and with relatively few errors. Because of the massive data sets it can process, AI can also give enterprises insights into their operations they might not have been aware of. The rapidly expanding population of generative AI tools will be important in fields ranging from education and marketing to product design.

Indeed, advances in AI techniques have not only helped fuel an explosion in efficiency, but opened the door to entirely new business opportunities for some larger enterprises. Prior to the current wave of AI, it would have been hard to imagine using computer software to connect riders to taxis, but Uber has become a Fortune 500 company by doing just that.

AI has become central to many of today's largest and most successful companies, including Alphabet, Apple, Microsoft and Meta, where AI technologies are used to improve operations and outpace competitors. At Alphabet subsidiary Google, for example, AI is central to its search engine, Waymo's self-driving cars and Google Brain, which invented the transformer neural network architecture that underpins the recent breakthroughs in natural language processing.

1.1.3 What are the Advantages and Disadvantages of Artificial Intelligence?

Artificial neural networks and deep learning AI technologies are quickly evolving, primarily because AI can process large amounts of data much faster and make predictions more accurately than humanly possible.

While the huge volume of data created on a daily basis would bury a human researcher, AI applications using machine learning can take that data and quickly turn it into actionable information. As of this writing, a primary disadvantage of AI is that it is expensive to process the large amounts of data AI programming requires. As AI techniques are incorporated into more products and services, organizations must also be attuned to AI's potential to create biased and discriminatory systems, intentionally or inadvertently.

Advantages of AI

The following are some advantages of AI.

- **Good at detail-oriented jobs:** AI has proven to be as good or better than doctors at diagnosing certain cancers, including breast cancer and melanoma.
- **Reduced time for data-heavy tasks:** AI is widely used in data-heavy industries, including banking and securities, pharma and insurance, to reduce the time it takes to analyse big data sets. Financial services, for example, routinely use AI to process loan applications and detect fraud.

- **Saves labor and increases productivity:** An example here is the use of warehouse automation, which grew during the pandemic and is expected to increase with the integration of AI and machine learning.
- **Delivers consistent results:** The best AI translation tools deliver high levels of consistency, offering even small businesses the ability to reach customers in their native language.
- **Can improve customer satisfaction through personalization:** AI can personalize content, messaging, ads, recommendations and websites to individual customers.
- **AI-powered virtual agents are always available:** AI programs do not need to sleep or take breaks, providing 24/7 service.

Disadvantages of AI

The following are some disadvantages of AI.

- Expensive.
- Requires deep technical expertise.
- Limited supply of qualified workers to build AI tools.
- Reflects the biases of its training data, at scale.
- Lack of ability to generalize from one task to another.
- Eliminates human jobs, increasing unemployment rates.

1.1.4 Strong AI vs. Weak AI

AI can be categorized as weak or strong.

Weak AI, also known as narrow AI, is designed and trained to complete a specific task. Industrial robots and virtual personal assistants, such as Apple's Siri, use weak AI.

Strong AI, also known as artificial general intelligence (AGI), describes programming that can replicate the cognitive abilities of the human brain. When presented with an unfamiliar task, a strong AI system can use fuzzy logic to apply knowledge from one domain to another and find a solution autonomously. In theory, a strong AI program should be able to pass both a Turing test and the Chinese Room argument.

1.1.5 What are the 4 Types of Artificial Intelligence?

ArendHintze, an assistant professor of integrative biology and computer science and engineering at Michigan State University, explained that AI can be categorized into four types, beginning with the task-specific intelligent systems in wide use today and progressing to sentient systems, which do not yet exist. The categories are as follows.

Type 1: Reactive machines. These AI systems have no memory and are task-specific. An example is Deep Blue, the IBM chess program that beat Garry Kasparov in the 1990s. Deep Blue can identify pieces on a chessboard and make predictions, but because it has no memory, it cannot use past experiences to inform future ones.

Type 2: Limited memory. These AI systems have memory, so they can use past experiences to inform future decisions. Some of the decision-making functions in self-driving cars are designed this way.

Type 3: Theory of mind. Theory of mind is a psychology term. When applied to AI, it means the system would have the social intelligence to understand emotions. This type of AI will be able to infer human intentions and predict behaviour, a necessary skill for AI systems to become integral members of human teams.

Type 4: Self-awareness. In this category, AI systems have a sense of self, which gives them consciousness. Machines with self-awareness understand their own current state. This type of AI does not yet exist.

1.2 BRIEF ABOUT MACHINE LEARNING

Machine learning (ML) is a type of artificial intelligence (AI) that allows software applications to become more accurate at predicting outcomes without being explicitly programmed to do so. Machine learning algorithms use historical data as input to predict new output values. Machine Learning is a discipline of AI that uses data to teach machines.

Recommendation engines are a common use case for machine learning. Other popular uses include fraud detection, spam filtering, malware threat detection, business process automation (BPA) and Predictive maintenance.

Intelligent Decision Formula

- Save the result of all actions
- Simulate all possible outcomes
- Compare the new action with the old ones
- Check if the new action is good or bad
- Choose the new action if it is less bad
- Do it all over again

1.2.1 Supervised Vs Unsupervised Learning

In supervised learning, the machine learns while being watched over. It includes a model that can make predictions using data that has been labelled. A dataset that has been labelled means that you already know the intended response. Supervised learning can be divided into classes: Classification and regression.

Classification: A classification algorithm is a supervised learning method that divides data into various classes using data training. New observations are categorised into classes or groups after being trained using data or observations in classification predictive modelling.

Regression: Regression analysis uses one or more independent variables to describe the relationship between a dependent (target) and independent (predictor) variables. More specifically, regression analysis enables us to comprehend how, while other independent variables are held constant, the value of the dependent variable changes in relation to an independent variable. It forecasts real, continuous values like temperature, age, salary, and cost, among others.

Some of the real-life applications of supervised learning include: risk assessment, image classification, fraud detection and visual recognition etc.

Unsupervised learning involves the computer learning on its own while using unlabelled data. In the unlabelled data, the machine looks for patterns and responds. It is further categorized as Clustering and Association.

Clustering is the technique of grouping together comparable groups of uncategorized data. This procedure makes sure that related data points are found and grouped together. The processing of data and the identification of groupings (natural clusters) depend heavily on clustering algorithms.

Association: As the data are not labelled, association rule is an example of unsupervised learning, where the algorithm tries to learn without a tutor. Association rules, a descriptive approach rather than a predictive one, are frequently employed to unearth intriguing relationships in huge datasets. Rules or regular item sets are common ways to represent relationships.

To find novel and intriguing connections among various objects in a collection, common patterns in transactional data, or any kind of relational database, association rules mining is used.

Some applications of unsupervised learning from real-life include market basket analysis, semantic clustering, delivery store optimization and identifying accident prone areas etc.

Reinforcement Learning: It gets the best of both worlds, that is, the best of both Supervised learning and Unsupervised learning. It is like learning with a critique. Here there is no exact feedback from the environment, rather there is critique feedback. The critique tells how close our solution is. Hence the model learns on its own based on the critique information. It is like supervised learning in that it receives feedback from the environment, but it is different in that it does not receive the desired output information, rather it receives critique information.

Reinforcement Learning in ML

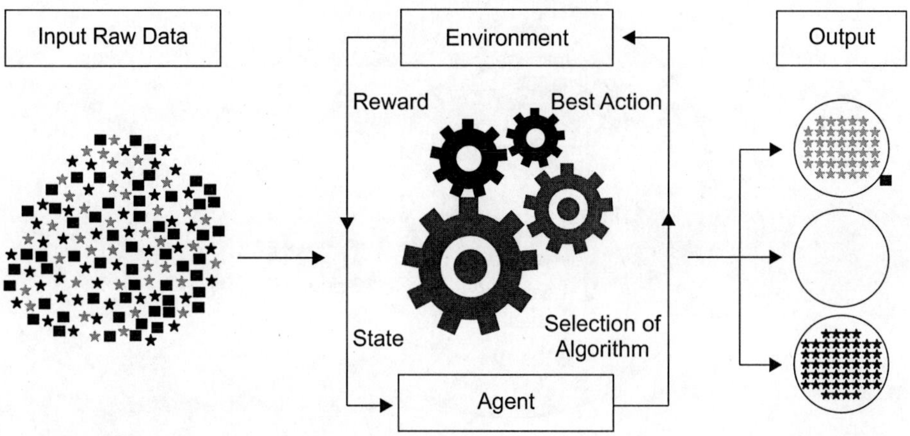

1.3 BRIEF ABOUT DEEP LEARNING

Deep learning is a subset of machine learning that enables computers to learn from examples in the same way that people do.

In contrast to hardwiring a computer programme to recognise and learn, machines are educated using images as examples. You have control over the factors that feed into it, not how it knows. Based on the photographs that were previously input, the computer recognises the object.

A synthetic version of a biological neuron was created by scientists and powers all deep learning machines.

Deep learning is a branch of machine learning which is based on artificial neural networks. It is capable of learning complex patterns and relationships within data. In deep learning, we don't need to explicitly program everything. It has become increasingly popular in recent years due to the advances in processing power and the availability of large datasets. Because it is based on artificial neural networks (ANNs) also known as deep neural networks (DNNs). These neural networks are inspired by the structure and function of the human brain's biological neurons, and they are designed to learn from large amounts of data.

Deep Learning is a subfield of Machine Learning that involves the use of neural networks to model and solve complex problems. Neural networks are modelled after the structure and function of the human brain and consist of layers of interconnected nodes that process and transform data.

The key characteristic of Deep Learning is the use of deep neural networks, which have multiple layers of interconnected nodes. These networks can learn complex representations of data by discovering hierarchical patterns and features in the data. Deep Learning algorithms can automatically learn and improve from data without the need for manual feature engineering.

Deep Learning has achieved significant success in various fields, including image recognition, natural language processing, speech recognition, and recommendation systems. Some of the popular Deep Learning architectures include Convolutional Neural Networks (CNNs), Recurrent Neural Networks (RNNs), and Deep Belief Networks (DBNs).

Training deep neural networks typically requires a large amount of data and computational resources. However, the availability of cloud computing and the development of specialized hardware, such as Graphics Processing Units (GPUs), has made it easier to train deep neural networks.

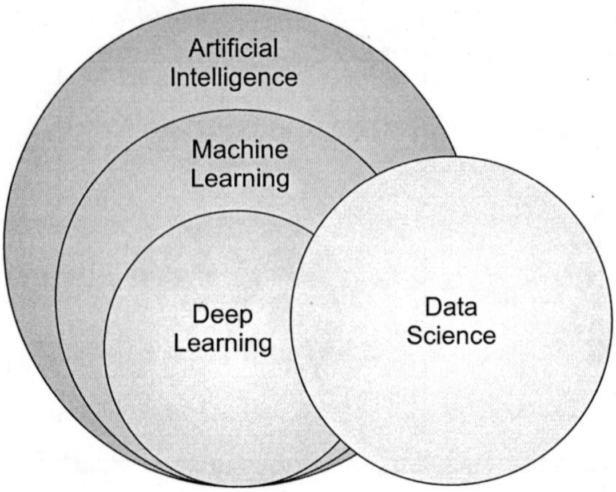

1.4 DIFFERENCES BETWEEN AI, MACHINE LEARNING AND DEEP LEARNING

AI, machine learning and deep learning are common terms in enterprise IT and sometimes used interchangeably, especially by companies in their marketing materials. But there are distinctions. The term AI, coined in the 1950s, refers to the simulation of human intelligence by machines. It covers an ever-changing set of capabilities as new technologies are developed. Technologies that come under the umbrella of AI include machine learning and deep learning.

Machine learning enables software applications to become more accurate at predicting outcomes without being explicitly programmed to do so. Machine learning algorithms use historical data as input to predict new output values. This approach became vastly more effective with the rise of large data sets to train on. Deep learning, a subset of machine learning, is based on our understanding of how the brain is structured. Deep learning's use of artificial neural networks structure is the underpinning of recent advances in AI, including self-driving cars and ChatGPT.

Difference between Machine Learning and Deep Learning

Machine Learning	Deep Learning
Apply statistical algorithms to learn the hidden patterns and relationships in the dataset.	Uses artificial neural network architecture to learn the hidden patterns and relationships in the dataset.
Can work on the smaller amount of dataset	Requires the larger volume of dataset compared to machine learning
Better for the low-label task.	Better for complex task like image processing, natural language processing, etc.
Takes less time to train the model.	Takes more time to train the model.
A model is created by relevant features which are manually extracted from images to detect an object in the image.	Relevant features are automatically extracted from images. It is an end-to-end learning process.
Less complex and easy to interpret the result.	More complex, it works like the black box interpretations of the result are not easy.
It can work on the CPU or requires less computing power as compared to deep learning.	It requires a high-performance computer with GPU.

1.5 INTRODUCTION TO NEURAL NETWORKS

Artificial systems called neural networks were influenced by biological neural networks. Neural networks are modelled after how the human brain processes information and are used to simulate some of the basic functions of the brain. Because of its speedy processing and response times, it is utilised to do a variety of real-time activities.

These systems acquire task-specific knowledge by being exposed to a variety of datasets and examples. The concept is that the system creates distinguishing qualities from the data it receives without being pre-programmed with knowledge of these datasets. The computer models for threshold logic are the foundation of neural networks. Algorithms and mathematics are used to create threshold logic. Either the study of the brain or the use of neural networks in artificial intelligence are the foundations for neural networks. The work has improved the theory of finite automata. A typical neural network consists of neurons, synapses, weights, biases, propagation function, and other elements.

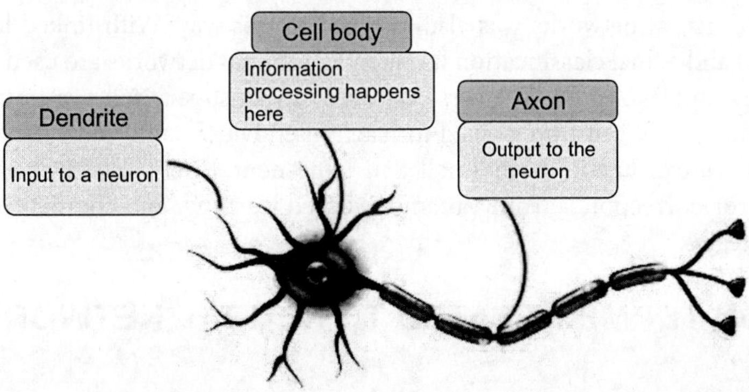

Dendrites

These are connected to other neurons, which send information or signals to them.

Cell Body

Cell bodies are where information processing takes place. These gather and process the information coming from all the different dendrites.

Axon

It transmits the output signal to a different neuron to facilitate information flow. Each of these flanges is joined to the dendrite or hairs of the one after it.

1.6 EVOLUTION OF NEURAL NETWORKS

The history of artificial neural networks goes back to the early days of computing. In 1943, mathematicians Warren McCulloch and Walter Pitts built a circuitry system intended to approximate the functioning of the human brain that ran simple algorithms.

It was not until around 2010 that research picked up again. The big data trend, where companies amass vast troves of data, and parallel computing gave data scientists the training data and computing resources needed to run complex artificial neural networks. In 2012, a neural network was able to beat human performance at an image recognition task as part of the ImageNet competition. Since then, interest in artificial neural networks as has soared and the technology continues to improve.

Neural plasticity is a topic covered by Hebbian learning in the evolution of neural networks. Hebbian learning involves long-term potentiation and is unsupervised. Exclusive-or circuits deal with if-then logic, while Hebbian learning works with pattern recognition. The exclusive-or problem that Hebbian learning was unable to handle was resolved through backpropagation. Additionally, this made multi-layer networks practical and effective. If a mistake was discovered, it was corrected at each layer by changing the weights at each node. Support vector machines, linear classifiers, and max-pooling were all developed as a result. Recurrent neural networks and back propagation-based feedforward networks are also impacted by the vanishing gradient problem. Deep learning is the term for this. For biophysical simulation and neurotrophic computing, hardware-based architectures are used. Convolution and large-scale component analysis are used to produce new class of neural network. Back-propagation for multi-layered feedforward neural networks was also resolved in this way. With linked layers (completely or sparsely connected) and a final classification layer, convolutional networks are used to alternate between convolutional layers and max-pooling layers. Without any unsupervised pre-training, the learning is completed. A weights vector must be trained for each filter, which is its equivalent. It must be ensured that the shift variance can handle both small and large neural networks. Development Networks is addressing this. Error-correction learning, memory-based learning, and competitive learning are a few other learning strategies.

1.7 COMMON TERMS RELATED TO NEURAL NETWORKS

Neurons

Neurons are the core processing unit of the neural network. Every neural network has interconnected neurons that receive input and product output. They resemble human brain neurons.

Layers

A neural network consists of three layers- the input layer, hidden layer, and output layer. The input layer is the layer where you feed the information. The hidden layer is where the computation or mathematical calculations happen. The output layer displays the output.

Weights and Bias

Weights refer to the strengths in the connection of neurons. Weights are generally initialized as random values. But gets adjusted during the training process (done to reduce errors in neural networks).

Besides weights, bias is also present in every neuron. Bias is the numeric value or the constant in the hidden layer. They are generally added to each input to determine if the output is above the threshold value. If the output exceeds a specified threshold value, the node gets activated and transmits the information to the outer layer.

It is important to remember that weight and bias are learning parameters of machine learning (ML) models. They are modified and used for training neural networks to perform complex tasks.

Building Block: Neuron

The fundamental building block of a neural network, the neuron, must be discussed first. A neuron receives inputs, performs mathematical operations on them, and outputs one result. A two-input neuron appears as follows:

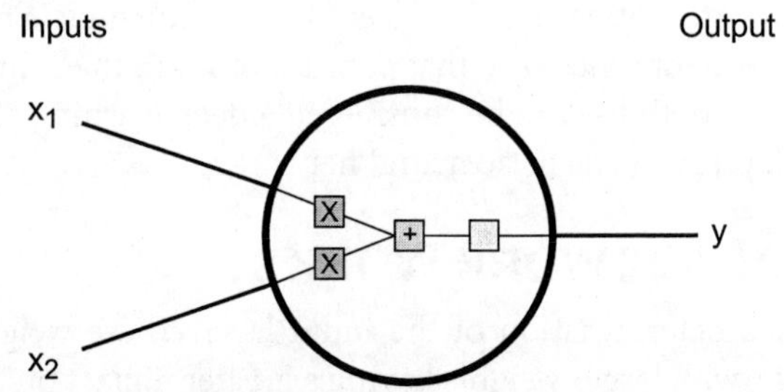

First, each input is multiplied by a weight:

$$x1 = x1*w1$$
$$x2 = x2*w2$$

Next, all the weighted inputs are added together with a bias b:

$(x1*w1) + (x2*w2) + b$

Finally, the sum is passed through an activation function:

$$y = f(x1*w1 + x2*w2 + b)$$

Combining Neurons

Simply said, a neural network is a collection of neurons joined together. Here is an example of a basic neural network:

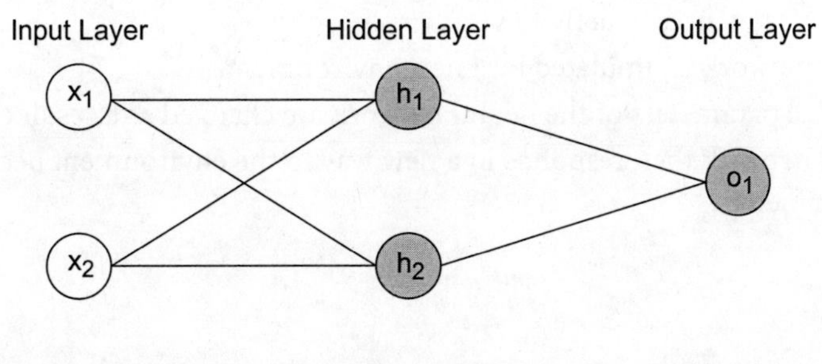

This network has two inputs, one neuron in the output layer and two neurons in the hidden layer (h1 and h2). This is a network since the outputs from h1 and h2 are the inputs for o1, as you can see.

Any layer between the input (first) layer and output (last) layer is a hidden layer. There may be several layers that are concealed!

1.8 COMPONENTS OF A NEURAL NETWORK

Input Layer: This layer is responsible for accepting input features. No computation is done at this layer; instead, nodes simply send information (features) to the hidden layer. It gives the network information from the outside world.

Hidden Layer: Since they are a component of the abstraction that any neural network provides, the nodes of this layer are not visible to the outside world. The features entered through the input layer are processed by the hidden layer in a variety of ways, and the output layer receives the results.

Output Layer: This layer is finally responsible for sharing the information that the network has learnt as output.

1.9 NEURAL NETWORKS VS. DEEP LEARNING

Deep Learning and neural networks tend to be used interchangeably in conversation, which can be confusing. As a result, it is worth noting that the "deep" in deep learning is just referring to the depth of layers in a neural network. A neural network that consists of more than three layers—which would be inclusive of the inputs and the output—can be considered a deep learning algorithm. A neural network that only has two or three layers is just a basic neural network.

1.10 HOW NEURAL NETWORK WORKS?

Weights are assigned after a determination of the input layer. These weights aid in determining the significance of each variable, with larger weights having a greater impact on the result than smaller ones. Next, each input is multiplied by its corresponding weight before being added together. The output is then determined by an activation function once the output has been passed through it. This "fires" (or activates) the node, sending data to the network's next layer, if the output rises beyond a predetermined threshold. As a result, the input of one node becomes the output of the following node. This neural network is a feedforward network since data is passed from one layer to the next layer throughout this procedure.

Predecessor neurons with activation $a_j(t)$, threshold ϕ_j, activation function f, and output function f_{out} will provide an input called $p_j(t)$ to the neuron. Connections are made up of weights, biases, and connections that govern how neuron i sends output to neuron j. Propagation calculates the input, outputs the output, and adds the weighted functions of the prior neurons. The change of the free parameters, i.e., weights and bias, is essentially what is meant by "learning" a neural network. The learning process consists of three main sequences of activities.

- The neural network is simulated by a new environment.
- Then the free parameters of the neural network are changed as a result of this simulation.
- The neural network then responds in a new way to the environment because of the changes in its free parameters.

1.11 TRAINING A NEURAL NETWORK

When we start off with our neural network, we initialize our weights randomly. Obviously, it will not give you very good results. In the process of training, we want to start with a bad performing neural network and wind up with network with high accuracy. In terms of loss function, we want our loss function to much lower in the end of training. Improving the network is possible, because we can change its function by adjusting weights. We want to find another function that performs better than the initial one.

The problem of training is equivalent to the problem of minimizing the loss function.

There are a lot of algorithms that optimize functions. These algorithms can gradient-based or not, in sense that they are not only using the information provided by the function, but also by its gradient. One of the simplest gradient-based algorithms

Steps in Training a Neural Network

1. First an ANN will require a **random weight initialization**
2. Split the dataset in **batches (batch size)**
3. Send the batches 1 by 1 to the GPU
4. Calculate the **forward pass** (what would be the output with the current weights)
5. Compare the calculated output to the expected output **(loss)**
6. Adjust the **weights** (using the **learning rate** increment or decrement) according to the **backward pass (backward gradient propagation)**.
7. Go back to square 2

1.12 GENERALIZATION

The classification and regression functions that are estimated using an MLP (or other neural network) are unknown — all we have is a training set, that gives input-output examples of the function. The role of neural network training is to identify this "mystery function", given only the training data. What the training process (e.g. backprop) does is to estimate the parameters of the function (i.e. the weights of the network) so that it replicates the data as well as possible — and generalizes to new data well. It turns out that obtaining the best generalization performance on new data is not usually the same solution as replicating the training data as well as possible. Consider the case when we have very few training patterns but a large network with many patterns. It will be relatively easy to manipulate the weights to reproduce the training set, but it does not seem likely that the resulting network will have learned the characteristics of new data. On the other hand, if we have very many training patterns, and we manage to train the network to replicate them, then it is more likely to respond correctly to new, unseen patterns. Our aim is to make such intuitions precise, and to develop approaches which can maximize the generalization performance of a network.

Evaluating Generalization: Training, Test and Validation Sets

The obvious way to obtain an estimate of how well a network generalizes is to test its performance on new data. However, we must be careful which data we use — if we keep on using the same test set, then although this data is not being used by the training algorithm, the fact we are trying to get the best performance on this particular data set may cause other factors (e.g. choice of learning rate) to be tuned to this "test set". To make the distinction explicit it is common to work with three data sets:

Training Set- This is the data that used by the training algorithm to adjust the weights of the network.

Validation (Development) Set- This data is used during training to assess how well the network is currently performing — the performance of the network on this data may be used to guide the training in some way (e.g. controlling the learning rate, deciding when to stop training, choosing between several trained networks).

Test (Evaluation) Set- This is the genuine test data — and, ideally, should be used once only, after training is complete.

Training and Generalization

Each training example that is presented to the network may be represented by a certain subset of the total set of functions available to the network. If the intersection of the function subsets relating to each data point is non-empty, then the training set can be learned perfectly by the network. (Note that finding a set of weights that corresponds to such a function is not guaranteed — this is the training problem.). In the case of an MLP learning a logic function (e.g. XOR) then this is the case after training. However, in pattern recognition it is not usually the case that a network is able to learn exactly all the training data — indeed it is not always desirable to do this.

Generalization is a measure that tells us how well the network performs on the actual problem once training is complete. This can be measured by looking at the performance of the network on evaluation data unseen during the training process. By definition, such data is not available when the network is being trained. Thus, we want to be able to predict the performance of the network on such data, and train the network to maximize the predicted performance. Since maximizing the generalization performance of the network involve producing the best possible performance on new data, a simple approach to estimate the generalization performance of networks is to evaluate their performance on a validation set.

The network is trained in the usual way, by minimizing the error function with respect to the training data set. The performance on an unseen test set, is estimated using a validation set. If we want to choose between different networks trained on the same data, then we choose the one that performs best on the validation set. This procedure is sometimes called a hold-out method, since the validation set may be regarded as data held out from the training set.

1.13 COMPETITIVE LEARNING IN ANN

It is concerned with unsupervised training in which the output nodes try to compete with each other to represent the input pattern. To understand this learning rule we will have to understand competitive net which is explained as follows –

Basic Concept of Competitive Network

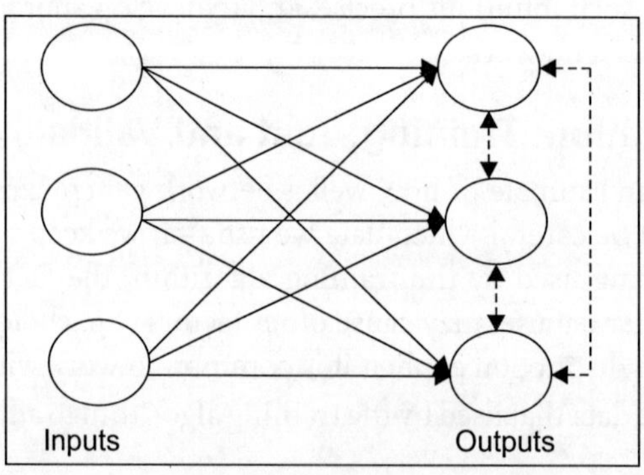

This network is just like a single layer feed-forward network having feedback connection between the outputs. The connections between the outputs are inhibitory type, which is shown by dotted lines, which means the competitors never support themselves.

Basic Concept of Competitive Learning Rule

As said earlier, there would be competition among the output nodes so the main concept is - during training, the output unit that has the highest activation to a given input pattern, will be declared the winner.

This rule is also called Winner-takes-all because only the winning neuron is updated and the rest of the neurons are left unchanged.

Mathematical Formulation

Following are the three important factors for mathematical formulation of this learning rule – Condition to be a winner

Suppose if a neuron $y_k$wants to be the winner, then there would be the following condition

y_k={1 if $v_k>v_j$forall j, j≠k

0 otherwise

}

It means that if any neuron, say, y_k wants to win, then its induced local field the output of the summation unit, say vk, must be the largest among all the other neurons in the network.

Condition of the Sum Total of Weight

Another constraint over the competitive learning rule is the sum total of weights to a particular output neuron is going to be 1. For example, if we consider neuron k then Σwkj=1for all k

Change of Weight for the Winner

If a neuron does not respond to the input pattern, then no learningtakes placein that neuron.However, if a particular neuron wins, then the corresponding weights areadjusted as follows –

Δwkj={−α(xj−wkj), if neuron k wins

0, if neuron k losses

Here α is the learning rate.

This clearly shows that we are favouring the winning neuron by adjusting its weight and if a neuron is lost, then we need not bother to re-adjust its weight. So, in short, Competitive learning is a form of unsupervised learning in artificial neural networks, in which nodes compete for the right to respond to a subset of the input data. A variant of Hebbian learning, competitive learning works by increasing the specialization of each node in the network. It is well suited to finding clusters within data.

1.14 ACTIVATION FUNCTION AND ITS USE

By calculating the weighted total and then adding bias to it, the activation function determines whether a neuron should be stimulated or not. The activation function's objective is to add non-linearity to a neuron's output.

We are aware that the neurons in the neural network function in accordance with weight, bias, and their respective activation functions. The weights and biases of the neurons in a neural network would be updated based on the output error. Back-propagation is the name of this procedure. Back-propagation is made possible by activation functions since they provide the gradients and error needed to update the weights and biases.

Activation functions can be divided into two classes: linear and non-linear.

Linear Activation Function: The activation is proportionate to the input in a linear activation function, also referred to as "no activation" or the "identity function" (multiplied by 1.0). The function just spits out the value it was given, doing nothing to the weighted sum of the input.

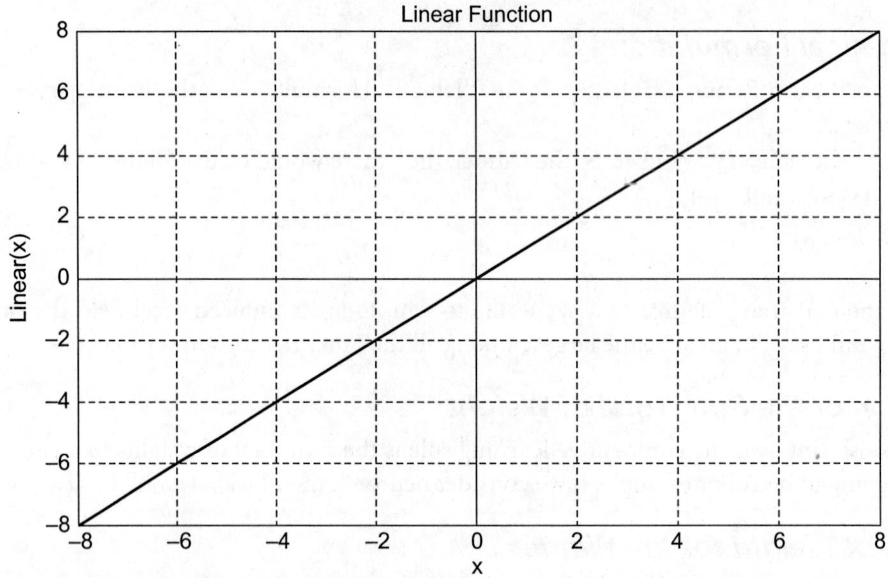

Non-Linear Activation Function: The most often utilised activation functions are nonlinear activation functions. It facilitates the model's generalisation or adaptation to a variety of data and facilitates output differentiation. The range or curves of the nonlinear activation functions serve as the basic basis for categorising the data.

Types of non-linear activation functions

Sigmoid: It is a non-linear activation function with S-shaped graph. Its equation is given as $1/(1 + e^{-x})$.

The sigmoid function is generally used in a classification's output nodes, where the outcome can only be either 0 or 1. Since the sigmoid function's value only has a range of 0 to 1, it is simple to assume that the output will be 1 if the value is greater than 0.5 and 0 if it is not.

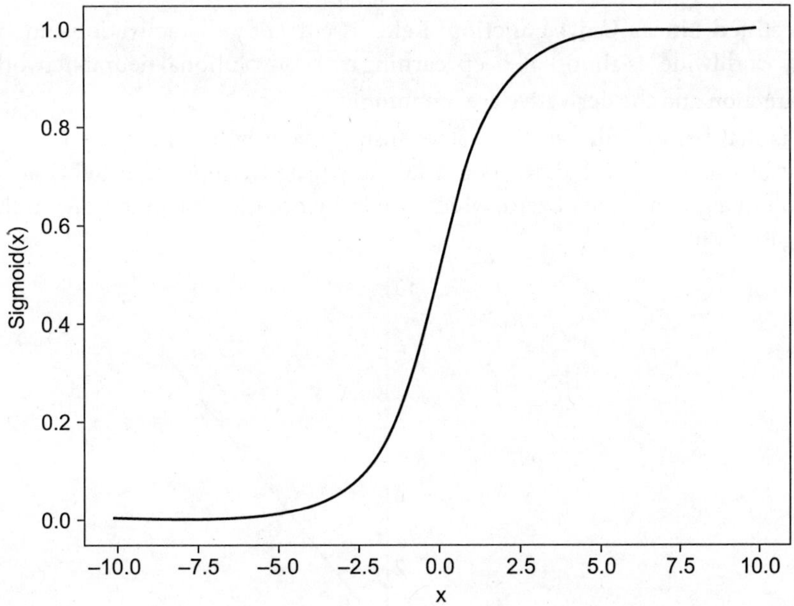

Tanh Function: Tangent hyperbolic function is the activation that regularly outperforms sigmoid function. It is a sigmoid function that has been modified mathematically. Each can be compared to and derived from the other.

$$f(x) = \tanh(x) = \frac{2}{(1+e^{-2x})} - 1 \quad \text{or} \quad \tanh(x) = 2 * \text{sigmoid}(2x) - 1$$

It is a non-linear function in which the values range from -1 to +1. The mean again for the hidden layer of a neural network will be zero or extremely close to it because its values normally range from -1 to one. As a result, the mean is close to zero, which centres the data. This makes learning for the layer below much easier.

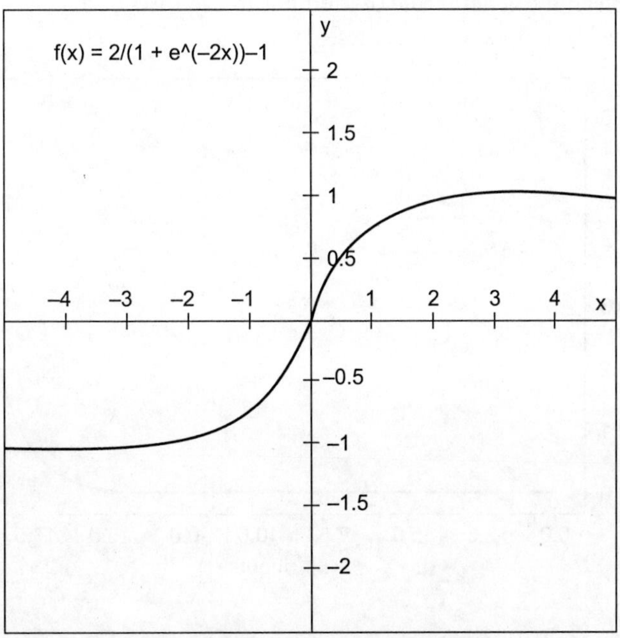

RELU (Rectified Linear Unit) Function: ReLU is currently the activation function that is used most frequently worldwide. as almost all deep learning and convolutional neural network systems use it.

Both the function and the derivative are monotonic.

The issue is that because all negative values instantaneously become zero, the model is less able to accurately fit or learn from the data. As a result, any negative input to a ReLU activation function will always result in a graph value of zero, which will influence the final graph due to the inappropriate mapping of negative values.

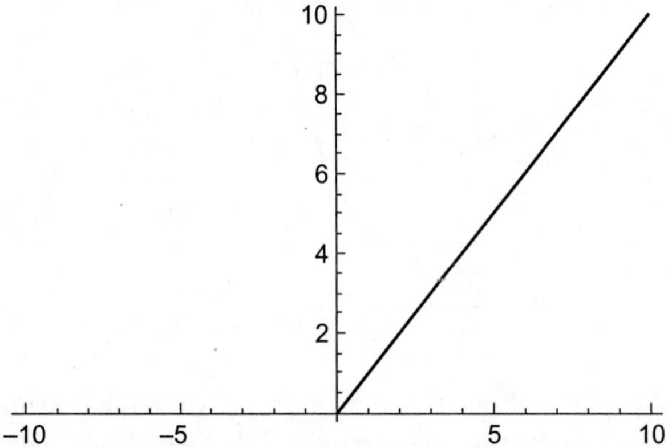

Softmax Function: The softmax function is useful for handling multiclass classification challenges even though it is a subclass of the sigmoid function, it is used a lot when overseeing multiple classes. The softmax was generally present in the output nodes of image classification problems. All outputs for each category would be constrained to fall between 0 and 1 by the softmax function, which would split by the sum of the outputs.

The softmax function is most effectively used in the classifier's output unit, which is where we are actually seeking to compute the probabilities to classify each input.

If we are truly unclear, the general rule of thumb is to use RELU, which is a common perceptron in hidden layers and is used in most situations these days.

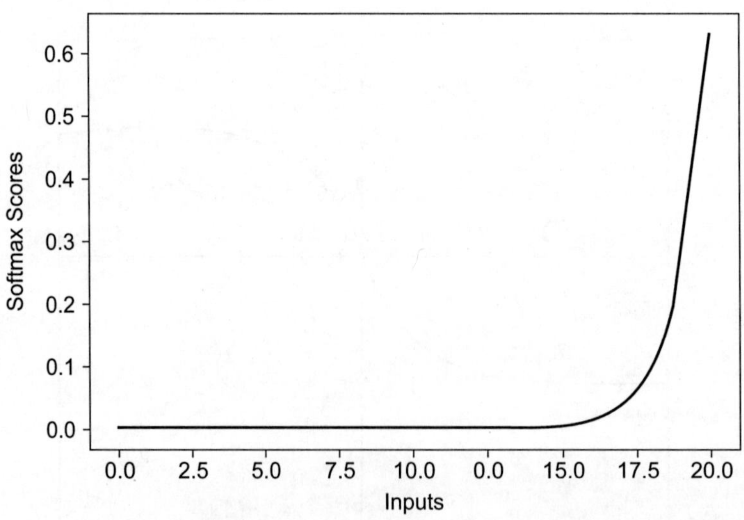

Requirement of a non-linear activation function: Without an activation function, a neural network is essentially just a linear regression model. The activation function transforms the input in a non-linear way, enabling it to learn and carry out more difficult tasks.

1.15 TYPES OF NEURAL NETWORKS

Perceptron: One of the earliest and most basic models of a neuron is the perceptron model, developed by Minsky and Papert. The tiniest neural network component, it performs specific computations to find features or business information in the incoming data. It accepts weighted inputs and uses an activation function to produce the desired output. Another name for a perceptron is a TLU (threshold logic unit).

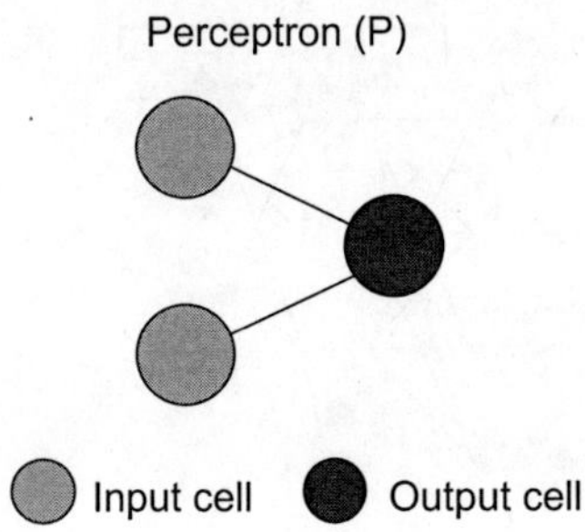

Perceptron

Feed Forward Neural Network: Multiple neurons and hidden layers that are coupled to one another make up Feed Forward (FF) networks. Because the data only flow forward and there is no backward propagation, these are referred to as "feed-forward" systems. Depending on the application, the network may not always have hidden levels.

More layers provide more potential for weights to be customised. Consequently, the network's capacity for learning will increase. Since there is no backpropagation, weights are not changed. The activation function, which serves as a threshold value, receives the output from multiplying the weights by the inputs. Their applications include classification, pattern recognition, face recognition and many more.

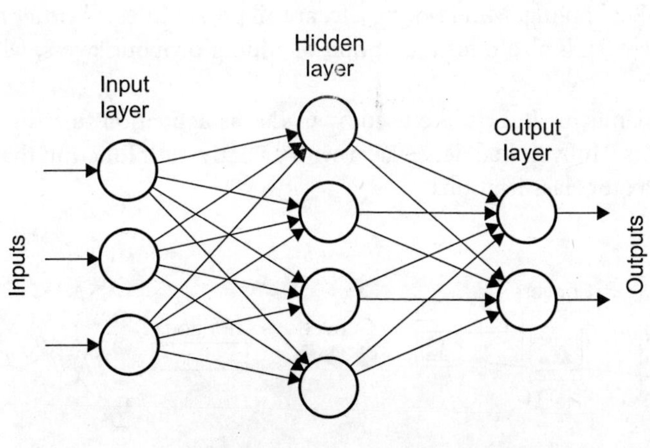

Feed Forward Neural Network

Multilayer Perceptron: It acts as a point of entry into more intricate neural networks where input data passes via several artificial neuronal layers. It is a fully connected neural network since every node is connected to every neuron in the layer below. There are input and output layers with many hidden layers, for a total of at least three layers. It propagates in both directions, or backward and forward, respectively.

Inputs are multiplied by weights and supplied to the activation function where they are changed in backpropagation to lessen the loss. Weights are, to put it simply, machine-learned values from neural networks. Depending on the discrepancy between training inputs and projected outputs, they self-adjust. Softmax is utilised as the output layer activation function after nonlinear activation functions.

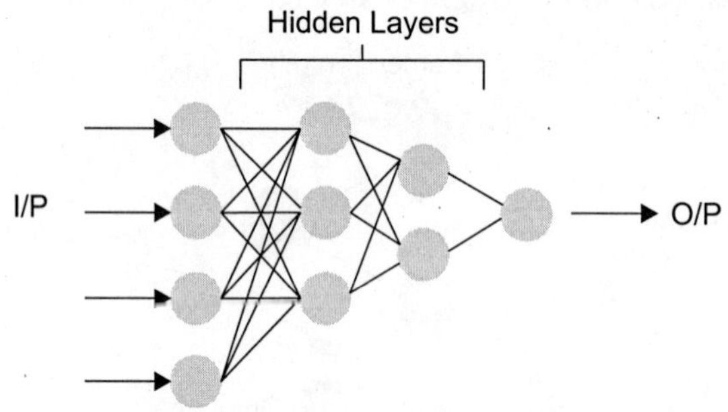

Multilayer Perceptron

Convolutional Neural Network: Convolution Neural Networks (CNN) are the most popular neural networks for image classification. Multiple convolution layers of CNN are responsible for extracting significant features from the image. The latter layers oversee more high-level features, whereas the earlier levels take care of low-level details.

Convolution operates on the input image using a custom matrix, sometimes known as filters, to produce maps. The backpropagation method is used to update these filters after a random initialization. The Canny Edge Detector, which is used to locate the edges of any image, is one illustration of such a filter.

A pooling layer follows the convolution layer and oversees combining the maps created by the convolutional layer. Max Pooling, Min Pooling, etc. are all possibilities. In order to avoid overfitting and speed up convergence, CNNs also offer the option of adding dropout layers, which disable or turn off specific neurons.

Rectified Linear Units, or ReLUs, are used by CNNs as activation functions in the hidden layers. The CNNs' final layer is a fully linked dense layer with an activation function that mostly uses ReLU for regression and Softmax for classification.

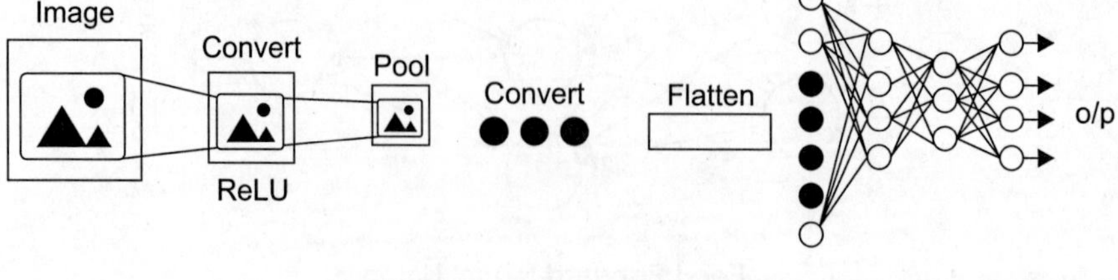

Convolutional Neural Network

Recurrent Neural Network: Recurrent neural networks are built to preserve layer output and feed it back to the input to aid with layer prediction. The first layer is often a feed forward neural network, followed by a recurrent neural network layer where a memory function remembers part of the information it had in the previous time step. In this situation, forward propagation is utilised. It keeps the data necessary for later usage. If the forecast is inaccurate, modest adjustments are made using the learning rate. As a result, it steadily gets better at making the correct prediction during backpropagation.

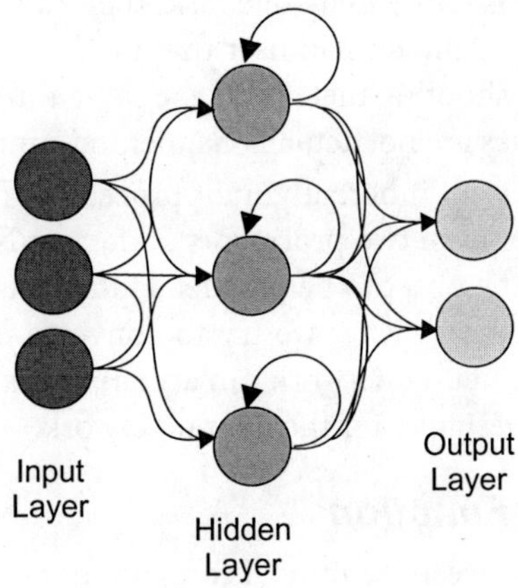

Recurrent Neural Network

Long Short -term Memory Networks: By including a unique memory cell that can store data for extended periods of time, LSTM neural networks get around the problem of Vanishing Gradient in RNNs. To determine which output should be used or ignored, LSTM uses gates. Input, output, and forget gates are the three gates it utilises. The input gate regulates what data is stored in memory. The forget gate regulates when to dump/forget the data that is not needed, while the output gate regulates the data that is passed to the next layer.

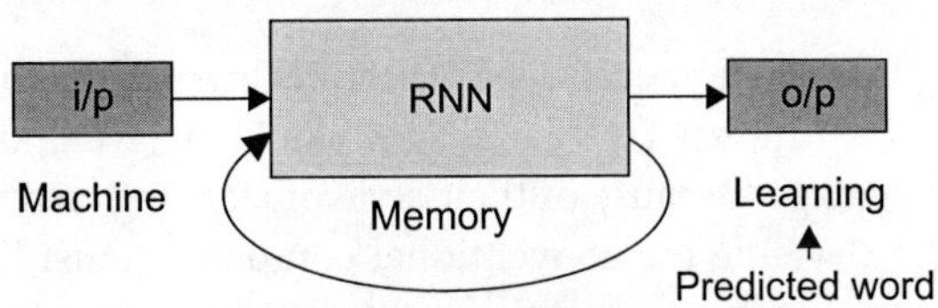

LSTM Network

1.16 WHY ARE NEURAL NETWORKS IMPORTANT?

Neural networks are a robust tool that businesses use to solve complex business problems. Companies use this form of network to identify patterns and predict rare events like fraud detection.

These networks can develop a relationship between non-linear and complex inputs and outputs. This makes them perfect for projects that require data-based decisions to achieve success. They are also used in areas such as:

- Quality control
- Voice recognition or natural language processing
- Healthcare for disease diagnosis
- Targeted marketing

1.17 COMPARISON BETWEEN CONVENTIONAL COMPUTERS AND NEURAL NETWORKS

Parallel Processing

One of the major advantages of the neural network is its ability to do many things at once. With traditional computers, processing is sequential--one task, then the next, then the next, and so on. The idea of threading makes it appear to the human user that many things are happening at one time. For instance, the Netscape throbber is shooting meteors at the same time that the page is loading. However, this is only an appearance; processes are not actually happening simultaneously.

The artificial neural network is an inherently multiprocessor-friendly architecture. Without much modification, it goes beyond one or even two processors of the von Neumann architecture. The artificial neural network is designed from the onset to be parallel. Humans can listen to music at the same time they do their homework--at least, that's what we try to convince our parents in high school. With a massively parallel architecture, the neural network can accomplish a lot in less time. The tradeoff is that processors have to be specifically designed for the neural network.

The Ways in Which They Function

Another fundamental difference between traditional computers and artificial neural networks is the way in which they function. While computers function logically with a set of rules and calculations, artificial neural networks can function via images, pictures, and concepts.

Based upon the way they function, traditional computers have to learn by rules, while artificial neural networks learn by example, by doing something and then learning from it. Because of these fundamental differences, the applications to which we can tailor them are extremely different. We will explore some of the applications later in the presentation.

Self-programming

The "connections" or concepts learned by each type of architecture is different as well. The von Neumann computers are programmable by higher level languages like C or Java and then translating that down to the machine's assembly language. Because of their style of learning, artificial neural networks can, in essence, "program themselves." While the conventional computers must learn only by doing different sequences or steps in an algorithm, neural networks are continuously adaptable by truly altering their own programming. It could be said that conventional computers are limited by their parts, while neural networks can work to become more than the sum of their parts.

Speed

The speed of each computer is dependent upon different aspects of the processor. Von Neumann machines requires either big processors or the tedious, error-prone idea of parallel processors, while neural networks require the use of multiple chips custom built for the application.

1.18 ADVANTAGES OF ARTIFICIAL NEURAL NETWORKS

1. Parallel processing abilities mean the network can perform more than one job at a time.
2. Information is stored on an entire network, not just a database.

3. The ability to learn and model nonlinear, complex relationships helps model the real-life relationships between input and output.
4. Fault tolerance means the corruption of one or more cells of the ANN will not stop the generation of output.
5. Gradual corruption means the network will slowly degrade over time, instead of a problem destroying the network instantly.
6. The ability to produce output with incomplete knowledge with the loss of performance being based on how important the missing information is.
7. No restrictions are placed on the input variables, such as how they should be distributed.
8. Machine learning means the ANN can learn from events and make decisions based on the observations.
9. The ability to learn hidden relationships in the data without commanding any fixed relationship means an ANN can better model highly volatile data and non-constant variance.
10. The ability to generalize and infer unseen relationships on unseen data means ANNs can predict the output of unseen data.

1.19 DISADVANTAGES OF ARTIFICIAL NEURAL NETWORKS

1. The lack of rules for determining the proper network structure means the appropriate artificial neural network architecture can only be found through trial and error and experience.
2. The requirement of processors with parallel processing abilities makes neural networks hardware-dependent.
3. The network works with numerical information; therefore, all problems must be translated into numerical values before they can be presented to the ANN.
4. The lack of explanation behind probing solutions is one of the biggest disadvantages in ANNs. The inability to explain the why or how behind the solution generates a lack of trust in the network.

1.20 APPLICATIONS OF NEURAL NETWORKS

1. **Facial Recognition:** Facial recognition systems are effective surveillance tools. Recognition software compares digital photographs to human faces and matches them. They are utilised in offices for restricted access. The systems then verify a human face and compare it to the list of IDs stored in their database.
2. **Stock market Prediction:** Market risks are there for investments. The very unpredictable stock market makes it practically hard to anticipate future changes. Before neural networks, the constantly shifting bullish and bearish phases were unpredictable. But what caused the change? Naturally, neural networks...
3. **Social media**: Whatever the cliche, social media has changed the mundane, everyday course of existence. Artificial neural networks are employed to research how social media users behave. Data exchanged daily through virtual dialogues is compiled and analysed for market competition.
4. **Aerospace:** The term "aerospace engineering" is broad and includes advancements in both aeroplanes and spacecraft. Some of the important areas that neural networks have taken over are fault diagnostics, high performance auto piloting, protecting the aircraft control systems, and modelling important dynamic simulations. lag in time It is possible to simulate nonlinear time dynamic systems using neural networks.

Delay in time for feature recognition that is independent of position, neural networks are used. Thus, the method based on time delay neural networks is capable of pattern recognition. By copying the original data from feature units, neural networks automatically create patterns that can be recognised.

5. **Defence:** Every country's defence sector is its foundation. The effectiveness of a nation's military operations determines its standing in the international community. The defensive strategies of nations with advanced technology are also influenced by neural networks. Japan, the United States of America, and Britain are among the nations that use artificial neural networks to create active defensive plans.

   Logistics, the analysis of armed attacks, and item location all involve neural networks. In addition, they are utilised to pilot automated drones and patrol the seas. Artificial intelligence is giving the defence industry the much-needed boost it needs to advance its technology.

6. **Healthcare:** The proverb "Health is Wealth" is quite old. People today are taking use of technology's benefits in the healthcare industry. Convolutional neural networks are currently used in the medical field for ultrasound, CT scans, and X-ray detection.

7. **Signature and handwriting analysis:** The self-explanatory word, "Signature Verification," refers to the process of confirming a person's signature. To double-check a person's identity, banks and other financial institutions utilise signature verification.

   Typically, the signatures are examined using a signature verification programme. Signature verification is a crucial component that aims to carefully evaluate the authenticity of signed papers because instances of forgery are rather widespread in financial organisations.

   The signatures are validated using artificial neural networks. ANN are taught to distinguish between authentic and fake signatures. Both offline and online signatures can be verified using ANNs.

8. **Weather forecasting:** Before the advent of artificial intelligence, the meteorological department's forecasts were never correct. The main goal of weather forecasting is to foresee future weather conditions in advance. Weather forecasts are now also used to forecast the likelihood of natural disasters.

1.21 Use Cases of Neural Networks

Artificial Neural Networks can be used in a number of ways. They can classify information, cluster data, or predict outcomes. ANN's can be used for a range of tasks. These include analyzing data, transcribing speech into text, powering facial recognition software, or predicting the weather.

Top Companies using Artificial Neural Network(ANN)

- Nvidia Corp. (NVDA)
- Alphabet (GOOG, GOOGL)
- Salesforce.com (CRM)
- Amazon.com (AMZN)
- Microsoft Corp. (MSFT)
- Twilio (TWLO)
- IBM (IBM)
- Facebook (FB)

1.22 FUTURE OF NEURAL NETWORKS

With the rapid pace that AI and machine learning are being adopted by companies today, we could see more advancements in the applications of neural networks in the foreseeable future. AI and machine learning will offer a wealth of personalized choices for users worldwide. For example, all mobile and web applications try to give you an enhanced customized experience based on your search history, and neural networks can make that possible.

Hyper-intelligent virtual assistants will make life easier. If you have ever used Google assistant, Siri, or any other products, you can see how they are slowly evolving. They may even predict your email responses in the future!

We can also expect intriguing discoveries on algorithms to support learning methods. However, we are just in the infant stage of applying artificial intelligence and neural networks to the real world.

Neural networks will be a lot faster in the future, and neural network tools can get embedded in every design surface. We already have a little mini neural network that plugs into an inexpensive processing board or even into your laptop. Instead of the software, focusing on the hardware would make such devices even faster.

Neural networks will also find their way into the fields of medicine, agriculture, physics, research, and anything else you can imagine. Neural networks will also find its way into the fields of medicine, agriculture, physics, research, and anything else you can imagine.

1.23 CONCLUSION

Neural network is a vast subject. Many data scientists solely focus on only Neural network techniques.

In this chapter we have discussed the introductory concepts. Neural Networks has much more advanced techniques. There are many algorithms other than back propagation.

Neural networks particularly work well on some particular class of problems like image recognition. The neural networks algorithms are very calculation intensive. They require highly efficient computing machines. Large datasets take significant amount of runtime on R. We need to try different types of options and packages.

Currently there is a lot of exciting research going on, around neural networks.

Review Questions

Solved Examples

Q.1. What do you mean by perceptron?

Ans. A perceptron also called an **artificial neuron** is a neural network unit that does certain computations to detect features.

It is a single-layer neural network used as a linear classifier while working with a set of input data. Since perceptron uses classified data points which are already labelled, it is a **supervised learning algorithm**. This algorithm is used to enable neurons to learn and process elements in the training set one at a time.

Q.2. What are the different types of perceptrons?

Ans. There are two types of perceptrons:

1. **Single-Layer Perceptrons:** Single-layer perceptrons can learn only linearly separable patterns.
2. **Multilayer Perceptrons:** Multilayer perceptrons, also known as **feedforward neural networks** having two or more layers have a higher processing power.

Q.3. What is the use of the loss functions?

Ans. The loss function is used as a measure of accuracy to identify whether our neural network has learned the patterns accurately or not with the help of the training data.

This is completed by comparing the training data with the testing data.

Therefore, the loss function is considered as a primary measure for the performance of the neural network. In Deep Learning, a good-performing neural network will always have a low value of the loss function when training happens.

Q.4. What is the role of the activation functions in neural networks?

Ans. The reason for using activation functions in neural networks are as follows:

1. The idea behind the activation function is to introduce nonlinearity into the neural network so that it can learn more complex functions.
2. Without the Activation function, the neural network behaves as a linear classifier, learning the function which is a linear combination of its input data.
3. The activation function converts the inputs into outputs.
4. The activation function is responsible for deciding whether a neuron should be activated i.e, fired or not.
5. To make the decision, firstly it calculates the weighted sum and further adds bias with it.
6. So, the basic purpose of the activation function is to introduce non-linearity into the output of a neuron.

Q.5. List down the names of some popular activation functions used in neural networks.

Ans. Some of the popular activation functions that are used while building the deep learning models are as follows:

- Sigmoid function
- Hyperbolic tangent function

- Rectified linear unit (RELU) function
- Leaky RELU function
- Maxout function
- Exponential Linear unit (ELU) function

Unsolved Questions

1. What is the difference between a feedforward neural network and recurrent neural network?
2. How human brain works?
3. What Are Hyperparameters?
4. How Are Weights Initialized in a Network?
5. What Are Vanishing and Exploding Gradients?

Multiple Choice Questions

Q.1. What is an Artificial Neural Network (ANN)?

(*a*) A computational model inspired by the human brain.
(*b*) A machine learning algorithm used for image processing
(*c*) A statistical analysis technique for data clustering.
(*d*) A programming language for neural network implementation

Q.2. What is the basic building block of an Artificial Neural Network?

(*a*) Neuron (*b*) Activation function
(*c*) Gradient descent (*d*) Loss function

Q.3. What is the purpose of the activation function in an ANN?

(*a*) It determines the output of a neuron
(*b*) It introduces non-linearity to the network
(*c*) It enables the network to learn complex patterns
(*d*) All of the above

Q.4. Which layer of an ANN is responsible for making predictions or producing the final output?

(*a*) Input layer (*b*) Hidden layer
(*c*) Output layer (*d*) All layers contribute equally

Q.5. Who is introduced neural networks?

(*a*) Claude Shannon (*b*) Vannevar Bush
(*c*) Warren Sturgis McCulloch (*d*) John von Neumann

Answer Key

1. (*a*) 2. (*a*) 3. (*d*) 4. (*c*) 5. (*c*)

Fill in the Blanks

1. ______ is the process of implementing Neural Networks.
2. ______ is the science of getting machines to interpret, process and analyse data.

3. ______ are the building blocks of the nervous system.
4. Neural networks allow programs to recognize ______ and solve common problems in artificial intelligence, machine learning and deep learning.
5. Neural networks are used to convert handwritten characters into ______ characters that a machine can recognize.

Answer Key

1. Forward Propagation
2. Artificial Intelligence
3. Neurons
4. Patterns
5. Digital

Solved Numerical Problems

Q.1. Which Boolean function is represented by the below figure, given that X_1 and X_2 are binary?

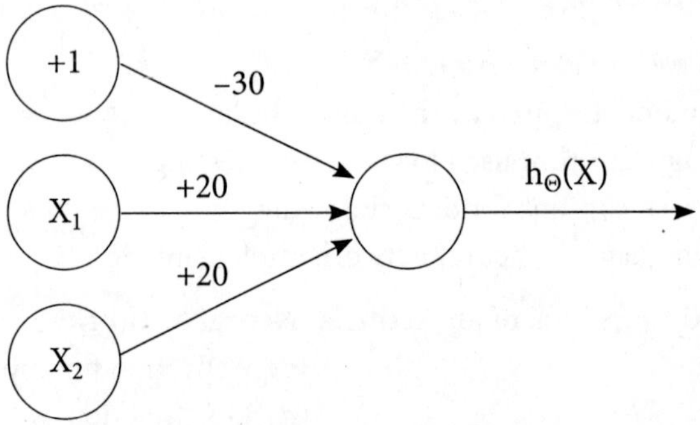

Solution: The given figure shows the AND function. Given bias B = +1, weights $\Theta_0 = -30$, $\Theta_1 = +20$ and $\Theta_2 = +20$. We have, $h_\Theta(X) = f(B\Theta_0 + X_1\Theta_1 + X_2\Theta_2)$. Then for the four input values,

X_1	X_2	$h_\Theta(X)$
0	0	f(1 * –30 + 0 * 20 + 0 * 20) = f(–30) ≈ 0
0	1	f(1 * –30 + 0 * 20 + 1 * 20) = f(–10) ≈ 0
1	0	f(1 * –30 + 1 * 20 + 0 * 20) = f(–10) ≈ 0
1	1	f(1 * –30 + 1 * 20 + 1 * 20) = f(10) ≈ 1

So only (1, 1) gives positive output as in AND function.

Q.2. What will be the hypotheses outputs for the below NOT function?

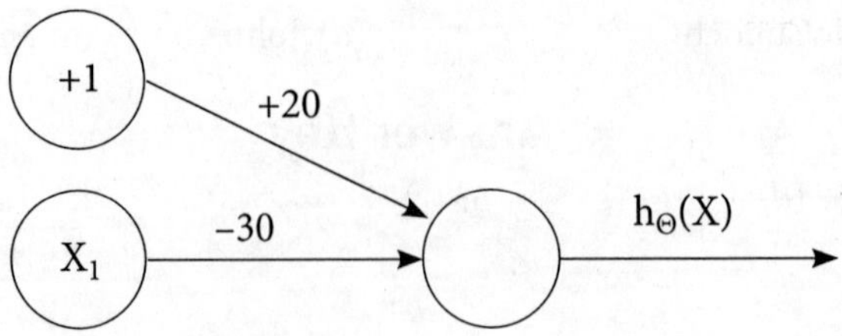

Solution: The given figure shows the NOT function. Given bias B = +1, weights $\Theta_0 = +20$ and $\Theta1 = -30$. We have, $h_\Theta(X) = f(B\Theta_0 + X_1\Theta_1)$. Then for the two input values,

X1	hΘ(X)
0	f(1 * 20 + 0 * -30) = f(20) ≈ 1
1	f(1 * 20 + 1 * -30) = f(-10) ≈ 0

Q.3. Which Boolean function is represented by the below figure, given that X_1 and X_2 are binary?

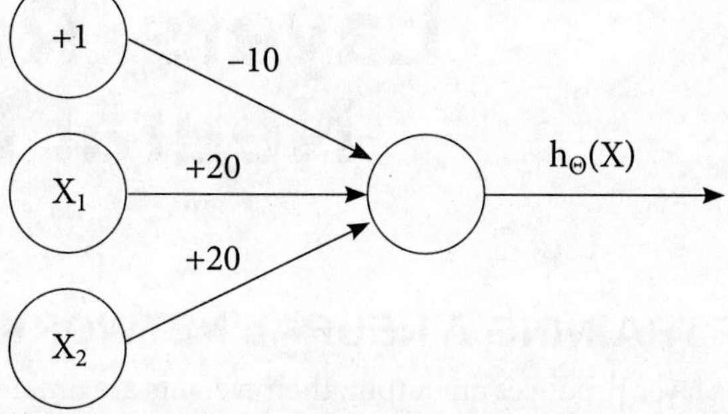

Solution: The given figure shows the OR function. Given bias B = +1, weights $\Theta_0 = -10$, $\Theta_1 = +20$ and $\Theta_2 = +20$. We have, $h_\Theta(X) = f(B\Theta_0 + X_1\Theta_1 + X_2\Theta_2)$. Then for the four input values,

X_1	X_2	$h_\Theta(X)$
0	0	f(1 * –10 + 0 * 20 + 0 * 20) = f(–10) ≈ 0
0	1	f(1 * –10 + 0 * 20 + 1 * 20) = f(10) ≈ 0
1	0	f(1 * –10 + 1 * 20 + 0 * 20) = f(10) ≈ 0
1	1	f(1 * –10 + 1 * 20 + 1 * 20) = f(30) ≈ 1

So only (0, 0) give negative value as in OR.

❑❑❑

2 Training a Neural Network, How to Determine Hidden Layers, Recurrent Neural Network

2.1 MEANING OF TRAINING A NEURAL NETWORK

Although every neuron in a layer produces an output, their weights are different for the layer below. As a result, if a neuron in a layer notices a certain pattern, it may not have as much of an impact on the overall picture and may even be muted entirely. We refer to this as "weighting," where a high weight denotes the importance of the input and a low weight, naturally, indicates that it should be disregarded. Each Neuron-to-Neuron Neural Connection will have a corresponding Weight.

And this is where neural network adaptability's power lies: Weights will be changed during the workout to suit the goals we have established (recognise a dog for a dog and a cat for a cat). In layman's terms: Gradient Backward Propagation is a feedback loop that is used in neural network training to determine the proper Weights of the Neural Connections.

2.2 TRAINING AN ARTIFICIAL NEURAL NETWORK

The output nodes can be given "correct" values by assigning "1" to the node corresponding to the proper class and "0" to the other nodes because during the training phase, the correct class for each record is known (this is known as supervised training). (In actuality, it has been discovered that using 0.9 and 0.1 as the respective numbers is preferable.) Thus, it is possible to compute an error term for each node (the "Delta" rule) by comparing the network's estimated values for the output nodes to these "correct" values. The weights in the hidden layers are then modified using these error terms in the hopes that the output values will be more closely aligned with the "correct" values.

The Iterative Learning Process: The iterative learning process used by neural networks, in which data cases (rows) are presented to the network one at a time and the weights corresponding to the input values are changed each time, is a critical component of these systems. The procedure frequently starts afresh once all the instances have been presented. The network gains knowledge during this learning phase by modifying the weights in order to anticipate the right class label of input data. Due to links between the units, neural network learning is also known as "connectionist learning." Neural networks can classify patterns for which they have not been taught, as well as a high tolerance for noisy input. The proposed back-propagation method is the most widely used neural network algorithm in 1980s.

A network is prepared to be taught once it has been set up for a specific purpose. The starting weights (explained in the following section) are selected at random to begin this process. The training or learning process then starts.

Utilising the weights and functions from the hidden layers, the network processes each record in the training data individually before comparing the results to the desired results. The system then updates the weights for use with the following record to be processed as errors are propagated back through the system. As the weights are adjusted again and over, this process repeats. The same set of data is processed numerous times throughout a network's training phase when the connection weights are determined.

The learning (training) process of a neural network is an iterative process in which the calculations are carried out forward and backward through each layer in the network until the loss function is minimized.

Be aware that not all networks can learn. This can be the case because the input data lack the precise information needed to produce the desired outcome. Additionally, networks do not converge if there is insufficient data to provide comprehensive learning. There should ideally be enough data to allow for the retention of a portion of the data as a validation set.

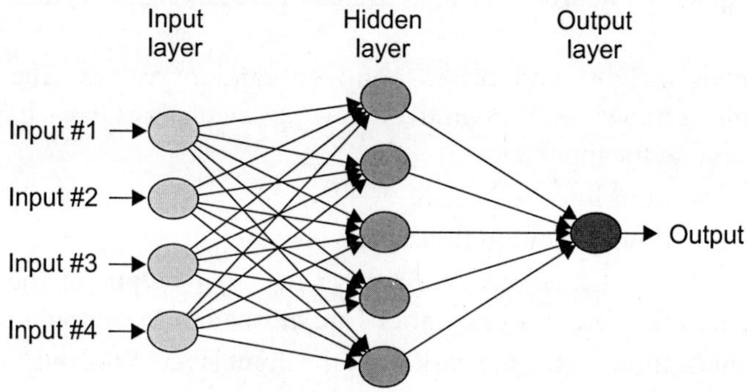

2.3 KEY STEPS FOR TRAINING A NEURAL NETWORK

1. **Pick a neural network architecture:** This implies that you shall be pondering primarily upon the connectivity patterns of the neural network including some of the following aspects:
   - **Number of input nodes:** The way to identify number of input nodes is identify the number of features.
   - **Number of hidden layers:** The default is to use the single or one hidden layer. This is the most common practice.
   - **Number of nodes in each of the hidden layers:** In case of using multiple hidden layers, the best practice is to use same number of nodes in each hidden layer. In general practice, the number of hidden units is taken as comparable number to that of number of input nodes. That means one could take either the same number of hidden nodes as input nodes or maybe twice or thrice the number of input nodes.
   - **Number of output nodes:** The way to identify number of output nodes is to identify the number of output classes you want the neural network to process.
   - **Random initialization of weights:** The weights are randomly intialized to value in between 0 and 1, or rather, very close to zero.
2. Implementation of forward propagation algorithm to calculate hypothesis function for a set on input vector for any of the hidden layer.

3. Calculation of the loss function
4. Implementation of back propagation algorithm to compute the error vector related with each of the nodes.

The entire learning process can be divided into three main parts:

1. Forward propagation (Forward pass)
2. Calculation of the loss function
3. Backward propagation (Backward pass/Backpropagation)

2.3.1 Forward Propagation

Multiple neurons (perceptron), which are stacked into layers, make up a neural network. Through the network's parameters (shown as arrows), connections between the levels were made. Weights and biases serve as the parameters.

Biases affect how quickly a neuron fires or activates whereas weights regulate the relative relevance of each input.

We begin by giving weights and biases non-zero random values. The network's parameter initialization is what this is known as. We run the following calculations in each network neuron based on these assigned values and the input data.

- Calculation of neuron's linear function.
- Calculation of neuron's activation function.

The network does these calculations. We receive the final output of the forward propagation component in the first iteration after the calculations are finished in the output layer node(s).

Calculations are made through the network from the input layer to the output layer (left to right) in forward propagation.

2.3.2 Calculation of Loss Function

The anticipated value is the output that is produced at the end of the forward propagation process. To evaluate the effectiveness of the neural network, this value should be contrasted with the corresponding ground-truth value (actual value). The loss function, also known as the objective function or cost function, is used in this situation.

Between the expected values and the ground truth values, the loss function calculates a score called the loss score. This is often referred to as the model mistake. The model's performance in each iteration is captured by the loss function. To update the parameters in the backpropagation section, we use the loss score as a feedback signal.

The loss function's optimum value is zero (zero). In order to improve the model's predictions and bring them closer to the actual values, we want to minimise the loss function as closely as possible to 0 in each iteration.

Here is a list of commonly used loss functions in neural network training.

1. **Mean Squared Error (MSE)** — This is used to measure the performance of regression problems.
2. **Mean Absolute Error (MAE)** — This is used to measure the performance of regression problems.
3. **Mean Absolute Percentage Error** — This is used to measure the performance of regression problems.

4. **Huber Loss** — This is used to measure the performance of regression problems.
5. **Binary Cross-entropy (Log Loss)** — This is used to measure the performance of binary (two-class) classification problems.
6. **Multi-class Cross-entropy/Categorical Cross-entropy** — This is used to measure the performance of multi-class (more than two classes) classification problems.

2.3.3 Backward Propagation

The predicted values are far from the ground truth values in the initial iteration; hence the distance score will be high. This is since we initially gave the network's parameters (weights and biases) arbitrary values. Those are not the ideal values. In order to minimise the loss function, we must therefore update the values of these parameters. Parameter learning or optimisation is the process of updating network parameters, and it is carried out using an optimisation method (optimizer) that uses backpropagation.

Finding the global minima, or regions with the lowest values of the loss function, is the goal of the optimisation algorithm. Finding the global minimum of a complex loss function while avoiding all local minima is a significant difficulty for an optimisation method. The minimal value for the loss function will not be obtained if the procedure is stopped at a local minimum. As a result, our model will not work well.

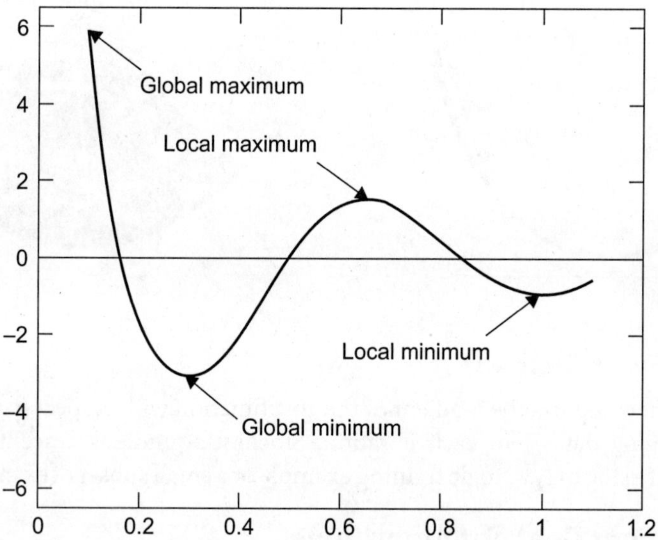

The partial derivatives (gradients) of the loss function with respect to the model parameters in each layer are computed in the backward propagation. Utilising calculus' chain rule, this is accomplished.

The slope of the loss function, which is its derivative, tells us which direction to consider while updating (changing) the values of the model parameters.

Keras libraries for neural networks offer automatic differentiation. This indicates that the libraries automatically generate all the derivates required for backpropagation when you define the neural network architecture.

Calculations are made through the network from the output layer to the input layer (right to left) in backward propagation.

Here is a list of commonly used optimizers in neural network training.

- Gradient Descent
- StocasticcGradeint Descent (SGD)
- Adam
- Adagrad
- Adadelta
- Adamax
- Nadam
- Ftrl
- Root Mean Squared Propagation (RMSProp)

Gradient Descent

Gradient descent is one of the famous ways to calculate the local minimum.

By Changing the weights, we are moving towards the minimum value of the error function. The weights are changed by taking steps in the negative direction of the function gradient(derivative).

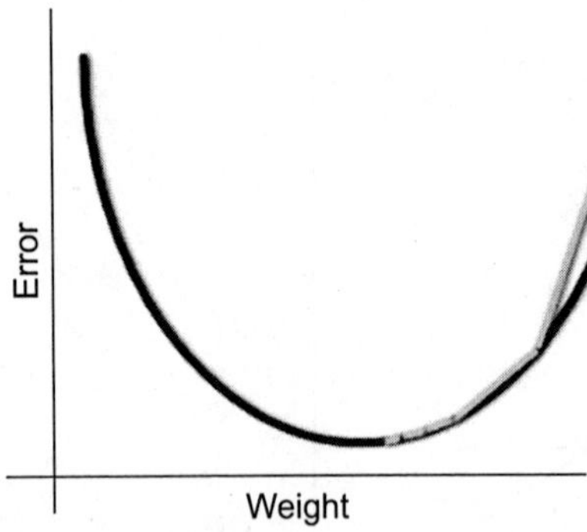

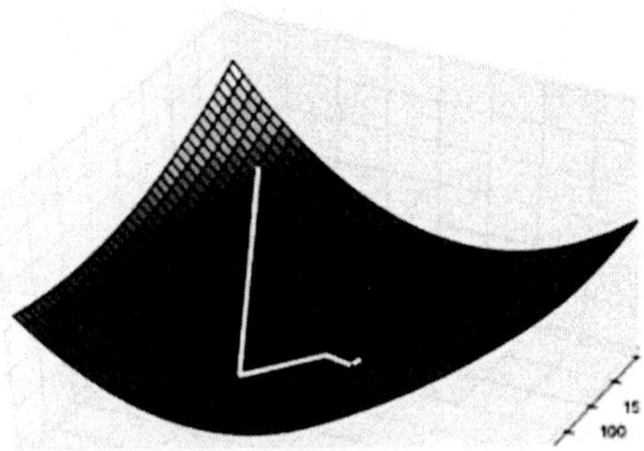

Stochastic Gradient Descent

Batch gradient descent computes the gradient of the cost function with respect to the model parameters using the entire training dataset in each iteration. Stochastic gradient descent, on the other hand, computes the gradient using only a single training example or a small subset of examples in each iteration.

Stochastic Gradient Descent Algorithms

Stochastic gradient descent algorithms are a modification of gradient descent. In stochastic gradient descent, you calculate the gradient using just a random small part of the observations instead of all of them. In some cases, this approach can reduce computation time.

Online stochastic gradient descent is a variant of stochastic gradient descent in which you estimate the gradient of the cost function for each observation and update the decision variables accordingly. This can help you find the global minimum, especially if the objective function is convex.

Batch stochastic gradient descent is somewhere between ordinary gradient descent and the online method. The gradients are calculated and the decision variables are updated iteratively with subsets of all observations, called minibatches. This variant is very popular for training neural networks.

You can imagine the online algorithm as a special kind of batch algorithm in which each minibatch has only one observation. Classical gradient descent is another special case in which there is only one batch containing all observations.

Minibatches in Stochastic Gradient Descent

As in the case of the ordinary gradient descent, stochastic gradient descent starts with an initial vector of decision variables and updates it through several iterations. The difference between the two is in what happens inside the iterations:

- Stochastic gradient descent randomly divides the set of observations into minibatches.
- For each minibatch, the gradient is computed and the vector is moved.
- Once all minibatches are used, you say that the iteration, or epoch, is finished and start the next one.

This algorithm randomly selects observations for minibatches, so you need to simulate this random (or pseudorandom) behaviour. You can do that with random number generation. Python has the built-in random module, and NumPy has its own random generator. The latter is more convenient when you work with arrays.

ADAM

Adaptive Moment Estimation is an algorithm for optimization technique for gradient descent. The method is really efficient when working with large problem involving a lot of data or parameters. It requires less memory and is efficient. Intuitively, it is a combination of the 'gradient descent with momentum' algorithm and the 'RMSP' algorithm.

Adam optimizer involves a combination of two gradient descent methodologies:

This algorithm is used to accelerate the gradient descent algorithm by taking into consideration the 'exponentially weighted average' of the gradients. Using averages makes the algorithm converge towards the minima in a faster pace.

ADAGRAD

Adagrad stands for Adaptive Gradient Optimizer. There were optimizers like Gradient Descent, Stochastic Gradient Descent, mini-batch SGD, all were used to reduce the loss function with respect to the weights. The weight updating formula is as follows:

$$(\mathrm{w})_{\text{new}} = (w)_{\text{old}} - \eta \frac{\partial L}{dw(\text{old})}$$

Based on iterations, this formula can be written as:

$$w_t = w_{t-1} - \eta \frac{\partial L}{\partial w(t-1)}$$

where $w(t)$ = value of w at current iteration

$\mathrm{w}(t-1)$ = value of w at previous iteration and η = learning rate.

In SGD and mini-batch SGD, the value of η used to be the same for each weight, or say for each parameter. Typically, $\eta = 0.01$. But in Adagrad Optimizer the core idea is that each weight has a different learning rate (η). This modification has great importance, in the real-world dataset, some features are sparse and some are dense (most of the features will be noon-zero), so keeping the same value of learning rate for all the weights is not good for optimization. The weight updating formula for adagrad looks like:

$$w_t = w_{t-1} - \eta_t' \frac{\partial L}{\partial w(t-1)}$$

where alpha(t) denotes different learning rates for each weight at each iteration.

$$\eta'_t = \frac{\eta}{\text{sqrt}(\alpha_t + \in)}$$

Here, η is a constant number, epsilon is a small positive value number to avoid divide by zero error if in case alpha(t) becomes 0 because if alpha(t) become zero then the learning rate will become zero which in turn after multiplying by derivative will make $w_{(\text{old})} = w_{(\text{new})}$, and this will lead to small convergence.

$$\alpha_t = \sum_{i=1}^{t} g_i^2$$

$$g_i = \frac{\partial L}{\partial w(\text{old})}$$

g_i is derivative of loss with respect to weight and gi will always be positive since it is a square term, which means that alpha(t) will also remain positive, this implies that alpha(t) >= alpha(t – 1).

It can be seen from the formula that as alpha(t) and is inversely proportional to one another, this implies that as **alpha(t)** will increase, will decrease. This means that as the number of iterations will increase, the learning rate will reduce adaptively, so you no need to manually select the learning rate.

ADADELTA

Adadelta optimization is a stochastic gradient descent method that is based on adaptive learning rate per dimension to address two drawbacks:

The continual decay of learning rates throughout training.

The need for a manually selected global learning rate.

Adadelta is a more robust extension of Adagrad that adapts learning rates based on a moving window of gradient updates, instead of accumulating all past gradients. This way, Adadelta continues learning even when many updates have been done. Compared to Adagrad, in the original version of Adadelta you do not have to set an initial learning rate.

ADAMAX

Adamax, a variant of Adam based on the infinity norm, is a first-order gradient-based optimization method. Due to its capability of adjusting the learning rate based on data characteristics, it is suited to learn time-variant process, e.g., speech data with dynamically changed noise conditions.

NADAM

Nesterov-accelerated Adaptive Moment Estimation, or the Nadam, is an extension of the Adam algorithm that incorporates Nesterov momentum and can result in better performance of the optimization algorithm.

The update rule is of the form:

$$\theta_{t+1} = \theta_t - \frac{\eta}{\sqrt{\hat{v}_t + \epsilon}}\left(\beta_1 \hat{m}_t + \frac{(1-\beta_t)g_t}{1-\beta_1^t}\right)$$

FTRL

"Follow The Regularized Leader" (FTRL) is an optimization algorithm developed at Google for click-through rate prediction in the early 2010s. It is most suitable for shallow models with large and sparse feature spaces. The algorithm is described by McMahan et al., 2013.

RMSPROP

The RMSprop optimizer is like the gradient descent algorithm with momentum. The RMSprop optimizer restricts the oscillations in the vertical direction. Therefore, we can increase our learning rate and our algorithm could take larger steps in the horizontal direction converging faster. The difference between RMSprop and gradient descent is on how the gradients are calculated. The following equations show how the gradients are calculated for the RMSprop and gradient descent with momentum. The value of momentum is denoted by beta and is usually set to 0.9.

Optimizers are the extended class, which include added information to train a specific model. The optimizer class is initialized with given parameters but it is important to remember that no Tensor is needed. The optimizers are used for improving speed and performance for training a specific model.

2.3.4 Classification by Back Propagation

Classification by backpropagation is a type of supervised learning algorithm that is used to train a neural network to classify data into different classes. The backpropagation algorithm is based on the idea of adjusting the weights and biases of a network in order to minimize the error between the predicted output and the actual output.

The backpropagation algorithm works by taking a set of training examples and feeding them through the neural network. The output of the network is compared to the desired output, and the error is calculated using a cost function such as mean squared error

The error is then propagated backwards through the network, with each neuron in the network adjusting its weights and biases based on its contribution to the error. This is done using a gradient descent algorithm, where the weights and biases are adjusted in the direction that reduces the error.

The backpropagation algorithm is an iterative process that continues until the error is minimized or until a predetermined number of iterations is reached. The final set of weights and biases is then used to classify new data.

Some key characteristics of classification by backpropagation include:

- Backpropagation can be used to train neural networks with multiple layers, known as deep learning networks. These networks can learn more complex features and relationships in the data, but may require more training data and computational resources.
- Backpropagation can handle both numerical and categorical input data, as long as the data is pre-processed and normalized appropriately.
- Backpropagation can suffer from overfitting, where the network becomes too specialized to the training data and performs poorly on new data. Regularization techniques such as dropout or early stopping can be used to prevent overfitting.

- Backpropagation requires a large amount of training data and may not perform well on small datasets. It also requires careful tuning of hyperparameters such as learning rate and batch size to achieve good performance.
- Backpropagation is a powerful and flexible algorithm that has been used for a wide range of classification tasks, including image recognition, natural language processing, and speech recognition.

Here are some additional points on classification by backpropagation

- Backpropagation is a type of feedforward neural network, which means that data flows through the network in one direction from the input layer to the output layer.
- The input layer of a neural network typically consists of one neuron for each input feature, while the output layer consists of one neuron for each output class.
- The number and size of hidden layers in the network can be adjusted depending on the complexity of the data and the task at hand. However, adding more layers can increase the risk of overfitting and may require more training data.
- The backpropagation algorithm can be computationally expensive and may require significant computational resources for large datasets. To address this, researchers have developed techniques such as mini-batch gradient descent and stochastic gradient descent that can speed up the training process.

Algorithm: Backpropagation. Neural network learning for classification or numeric prediction, using the backpropagation algorithm.

Input:

- *D*, a data set consisting of the training tuples and their associated target values;
- *l*, the learning rate;
- network, a multilayer feed-forward network.

Output: A trained neural network.

Method

1. Initialize all weights and biases in network.
2. While terminating condition is not satisfied {
3. for each training tuple *X* in *D*{
4. // Propagate the inputs forward:
5. for each input layer unit j {
6. $O_j = I_j$; // output of an input unit is its actual input value
7. for each hidden or output layer unit *j* :
8. $I_j = \sum_i w_{ij} O_i + \theta_j$; // compute the net input of unit *j* with respect to the previous layer, *i*
9. $O_j = \dfrac{1}{1+e^{-I_j}}$; // compute the output of each unit *j*
10. // Backpropagate the errors:
11. for each unit *j* in the output layer
12. $\text{Err}_j = O_j(1 - O_j)(T_j - O_j)$; // compute the error

```
for each unit j in the hidden layers, from the last to first hidden layer
Err_j = O_j(1 – O_j)Σ_k Err_k w_jk; // compute the error with respect to the next higher layer, k
for each weight w_ij in network {
Δw_ij = (l)Err_j O_i; // weight increment
w_ij = w_ij + Δw_ij; } // weight update
for each bias θ_j in network {
Δθ_j = (l) Err_j; // bias increment
θ_j = θ_j + Δθ_j; } // bias update
}}
```

Initialize the weights: The weights in the network are initialized to small random numbers (e.g., ranging from −1.0 to 1.0, or −0.5 to 0.5). Each unit has a bias associated with it, as explained later. The biases are similarly initialized to small random numbers. Each training tuple, X, is processed by the following steps.

- Propagate the inputs forward: First, the training tuple is fed to the network's input layer. The inputs pass through the input units, unchanged. That is, for an input unit, j, its output, O_j, is equal to its input value, I_j.
- Next, the net input and output of each unit in the hidden and output layers are computed. The net input to a unit in the hidden or output layers is computed as a linear combination of its inputs.

To help illustrate this point, a hidden layer or output layer unit is shown in figure.

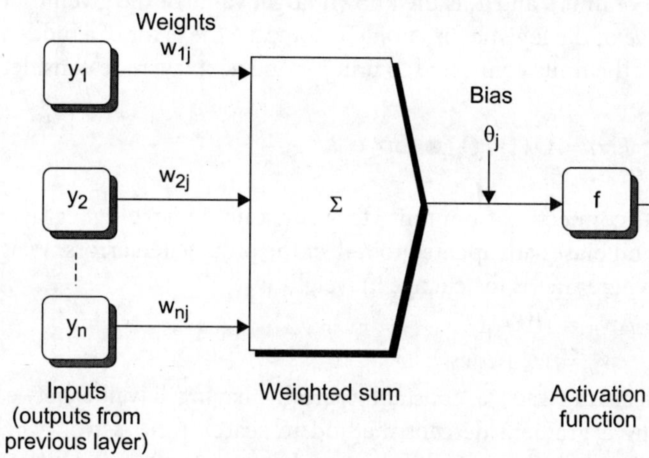

Hidden or output layer unit *j*: The inputs to unit j are outputs from the previous layer. These are multiplied by their corresponding weights to form a weighted sum, which is added to the bias associated with unit j. A non-linear activation function is applied to the net input. (For ease of explanation, the inputs to unit j are labeled $y_1, y_2, ..., y_n$. If unit j were in the first hidden layer, then these inputs would correspond to the input tuple $(1_1, x_2, ..., x_n)$).

- Each such unit has a number of inputs to it that are, in fact, the outputs of the units connected to it in the previous layer. Each connection has a weight. To compute the net input to the unit, each input connected to the unit is multiplied by its corresponding weight, and this is summed. Given a unit, j in a hidden or output layer, the net input, I_j, to unit j is

$$I_j = \sum_i w_{ij} O_i + \theta_j$$

where w_{ij} is the weight of the connection from unit i in the previous layer to unit j; O_i is the output of unit i from the previous layer; and θ_j is the bias of the unit. The bias acts as a threshold in that it serves to vary the activity of the unit. Each unit in the hidden and output layers takes its net input and then applies an activation function to it, as illustrated in above figure. The function symbolizes the activation of the neuron represented by the unit. The logistic, or sigmoid, function is used. Given the net input I_j to unit j, then O_j, the output of unit j, is computed as

$$O_j = \frac{1}{1+e^{-I_j}}$$

This function is also referred to as a squashing function, because it maps a large input domain onto the smaller range of 0 to 1. The logistic function is nonlinear and differentiable, allowing the back propagation to model classification problems that are linearly inseparable. We compute the output values, O_j, for each hidden layer, up to and including the output layer, which gives the network's prediction. In practice, it is a good idea to cache (i.e., save) the intermediate output values at each unit as they are required again later when backpropagating the error. This trick can substantially reduce the amount of computation required.

Backpropagate the error: The error is propagated backward by updating the weights and biases to reflect the error of the network's prediction. For a unit j in the output layer, the error Errj is computed by

$$Err_j = O_j(1 - O_j)(T_j - O_j)$$

where O_j is the actual output of unit j, and T_j is the known target value of the given training tuple. Note that $O_j(1 - O_j)$ is the derivative of the logistic function. To compute the error of a hidden layer unit j, the weighted sum of the errors of the units connected to unit j in the next layer are considered. The error of a hidden layer unit j is

$$Err_j = O_j(1 - O_j) \underset{k}{\bullet} Err_k w_j k$$

where $w_j k$ is the weight of the connection from unit j to a unit k in the next higher layer, and Err_k is the error of unit k. The weights and biases are updated to reflect the propagated errors. Weights are updated by the following equations, where Δw_{ij} is the change in weight w_{ij}

$$\Delta w_{ij} = (l) Err_j O_i$$

$$w_{ij} = w_{ij} + \Delta w_{ij}$$

The variable l is the learning rate, a constant typically having a value between 0.0 and 1.0. Backpropagation learns using a gradient descent method to search for a set of weights that fits the training data so as to minimize the mean squared distance between the network's class prediction and the known target value of the tuples. Biases are updated by the following equations, where $\Delta\theta_j$ is the change in bias θ_j:

$$\Delta\theta_j = (l) Err_j$$

$$\theta_j = \theta_j + \Delta\theta_j$$

Note that here we are updating the weights and biases after the presentation of each tuple. This is referred to as case updating. Alternatively, the weight and bias increments could be accumulated in variables, so that the weight and biases are updated after all the tuples in training set have been presented. This later strategy is called epoch updating, where one iteration through the training set is an epoch. In theory, the mathematical derivation of backward propagation employs epoch updating, yet in practice, case updating is more common because it trends to yield more accurate results.

Terminating Condition

Training stops when:

- All Δw_{ij} in the previous epoch are so small as to below some specified threshold, or
- The percentage of tuples misclassified in the previous epoch is below some threshold, or
- A prespecified number of epochs has expired.

In practice, several hundreds of thousands of epochs may be required before the wights will converge.

Sample calculations for learning by the backpropagation algorithm. Figure below shows a multilayer feed-forward neural network. Let the learning rate be 0.9. The initial weight and bias values of the network are given in Table 1, along with the first training tuple, X = (1, 0, 1), with a class label of 1. This example shows the calculations for backpropagation, given the first training tuple, X. The tuple is fed into the network, and the net input and output of each unit are computed. These values are shown in Table 2. The error of each unit is computed and propagated backward. The error values are shown in Table 3. The weight and bias updates are shown in Table 4.

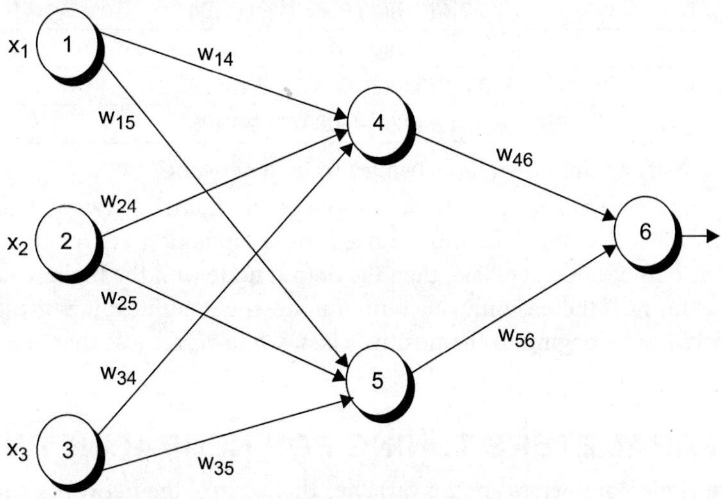

Example of a Multilevel Feedforward neural network.

Table 1. Initial input, weight, and bias values

x_1	x_2	x_3	w_{14}	w_{15}	w_{24}	w_{25}	w_{34}	w_{35}	w_{46}	w_{56}	θ_4	θ_5	θ_6
1	01	0.2	–0.3	0.4	0.1	–0.5	0.2	–0.3	–0.2	–0.4	0.2	0.1	

Table 2. Net input and output calculations

Unit, j	Net Input, I_j	Output, O_j
4	0.2 + 0 – 0.5 – 0.4 = –0.7	$1/(1 + e^{0.7}) = 0.332$
5	–0.3 + 0 + 0.2 + 0.2 = 0.1	$1/(1 + e^{-0.1}) = 0.525$
6	(–0.3)(0.332) – (0.2)(0.525) + 0.1 = –0.105	$1/(1 + e^{0.105}) = 0.474$

Table 3. Calculation of the error at each node

Unit, j	Err_j
4	(0.474)(1 – 0.474)(1 – 0.474) = 0.1311
5	(0.525)(1 – 0.525)(0.1311)(–0.2) = –0.0065
6	(0.332)(1 – 0.332)(0.1311)(–0.3) = –0.0087

Table 4. Calculations for weight and bias updating

Weight or Bias	New Value
w_{46}	–0.3 + (0.9)(0.1311)(0.332) = –0.261
w_{56}	–0.2 + (0.9)(0.1311)(0.525) = –0.138
w_{14}	0.2 + (0.9)(–0.0087)(1) = 0.192
w_{15}	–0.3 + (0.9)(–0.0065)(1) = –0.306
w_{24}	0.4 + (0.9)(–0.0087)(0) = 0.4
w_{25}	0.1 + (0.9)(–0.0065)(0) = 0.1
w_{34}	–0.5 + (0.9)(–0.0087)(1) = –0.508
w_{35}	0.2 + (0.9)(–0.0065)(1) = 0.194
θ_6	0.1 + (0.9)(0.1311) = 0.218
θ_5	0.2 + (0.9)(–0.0065) = 0.194
θ_4	–0.4 + (0.9)(–0.0087) = –0.408

"How can we classify an unknown tuple using a trained network?"

To classify an unknown tuple, X, the tuple is input to the trained network, and the net input and output of each unit are computed. (There is no need for computation and/or backpropagation of the error.) If there is one output node per class, then the output node with the highest value determines the predicted class label for X. If there is only one output node, then output values greater than or equal to 0.5 may be considered as belonging to the positive class, while values less than 0.5 may be considered negative.

2.4 HYPERPARAMETERS TUNING FOR NEURAL NETWORKS

Hyperparameters: Hyperparameters are the variables that control the network's structure (such as the number of hidden units) and its training (such as the learning rate).

Prior to training (and before weight and bias optimisation), hyperparameters are set.

Hyperparameters Related to Network Structure

Number of Hidden Layers and hidden units: Hidden layers are the layers between input layer and output layer.

"It is very easy. Simply keep adding layers until the test error stops getting better."

Layers in Neural Network also determine the result of the prediction model. A smaller number of layers is enough for a simpler problem, but a larger number of layers is needed to build a model for a more complicated problem. Inserting regularization layers in a neural network can help prevent overfitting.

Accuracy can be improved by using regularisation techniques on numerous hidden units within a layer. Underfitting may result from a smaller number of pieces.

Dropout: Dropout is a regularisation approach that reduces overfitting (increases validation accuracy), hence boosting generalizability.

- Use a dropout rate of 20%–50% of neurons on average, with 20% serving as a suitable starting point. A probability that is too low has little impact, and a probability that is too high prevents the network from learning enough.
- Utilise a wider network. Using dropout on a larger network will probably result in greater performance because it gives the model more chances to learn independent representations.

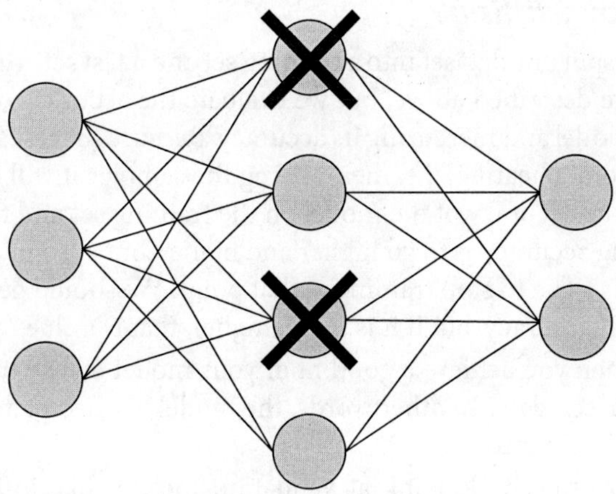

Dropout process

Network Weight Initialization: The activation function used on each layer should determine which weight initialization approach should be employed.

The distribution is mostly uniform.

Learning Rate: How rapidly a network updates its parameters depends on its learning rate.

Low learning rates cause the learning process to progress more slowly but smoothly. Though it might not converge, a higher learning rate accelerates learning.

A declining learning rate is typically desired.

Momentum: With the information of the past steps, momentum helps to choose the direction of the next step. It aids in stopping oscillations. The average range for momentum is 0.5 to 0.9.

Number of epochs: When training, the network is shown the entire training set a certain number of times, or epochs.

Increase the number of epochs until, due to overfitting, the validation accuracy begins to decline even while training accuracy increases.

Batch size: The number of sub samples provided to the network as part of the mini batch size is when parameter updating takes place.

32 could be a reasonable batch size default. Try 32, 64, 128, 256, and so on as well.

2.4.1 Overfitting

Overfitting describes the situation in which your model is over-optimized to accurately predict the training set, at the expense of generalizing to unknown data (which is the objective of learning in the first place). This can happen because the model greatly twists itself to perfectly conform to the training set, even capturing its underlying noise.

One way we can think of overfitting is that our algorithm is sort of "cheating." It is trying to convince you it has an artificially high score by orienting itself in such a way as to get minimal error on the known data. It would be as though you are trying to learn how fashion works but all you've seen is pictures of people at disco nightclubs in the 70s, so you assume all fashion everywhere consists of nothing but bell bottoms, denim jackets, and platform shoes. Perhaps you even have a close friend or family member whom this describes.

How can we avoid overfitting?

The simplest solution is to split our dataset into a training set and a test set. The training set is used for the optimization procedure we described above, but we evaluate the accuracy of our model by forwarding the test set to the trained model and measuring its accuracy. Because the test set is held out from training, this prevents the model from "cheating," i.e. memorizing the samples it will be quizzed on later. During training, we can monitor the accuracy of the model on the training set and test set. The longer we train, the more likely our training accuracy is to go higher and higher, but at some point, it is likely the test set will stop improving. This is a cue to stop training at that point. We should generally expect that training accuracy is higher than test accuracy, but if it is much higher, that is a clue that we have overfit.

Overfitting occurs when you achieve a good fit of your model on the training data, but it does not generalize well on new, unseen data. In other words, the model learned patterns specific to the training data, which are irrelevant in other data.

We can identify overfitting by looking at validation metrics like loss or accuracy. Usually, the validation metric stops improving after a certain number of epochs and begins to decrease afterward. The training metric continues to improve because the model seeks to find the best fit for the training data.

There are several manners in which we can reduce overfitting in deep learning models. The best option is to get more training data.

2.4.2 Underfitting

When a model has not learned the patterns in the training data well and is unable to generalize well on the new data, it is known as underfitting. An underfit model has poor performance on the training data and will result in unreliable predictions.

Underfitting causes an error rate not only to the training set, but also to unseen data. It most often occurs when there is insufficient data or the wrong type of data for the task at hand.

Techniques to Reduce Underfitting

- Increase model complexity.
- Increase the number of features, performing feature engineering.
- Remove noise from the data.
- Increase the number of epochs or increase the duration of training to get better results.

2.4.3 Cross Validation

Cross-validation is a technique in which we train our model using the subset of the data-set and then evaluate using the complementary subset of the data-set. The three steps involved in cross-validation are as follows:

- Reserve some portion of sample data-set.
- Using the rest data-set train the model.
- Test the model using the reserve portion of the data-set.

Methods of Cross Validation

Validation In this method, we perform training on the 50% of the given data-set and rest 50% is used for the testing purpose. The major drawback of this method is that we perform training on the 50% of the dataset, it may possible that the remaining 50% of the data contains some important information which we are leaving while training our model i.e., higher bias. LOOCV (Leave One Out Cross Validation) In this method, we perform training on the whole data-set but leaves only one data-point of the available data-set and then iterates for each data-point. It has some advantages as well as disadvantages also. An advantage of using this method is that we make use of all data points and hence it is low bias. The major drawback of this method is that it leads to higher variation in the testing model as we are testing against one data point. If the data point is an outlier it can lead to higher variation. Another drawback is it takes a lot of execution time as it iterates over 'the number of data points' times. K-Fold Cross Validation In this method, we split the data-set into k number of subsets (known as folds) then we perform training on the all the subsets but leave one(k-1) subset for the evaluation of the trained model. In this method, we iterate k times with a different subset reserved for testing purpose each time.

- It is always suggested that the value of k should be 10 as the lower value of k is takes towards validation and higher value of k leads to LOOCV method.

Advantages of Cross Validation

Overcoming Overfitting: Cross validation helps to prevent overfitting by providing a more robust estimate of the model's performance on unseen data.

Model Selection: Cross validation can be used to compare different models and select the one that performs the best on average.

Hyperparameter tuning: Cross validation can be used to optimize the hyperparameters of a model, such as the regularization parameter, by selecting the values that result in the best performance on the validation set.

Data Efficient: Cross validation allows the use of all the available data for both training and validation, making it a more data-efficient method compared to traditional validation techniques.

Disadvantages of Cross Validation:

Computationally Expensive: Cross validation can be computationally expensive, especially when the number of folds is large or when the model is complex and requires a long time to train.

Time-Consuming: Cross validation can be time-consuming, especially when there are many hyperparameters to tune or when multiple models need to be compared.

Bias-Variance Tradeoff: The choice of the number of folds in cross validation can impact the bias-variance tradeoff, i.e., too few folds may result in high variance, while too many folds may result in high bias.

2.4.4 Methods to find out Hyperparameters

- **Manual Search:** The developer should try out various combinations of hyperparameters for the model and choose the one that performs the best; there is no need for a special library for manual hyperparameter tuning. To find the model that performs the best, one can train models for all possible combinations of hyperparameter values. Another manual search method for hyperparameter optimisation is iteratively looping through several hyperparameter settings and analysing each combination.Manual Search is a bit tedious process and hence requires unnecessary manpower.
- **Grid Search:** An automated version of manual search hyperparameter optimisation is what Grid Search is. Although Grid Search requires several lines of code to implement, it is computationally inefficient due to the length of time required to optimise it. The GridSearchCV function accepts the training model and set of hyperparameters in dictionary format and returns the performing model and its scoring metric.
- **Random Search:** Grid Search tests all possible combinations of hyperparameters, which makes the computation more time-consuming. Randomised search trains a model using random combinations of hyperparameters. In comparison to grid search, less combinations are used overall to train the various models in randomised search.
- **Bayesian Optimization:** In order to quickly find optimised parameter values, Bayes Grid Search models the search space using the Bayesian optimisation technique. To reduce search time, it makes use of the structure of the search space. The Bayes Search technique samples new candidates based on their likelihood to produce superior outcomes from previous evaluation findings.

2.5 TRAINING NEURAL NETWORK IN PYTHON USING KERAS

Keras is a powerful and easy-to-use free open-source Python library for developing and evaluating deep learning models.

It is part of the TensorFlow library and allows you to define and train neural network models in just a few lines of code.

Now, we will understand how to create your first deep learning neural network model in Python using Keras.

The main steps include:

1. Load Data
2. Define Keras Model
3. Compile Keras Model
4. Fit Keras Model
5. Evaluate Keras Model
6. Tie It All Together
7. Make Predictions

To start code, you will need to have:

1. Python 2 or 3 installed and configured.
2. SciPy (including NumPy) installed and configured.
3. Keras and a backend (Theano or TensorFlow) installed and configured.

1. **Load Data**

   The first step is to define the functions and classes you intend to use in this tutorial.

   You will use the NumPy library to load your dataset and two classes from the Keras library to define your model.

   The imports required are listed below.

```
# first neural network with kerbs keras tutorial
from numpy import loadtxt
from tensorflow.keras.models import Sequential
from tensorflow.keras.layers import Dense
...
```

   You can now load your dataset.

2. **Define Keras Model**

   Models in Keras are defined as a sequence of layers.

   We create a Sequential model and add layers one at a time until we are happy with our network architecture.

   The first thing to get right is to ensure the input layer has the correct number of input features. This can be specified when creating the first layer with the input_shape argument and setting it to (8,) for presenting the eight input variables as a vector.

   How do we know the number of layers and their types?

   This is a tricky question. There are heuristics that you can use, and often the best network structure is found through a process of trial-and-error experimentation. Generally, you need a network large enough to capture the structure of the problem.

   In this example, let us use a fully-connected network structure with three layers.

   Fully connected layers are defined using the Dense class. You can specify the number of neurons or nodes in the layer as the first argument and the activation function using the activation argument.

   Also, you will use the rectified linear unit activation function referred to as ReLU on the first two layers and the Sigmoid function in the output layer.

   It used to be the case that Sigmoid and Tanh activation functions were preferred for all layers. These days, better performance is achieved using the ReLU activation function. Using a sigmoid on the output layer ensures your network output is between 0 and 1 and is easy to map to either a probability of class 1 or snap to a hard classification of either class with a default threshold of 0.5.

   You can piece it all together by adding each layer:

   The model expects rows of data with 8 variables (the input_shape=(8,) argument).

   The first hidden layer has 12 nodes and uses the relu activation function.

   The second hidden layer has 8 nodes and uses the relu activation function.

   The output layer has one node and uses the sigmoid activation function.

```
# define the keras model
model = Sequential ()
model.add(Dense(12, input_shape=(8,), activation='relu'))
model.add(Dense(8, activation='relu'))
model.add(Dense(1, activation='sigmoid'))
...
```

3. **Compile Keras Model**

Now that the model is defined, you can compile it.

Compiling the model uses the efficient numerical libraries under the covers (the so-called backend) such as Theano or TensorFlow. The backend automatically chooses the best way to represent the network for training and making predictions to run on your hardware, such as CPU, GPU, or even distributed.

When compiling, you must specify some additional properties required when training the network. Remember training a network means finding the best set of weights to map inputs to outputs in your dataset.

You must specify the loss function to use to evaluate a set of weights, the optimizer used to search through different weights for the network, and any optional metrics you want to collect and report during training.

In this case, use cross entropy as the loss argument. This loss is for a binary classification problem and is defined in Keras as "binary_crossentropy".

We will define the optimizer as the efficient stochastic gradient descent algorithm "adam ". This is a popular version of gradient descent because it automatically tunes itself and gives good results in a wide range of problems.

Finally, because it is a classification problem, you will collect and report the classification accuracy defined via the metrics argument.

```
# compile the keras model
model.compile(loss='binary_crossentropy', optimizer='adam', metrics=['accuracy'])
...
```

4. **Fit Keras Model**

You have defined your model and compiled it to get ready for efficient computation.

Now it is time to execute the model on some data.

You can train or fit your model on your loaded data by calling the fit() function on the model.

Training occurs over epochs, and each epoch is split into batches.

Epoch: One pass through all the rows in the training dataset

Batch: One or more samples considered by the model within an epoch before weights are updated

One epoch comprises one or more batches, based on the chosen batch size, and the model is fit for many epochs. For more on the difference between epochs and batches, see the post:

What is the Difference Between a Batch and an Epoch in a Neural Network?

The training process will run for a fixed number of epochs (iterations) through the dataset that you must specify using the epochs argument. You must also set the number of dataset rows that are considered before the model weights are updated within each epoch, called the batch size, and set using the batch_size argument.

This problem will run for a small number of epochs (150) and use a relatively small batch size of 10. These configurations can be chosen experimentally by trial and error. You want to train the model enough so that it learns a good (or good enough) mapping of rows of input data to the output classification. The model will always have some error, but the amount of error will level out after some point for a given model configuration. This is called model convergence.

```
...
# fit the keras model on the document
model.fit(X, y, epochs=150, batch_size=10)
...
```

This is where the work happens on your CPU or GPU.

5. **Evaluate Keras Model**

   You have trained our neural network on the entire dataset, and you can evaluate the performance of the network on the same dataset.

   This will only give you an idea of how well you have modelled the dataset (e.g., train accuracy), but no idea of how well the algorithm might perform on new data. This was done for simplicity, but ideally, you could separate your data into train and test datasets for training and evaluation of your model.

   You can evaluate your model on your training dataset using the **evaluate()** function and pass it the same input and output used to train the model.

   This will generate a prediction for each input and output pair and collect scores, including the average loss and any metrics you have configured, such as accuracy.

   The **evaluate()** function will return a list with two values. The first will be the loss of the model on the dataset, and the second will be the accuracy of the model on the dataset. You are only interested in reporting the accuracy so ignore the loss value.

```
...
# evaluate the keras model
_, accuracy = model.evaluate(X, y)
print(‘Accuracy: %.2f’ % (accuracy*100))
```

6. **Tie It All Together**

   You have just seen how you can easily create your first neural network model in Keras.

   Let us tie it all together into a complete code example.

```
from numpy import loadtxt
from tensorflow.keras.models import Sequential
from tensorflow.keras.layers import Dense
# load the dataset
dataset = loadtxt(‘pima-indians-diabetes.csv’, delimiter=‘,’)
# split into input (X) and output (y) variables
X = dataset[:,0:8]
y = dataset[:,8]
# define the keras model
model = Sequential()
model.add(Dense(12, input_shape=(8,), activation=‘relu’))
model.add(Dense(8, activation=‘relu’))
model.add(Dense(1, activation=‘sigmoid’))
# compile the keras model
```

```
model.compile(loss='binary_crossentropy', optimizer='adam', metrics=['accuracy'])
# fit the keras model on the dataset
model.fit(X, y, epochs=150, batch_size=10)
# evaluate the keras model
_, accuracy = model.evaluate(X, y)
print('Accuracy: %.2f' % (accuracy*100))
```

You can copy all the code into your Python file and save it as "**keras_first_network.py**" in the same directory as your data file "**pima-indians-diabetes.csv**". You can then run the Python file as a script from your command line (command prompt) as follows:

```
python keras_first_network.py
```

Running this example, you should see a message for each of the 150 epochs, printing the loss and accuracy, followed by the final evaluation of the trained model on the training dataset.

It takes about 10 seconds to execute on my workstation running on the CPU.

Ideally, you would like the loss to go to zero and the accuracy to go to 1.0 (e.g., 100%). This is not possible for any but the most trivial machine learning problems. Instead, you will always have some error in your model. The goal is to choose a model configuration and training configuration that achieve the lowest loss and highest accuracy possible for a given dataset.

```
768/768 [==============================] - 0s 63us/step – loss: 0.4817 – acc: 0.7708
Epoch 147/150
768/768 [==============================] - 0s 63us/step – loss: 0.4764 – acc: 0.7747
Epoch 148/150
768/768 [==============================] - 0s 63us/step – loss: 0.4737 – acc: 0.7682
Epoch 149/150
768/768 [==============================] - 0s 64us/step – loss: 0.4730 – acc: 0.7747
Epoch 150/150
768/768 [==============================] - 0s 63us/step – loss: 0.4754 – acc: 0.7799
768/768 [==============================] - 0s 38us/step
Accuracy: 76.56
```

Note: If you try running this example in an IPython or Jupyter notebook, you may get an error. The reason is the output progress bars during training. You can easily turn these off by setting **verbose=0** in the call to the **fit()** and **evaluate()** functions; for example:

```
# fit the keras model on the dataset without progress bars
model.fit(X, y, epochs=150, batch_size=10, verbose=0)
# evaluate the keras model
_, accuracy = model.evaluate(X, y, verbose=0)
...
```

Note: Your results may vary given the stochastic nature of the algorithm or evaluation procedure, or differences in numerical precision. Consider running the example a few times and compare the average outcome.

Review Questions

Solved Examples

Q.1. What do you mean by cost function?

Ans. While building deep learning models, our whole objective is to minimize the cost function.

A cost function explains how well the neural network is performing for its given training data and the expected output.

It may depend on the neural network parameters such as weights and biases. It provides the performance of a neural network.

Q.2. What do you mean by backpropagation?

Ans. The backpropagation algorithm is used to train multilayer perceptrons. It propagates the error information from the end of the network to all the weights inside the network. It allows the efficient computation of the gradient or derivatives.

Backpropagation can be divided into the following steps:

- It can forward the propagation of training data through the network to generate output.
- It uses target value and output value to compute error derivatives by concerning the output activations.
- It can backpropagate to calculate the derivatives of the error concerning output activations in the previous layer and continue for all the hidden layers.
- It uses the previously computed derivatives for output and all hidden layers to calculate the error derivative concerning weights.
- It updates the weights and repeats until the cost function is minimized.

Q.3. How to initialize weights and biases in neural networks?

Ans. Neural network initialization means initialized the values of the parameters i.e, weights, and biases. Biases can be initialized to zero but we cannot initialize weights with zero.

Weight initialization is one of the crucial factors in neural networks since bad weight initialization can prevent a neural network from learning the patterns.

On the contrary, a good weight initialization helps in giving a quicker convergence to the global minimum. As a rule of thumb, the rule for initializing the weights is to be close to zero without being too small.

Q.4. Why is zero initialization of weight, not a good initialization technique?

Ans. If we initialize the set of weights in the neural network as zero, then all the neurons at each layer will start producing the same output and the same gradients during backpropagation.

As a result, the neural network cannot learn anything at all because there is no source of asymmetry between different neurons. Therefore, we add randomness while initializing the weight in neural networks.

Q.5. Explain gradient descent and its types.

Ans. Gradient Descent is an optimization algorithm that aims to minimize the cost function or to minimize an error. Its main objective is to find the local or global minima of a function based on its convexity. This determines in which direction the model should go to reduce the error.

There are three types of gradient descent:

- Mini-Batch Gradient Descent
- Stochastic Gradient Descent
- Batch Gradient Descent

Q.6. Explain the different steps used in gradient descent algorithm.

Ans. The five main steps that are used to initialize and use the gradient descent algorithm are as follows:

- Initialize biases and weights for the neural network.
- Pass the input data through the network i.e, the input layer.
- Compute the difference or the error between the expected and the predicted values.
- Adjust the values i.e, weight updation in neurons to minimize the loss function.
- We repeat the same steps i.e, multiple iterations to determine the best weights for efficient working.

Unsolved Questions

1. How is one shot learning still not attainable for Artificial Neural Networks?
2. How to choose the features of neural networks?
3. What is the use of the Loss functions?
4. Why is zero initialization of weight, not a good initialization technique?
5. What do you mean by Optimizers?

Multiple Choice Questions

Q.1. What is the purpose of the backpropagation algorithm in ANN training?

(*a*) To update the weights and biases based on the prediction error
(*b*) To initialize the weights and biases of the network
(*c*) To determine the number of hidden layers and neurons
(*d*) None of the above

Q.2. Which of the following is a common loss function used in ANNs for binary classification?

(*a*) Mean Absolute Error (MAE) (*b*) Mean Squared Error (MSE)
(*c*) Binary Cross-Entropy (*d*) Categorical Cross-Entropy

Q.3. What is the purpose of regularization in ANN training?

(*a*) To prevent overfitting by adding a penalty term to the loss function
(*b*) To increase the model's capacity for learning complex patterns
(*c*) To speed up the training process by adjusting the learning rate
(*d*) None of the above.

Q.4. Which activation function is commonly used in the output layer for binary classification in ANNs?

(*a*) Sigmoid (*b*) ReLU (Rectified Linear Unit)
(*c*) Tanh (Hyperbolic Tangent) (*d*) Softmax

Q.5. Which of the following techniques can be used to prevent overfitting in ANN training?

(*a*) Dropout regularization (*b*) L1 and L2 regularization
(*c*) Early stopping (*d*) All of the above

Answer Key

1. (*a*) 2. (*c*) 3. (*a*) 4. (*a*) 5. (*d*)

Fill in the Blanks

1. In Adaline model _______ relation exists between output & activation value.
2. The activation function decides whether a neuron should be activated or not by calculating the _______ and further adding bias to it.
3. The father of machine learning is _______.
4. The most significant phase in genetic algorithm is _______.
5. Full form of PAC is _______.

Answer Key

1. Linear 2. Weighted sum 3. Geoffrey Everest Hinton.
4. Crossover 5. Probably Approximate Correct.

❑❑❑

3 Convolution Neural Network, Image Classification and CNN

3.1 INTRODUCTION TO CONVOLUTION NEURAL NETWORK

A convolutional neural network (CNN or ConvNet) is a network architecture for deep learning that learns directly from data. CNNs are particularly useful for finding patterns in images to recognize objects, classes, and categories. They can also be quite effective for classifying audio, time-series, and signal data. Image classification is one of the most important areas where CNN model has proved to be exceptionally good in terms of accuracy. Image classification refers to the abstraction of tagged pixels from the image to a separate class as a result of many methodologies being developed and compared in recent years.

For the computer to recognise the images, it must first receive training. The computer system needs to be further trained for diverse images. A technique for recognising the images called as DNN (Deep Neural Network) was introduced in the late 1950s. It is the more sophisticated nature of this method in computer vision. AI's (Artifical Intelligence) area of computer vision aims to give machines the ability to recognise images just like people can. The low-level features in the photos cannot be recognised using this method.

There are numerous sophisticated image classification methods that combine supervised and unsupervised learning. Fuzzy decision trees relates to unsupervised learning, while Artificial Neural Networks (ANN) and Support Vector Machines (SVM) are deployed in supervised learning.

Convolutional layers, which apply a series of filters to the input image, are the foundation of CNNs. By executing element-wise multiplications and aggregating the results into feature maps, these filters extract regional patterns or characteristics from the image. Usually, several filters are applied simultaneously, producing several feature maps that each represent a particular learnt feature. This convolutional technique gathers spatial information at various scales, including edges, textures, and forms.

To extract more sophisticated and abstract characteristics, several convolutional and pooling layers are stacked on top of one another. On top of the low-level features discovered in earlier levels, deeper layers capture high-level features. The network can learn increasingly complex representations because the number of filters often grows with network depth.

In many different domains, image classification using CNNs has shown impressive results, sometimes outperforming human skill. For a variety of applications, including object recognition, scene understanding, medical picture analysis, and others, CNNs have been employed. CNN image classification continues to push the limits of computer vision applications thanks to improvements in CNN designs, training methods, and the availability of large-scale labelled datasets.

3.2 CNN (CONVOLUTION NEURAL NETWORK)

Convolution Neural Network (CNN) was developed in 1990 in order to enable computers to recognize images. Using CNN, the features of an image are extracted. CNN (Convolution Neural Network) is a multilayer neural network that uses a unique form of mechanical approach to operate. The CNN (Convolution Neural Network) deep learning idea was used to extract new features from hyper spectral images (HSI). As the computer classifies the images with the aid of pixel recognition and must record their size and kind, it then performs numerous calculations using pixels to abstract the information of the images. Image analysis for remote sensing is frequently highlighted using the deep learning approach. The typical strategy for a CNN (Convolutional Neural Network) is to directly learn object attributes from a batch of hyperspectral data.

3.3 COMPONENTS OF CNN

A CNN is made up of numerous blocks of convolutional layers, sampling layers, output layers, and layers that are fully connected.

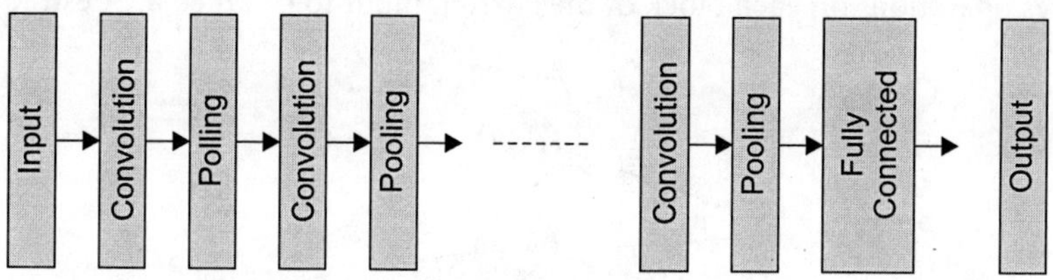

Fig. 1. Building block of a typical CNN

A. **Convolutional Layer:** The major component of a CNN is the convolutional layer, which takes a small portion of a huge image as a sample, compares it to a similar pattern in another area, and then passes that portion through all the points in the large image. We think of them as a location that we are travelling through. The kernel is configured using the back propagation technique when small portions of an image are passed over a larger picture.

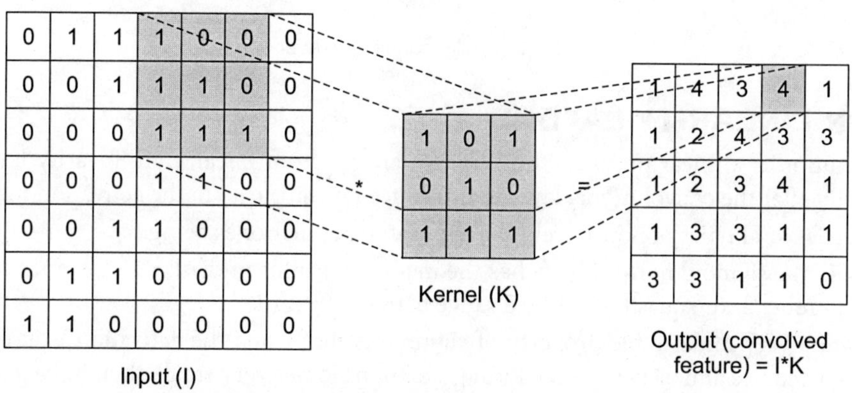

Fig. 2. Convolutional layer

B. **A Pooling Layer:** To pool an image is to sample it. It receives input from the more focused region of the convolutional output and generates an output. There are numerous different pooling methods, including mean, maximum, and average pooling. Nowadays, we employ the max pooling strategy, which takes the value of the pixel with the highest value and reduces the number of regions that need to be compared but results in areas that are diverse in size and shape.

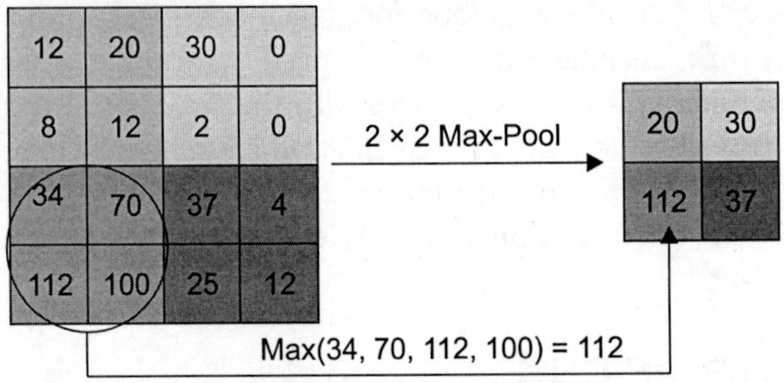

Fig. 3. Max pooling operation

C. **Fully Connected Layer:** A fully connected layer receives input from the preceding layer's output and executes operations on each block of the current input to produce the desired output.

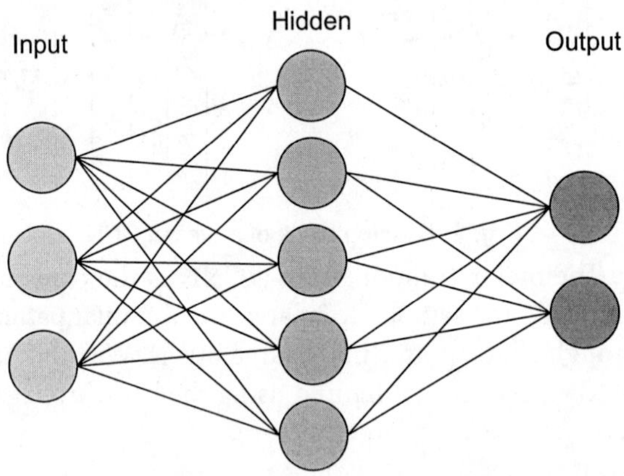

Fig. 4. Fully-connected layer

3.4 NON-LINEARITY LAYERS

Since convolution is a linear operation and images are far from linear, non-linearity layers are often placed directly after the convolutional layer to introduce non-linearity to the activation map.

There are several types of non-linear operations, the popular ones being:

1. **Sigmoid:** The sigmoid non-linearity has the mathematical form $\sigma(\kappa) = 1/(1 + e^{-\kappa})$. It takes a real-valued number and "squashes" it into a range between 0 and 1.

   However, a very undesirable property of sigmoid is that when the activation is at either tail, the gradient becomes almost zero. If the local gradient becomes very small, then in backpropagation it will effectively "kill" the gradient. Also, if the data coming into the neuron is always positive, then the output of sigmoid will be either all positives or all negatives, resulting in a zig-zag dynamic of gradient updates for weight.

2. **Tanh:** Tanh squashes a real-valued number to the range [−1, 1]. Like sigmoid, the activation saturates, but — unlike the sigmoid neurons — its output is zero centered.

3. **ReLU:** The Rectified Linear Unit (ReLU) has become very popular in the last few years. It computes the function $f(\kappa)=\max(0, \kappa)$. In other words, the activation is simply threshold at zero.

   In comparison to sigmoid and tanh, ReLU is more reliable and accelerates the convergence by six times.

   Unfortunately, a con is that ReLU can be fragile during training. A large gradient flowing through it can update it in such a way that the neuron will never get further updated. However, we can work with this by setting a proper learning rate.

3.5 MOTIVATION BEHIND CONVOLUTION

Convolution leverages three important ideas that motivated computer vision researchers: sparse interaction, parameter sharing, and equivariant representation. Let us describe each one of them in detail.

Trivial neural network layers use matrix multiplication by a matrix of parameters describing the interaction between the input and output unit. This means that every output unit interacts with every input unit. However, convolution neural networks have sparse interaction. This is achieved by making kernel smaller than the input e.g., an image can have millions or thousands of pixels, but while processing it using kernel, we can detect meaningful information that is of tens or hundreds of pixels. This means that we need to store fewer parameters that not only reduces the memory requirement of the model but also improves the statistical efficiency of the model.

If computing one feature at a spatial point (x1, y1) is useful then it should also be useful at some other spatial point say (x2, y2). It means that for a single two-dimensional slice i.e., for creating one activation map, neurons are constrained to use the same set of weights. In a traditional neural network, each element of the weight matrix is used once and then never revisited, while convolution network has shared parameters i.e., for getting output, weights applied to one input are the same as the weight applied elsewhere.

Due to parameter sharing, the layers of convolution neural network will have a property of equivariance to translation. It says that if we changed the input in a way, the output will also get changed in the same way.

Why ConvNets over Feed-Forward Neural Nets?

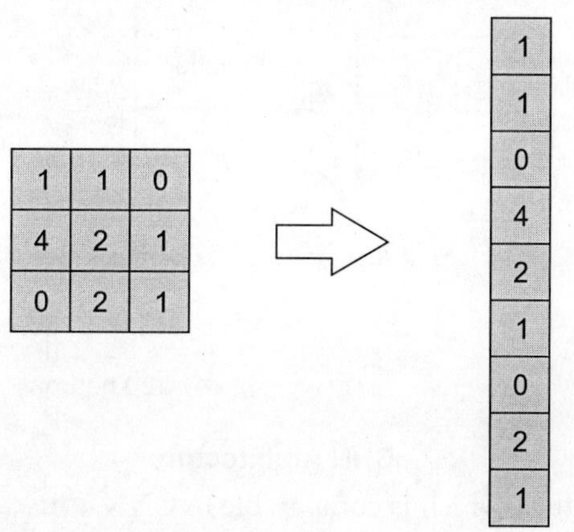

Fig 5. Flattening of a 3 × 3 image matrix into a 9 × 1 vector

An image is nothing but a matrix of pixel values, right? So why not just flatten the image (e.g., 3 × 3 image matrix into a 9 × 1 vector) and feed it to a Multi-Level Perceptron for classification purposes?

In cases of extremely basic binary images, the method might show an average precision score while performing prediction of classes but would have little to no accuracy when it comes to complex images having pixel dependencies throughout.

A ConvNet can successfully capture the Spatial and Temporal dependencies in an image through the application of relevant filters. The architecture performs a better fitting to the image dataset due to the reduction in the number of parameters involved and the reusability of weights. In other words, the network can be trained to understand the sophistication of the image better.

3.6 WORKING OF CNN

A popular class of deep learning models called convolutional neural networks (CNNs) is used to handle images and videos for tasks including object recognition, segmentation, and classification. CNNs are extremely successful for jobs involving grid-like structures, such as photographs, because they are specifically created to capture spatial and local dependencies in data. In this discussion, we'll examine how CNN layers function and how that affects the network's overall performance. The procedures below are used to classify the images using CNN after the SVM has been implemented successfully. The CNN architecture that was employed is shown below.

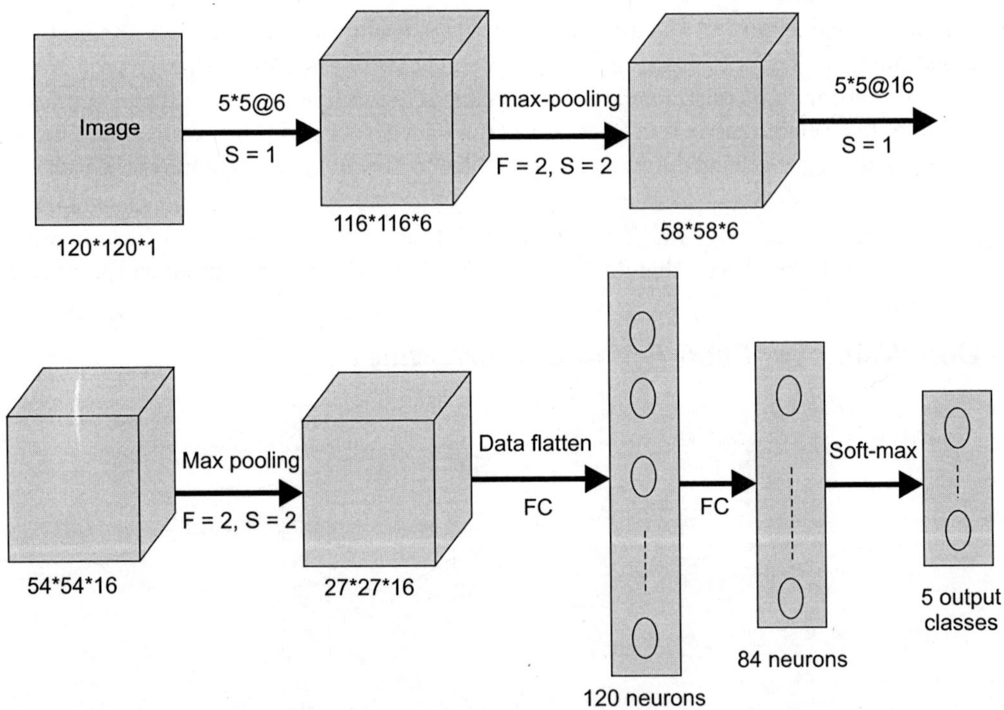

CNN Architecture

- The LeNet5 architecture, which is comparable to CNN, is used in this methodology.
- First, a filter is used to change the image's size and shape from 120 × 120 × 1 to 116 × 116 × 6.

- The output from the first stage is further reduced to 58 × 58 × 6 using a maximum pooling technique with two operations.
- The output of the maximum pooling is lowered to 27 × 27 × 16 using filters.
- After using the soft-max, the final result is divided into 5 classes of images.

After applying two operations, the result is flattened until we have a layer of 84 neurons that is fully connected.

Input Layer: The raw input data for a CNN, which is typically an image represented as a grid of pixels, is received by the input layer. The three colour channels (Red, Green, and Blue) that make up each pixel often create a 3D tensor with dimensions (height, width, and channels).

Convolution Layer: The fundamental component of CNNs is the convolutional layer. The input image is processed by a group of teachable filters, commonly referred to as kernels or feature detectors. Each filter is a tiny matrix that slides across the input image's spatial dimensions to scan it. The matrix then multiplies each element separately and aggregates the results into a feature map.

From the input image, the convolution technique extracts regional patterns or features. It is efficient at capturing spatial details at various scales, including edges, corners, and textures. It is possible to use numerous filters at once to create various feature maps that reflect various learnt features.

Activation Function: An activation function is used element-wise after the convolution procedure to add non-linearities to the network. The Rectified Linear Unit (ReLU), which sets negative values to zero while maintaining positive values, is the most often used activation function in CNNs. ReLU increases convergence during training and improves the network's capacity for learning intricate patterns.

Pooling Layer: By combining layers, it is possible to keep key features while reducing the width and height of the feature maps. The most popular pooling method is called MaxPooling, which downsamples the feature map by breaking each region of the feature map into smaller regions and choosing the maximum value inside each zone. The use of pools increases computational effectiveness, lowers overfitting, and offers a semblance of translation invariance.

Addition convolution and pooling Layers: To extract more complex and abstract features, multiple convolutional and pooling layers are stacked together in a CNN. Deeper layers capture high-level features built upon the low-level features detected in earlier layers. The number of filters typically increases with the depth of the network, allowing it to learn more sophisticated representations.

Fully Connected Layer: After several convolutional and pooling layers, the feature maps are usually flattened into a 1D vector. This vector is then connected to a fully connected layer (similar to those found in traditional artificial neural networks). The fully connected layer acts as a classifier, mapping the learned features to specific classes or labels through a series of weighted connections and applying an activation function, often softmax, to produce class probabilities.

Output Layer: The final prediction made by the CNN is provided by the output layer. The number of classes in the classification job is matched by the number of neurons in this layer. The chance that an input belongs to a particular class is represented by each neuron. The anticipated class label is chosen based on the highest probability.

3.7 BACKPROPOGATION AND TRAINING

The CNN learns to minimise a loss function that measures the difference between the predicted and real labels during the training phase in order to optimise the weights of its filters. This is accomplished by backpropagation, in which optimisation methods like stochastic gradient descent (SGD) are employed to calculate the gradient of the loss function and use it to update the filter weights.

Example showing the working of CNN.

Input Image

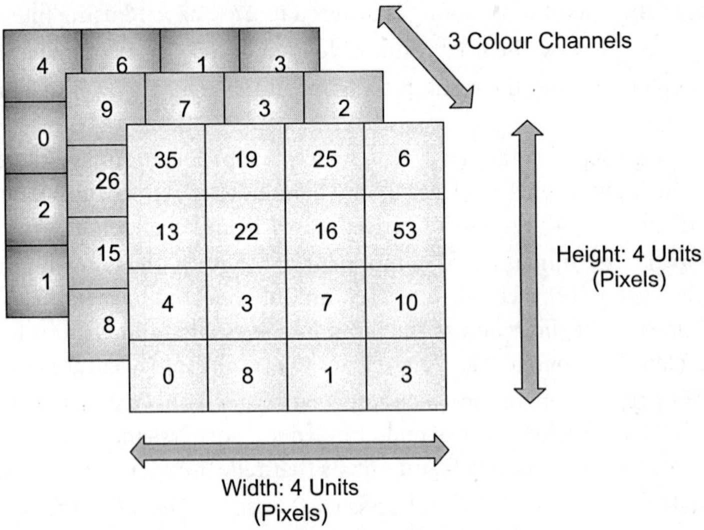

Fig. 6. 4 × 4 × 3 RGB Image

In the figure, we have an RGB image that has been separated by its three-color planes — Red, Green, and Blue. There are several such color spaces in which images exist — Grayscale, RGB, HSV, CMYK, etc.

You can imagine how computationally intensive things would get once the images reach dimensions, say 8K (7680×4320). The role of ConvNet is to reduce the images into a form that is easier to process, without losing features that are critical for getting a good prediction. This is important when we are to design an architecture that is not only good at learning features but also scalable to massive datasets.

Convolution Layer — The Kernel

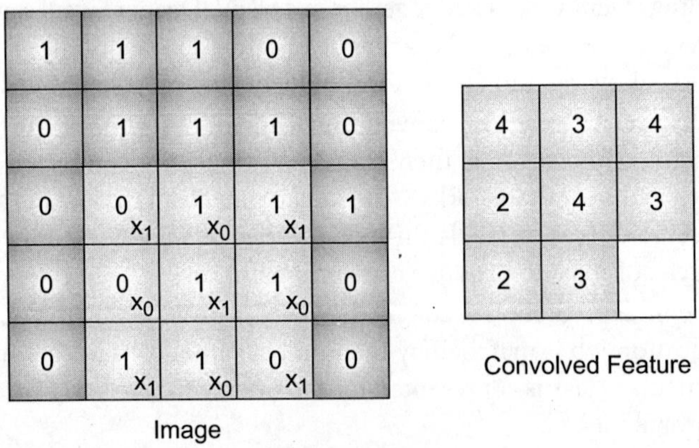

Fig. 7. Convoluting a 5 × 5 × 1 image with a 3 × 3 × 1 kernel to get a 3 × 3 × 1 convolved feature

Image Dimensions = 5 (Height) × 5 (Breadth) × 1 (Number of channels, e.g., RGB)

In the above demonstration, the green section resembles our 5 × 5 × 1 input image, I. The element involved in the convolution operation in the first part of a Convolutional Layer is called the Kernel/Filter, K, represented in color yellow. We have selected K as a 3 × 3 × 1 matrix.

$$\text{Kernel/Filter, } K = \begin{matrix} 1 & 0 & 1 \\ 0 & 1 & 0 \\ 1 & 0 & 1 \end{matrix}$$

The Kernel shifts 9 times because of Stride Length = 1 (Non-Strided), every time performing an elementwise multiplication operation (Hadamard Product) between K and the portion P of the image over which the kernel is hovering.

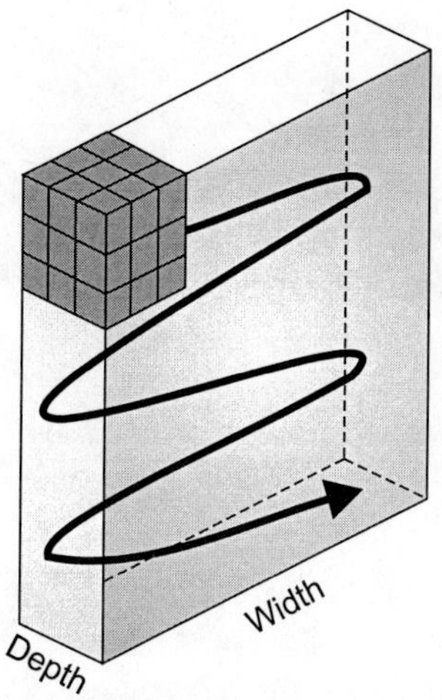

Fig. 9. Movement of the Kernel

The filter moves to the right with a certain Stride Value till it parses the complete width. Moving on, it hops down to the beginning (left) of the image with the same Stride Value and repeats the process until the entire image is traversed.

0	0	0	0	0	0	–
0	156	155	156	158	158	–
0	153	154	157	159	159	–
0	149	151	155	158	159	–
0	146	146	149	153	158	–
0	145	143	143	148	158	–
–	–	–	–	–	–	–

Input Channel #1(Red)

0	0	0	0	0	0	–
0	167	166	167	169	169	–
0	164	165	168	170	170	–
0	160	162	166	169	170	–
0	156	156	159	163	168	–
0	155	153	153	158	168	–
–	–	–	–	–	–	–

Input Channel #2(Green)

0	0	0	0	0	0	–
0	163	162	163	165	165	–
0	160	161	164	166	166	–
0	156	158	162	165	166	–
0	155	155	155	162	167	–
0	154	152	152	157	167	–
–	–	–	–	–	–	–

Input Channel #3(Blue)

–1	–1	1
0	1	–1
0	1	1

Kernel Channel #1

1	0	0
1	–1	–1
1	0	–1

Kernel Channel #2

0	1	1
0	1	0
1	–1	1

Kernel Channel #3

158 + –14 + 653 + 1 = 798

Bias = 1

Output

–25	466	466	475	–
295	787	798		–
				–
				–
–	–	–	–	–

Fig. 10. Convolution operation on a MxNx3 image matrix with a 3 × 3 × 3 Kernel

In the case of images with multiple channels (e.g., RGB), the Kernel has the same depth as that of the input image. Matrix Multiplication is performed between Kn and In stack ([K1, I1]; [K2, I2]; [K3, I3]) and all the results are summed with the bias to give us a squashed one-depth channel Convoluted Feature Output.

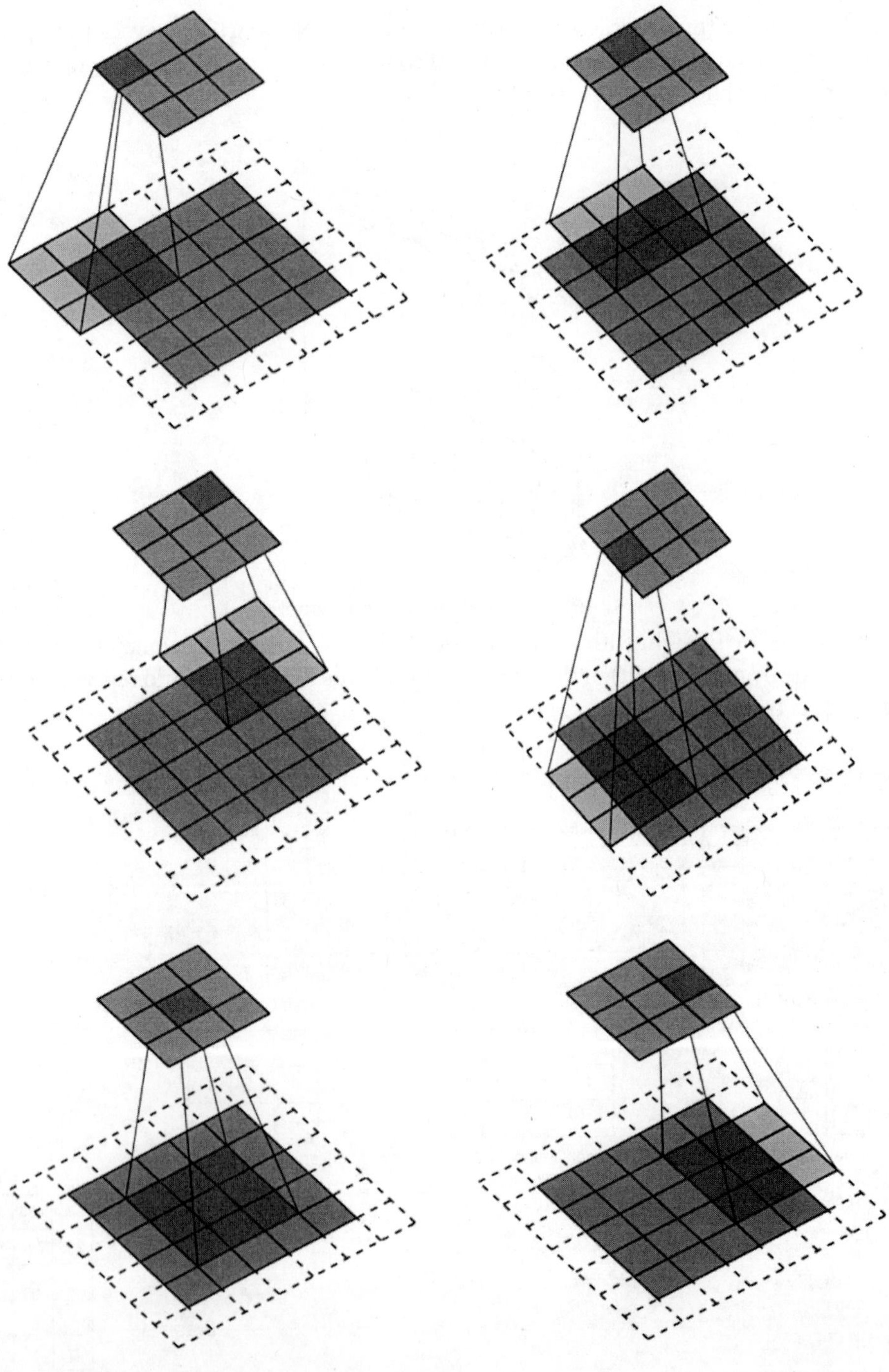

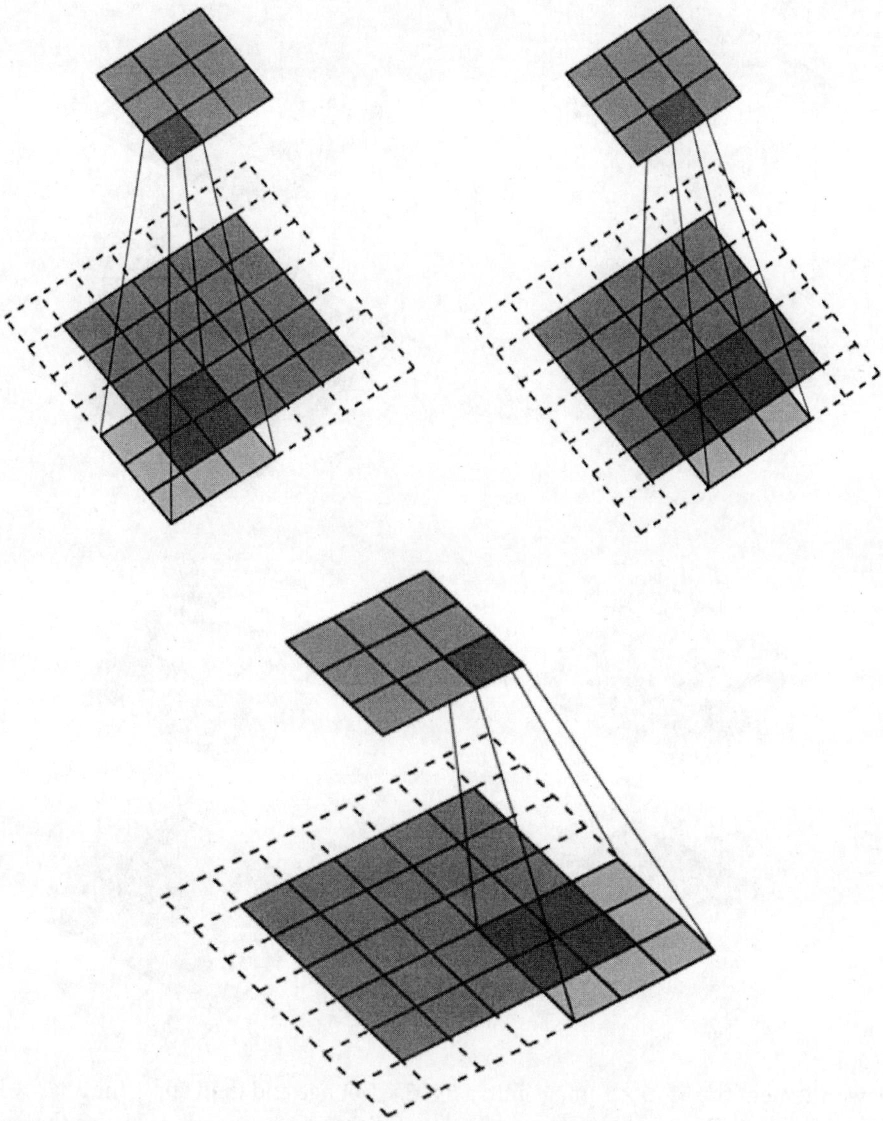

Fig 11. Convolution Operation with Stride Length = 2

The objective of the Convolution Operation is to extract the high-level features such as edges, from the input image. ConvNets need not be limited to only one Convolutional Layer. Conventionally, the first ConvLayer is responsible for capturing the Low-Level features such as edges, color, gradient orientation, etc. With added layers, the architecture adapts to the High-Level features as well, giving us a network that has a wholesome understanding of images in the dataset, similar to how we would.

There are two types of results to the operation — one in which the convolved feature is reduced in dimensionality as compared to the input, and the other in which the dimensionality is either increased or remains the same. This is done by applying Valid Padding in the case of the former, or Same Padding in the case of the latter.

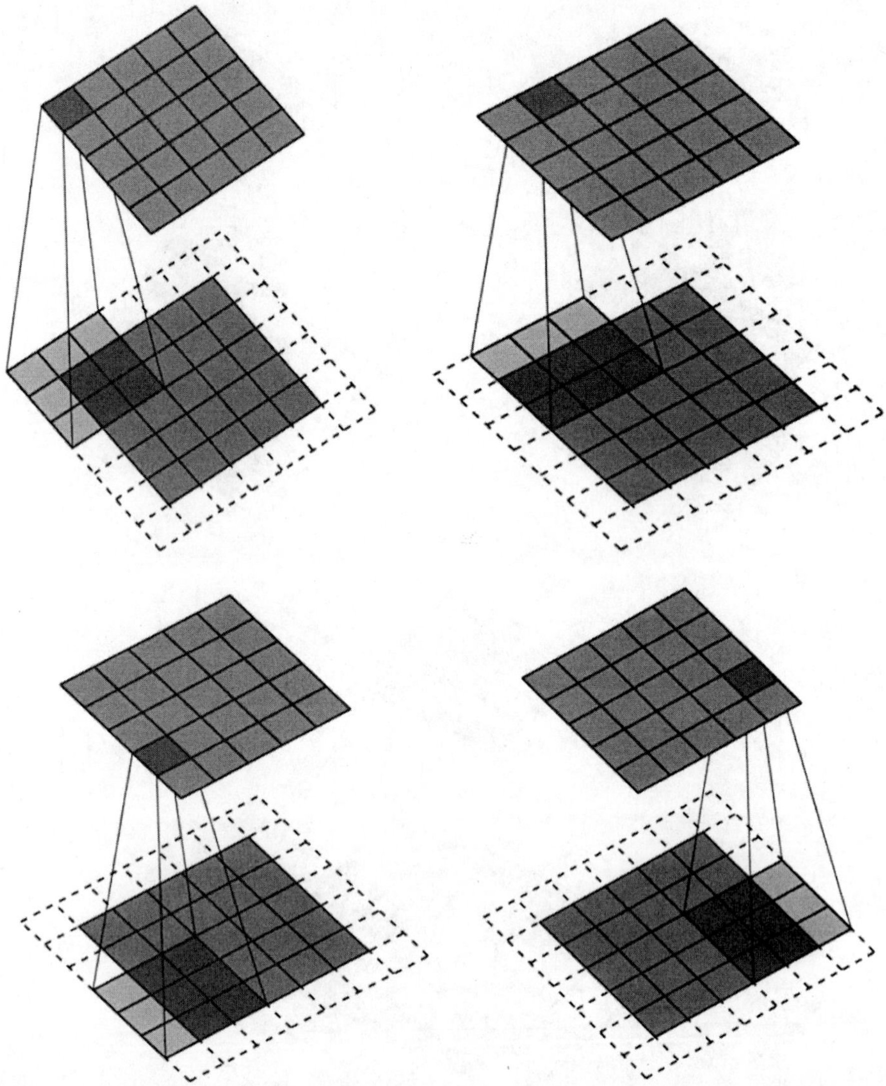

When we augment the 5 × 5 × 1 image into a 6 × 6 × 1 image and then apply the 3 × 3 × 1 kernel over it, we find that the convolved matrix turns out to be of dimensions 5 × 5 × 1. Hence the name — Same Padding.

On the other hand, if we perform the same operation without padding, we are presented with a matrix that has dimensions of the Kernel (3 × 3 × 1) itself — Valid Padding.

The following repository houses many such GIFs which would help you get a better understanding of how Padding and Stride Length work together to achieve results relevant to our needs.

Pooling Layer

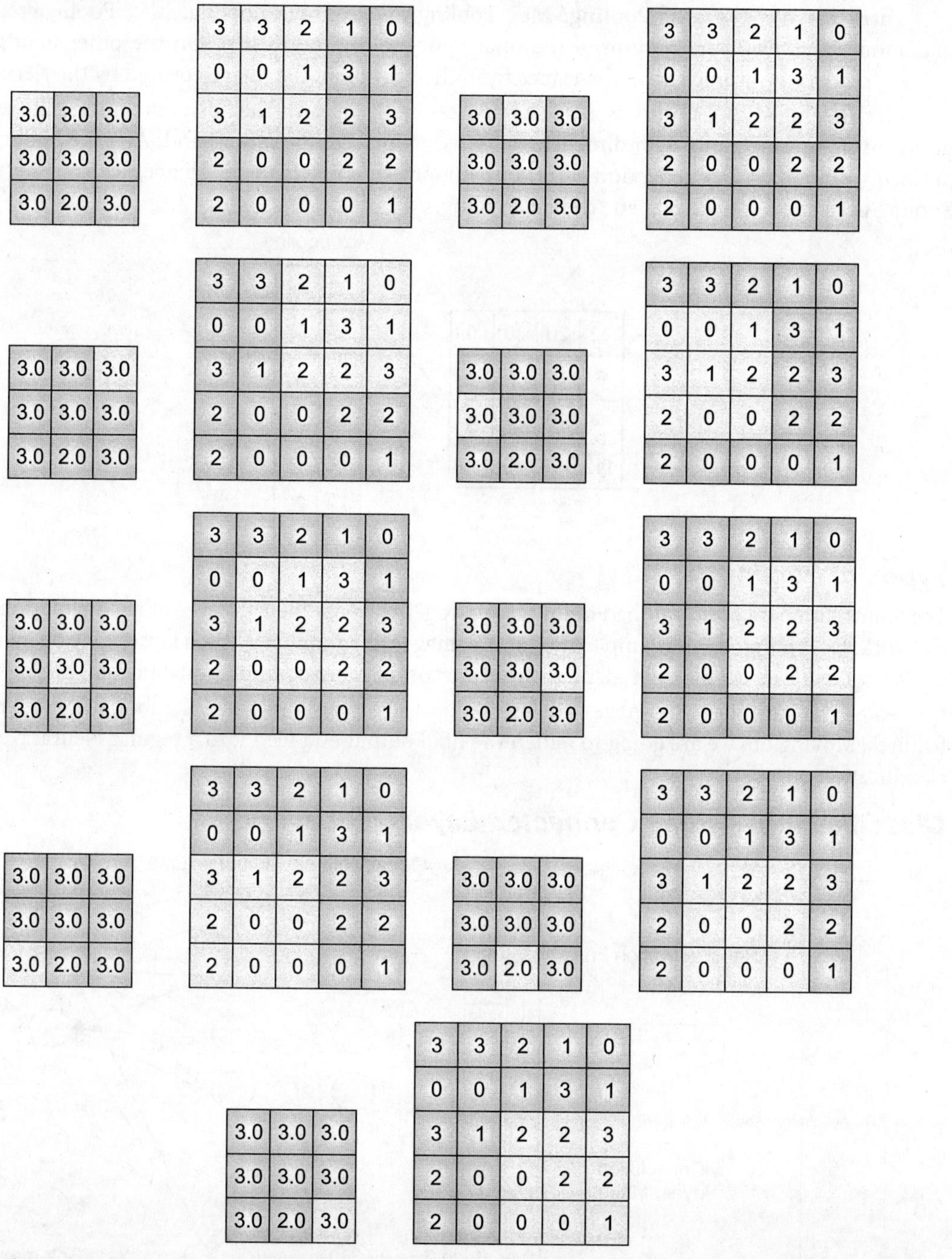

Like the Convolutional Layer, the Pooling layer is responsible for reducing the spatial size of the Convolved Feature. This is to decrease the computational power required to process the data through dimensionality reduction. Furthermore, it is useful for extracting dominant features which are rotational and positional invariant, thus maintaining the process of effectively training the model.

There are two types of Pooling: Max Pooling and Average Pooling. Max Pooling returns the maximum value from the portion of the image covered by the Kernel. On the other hand, Average Pooling returns the average of all the values from the portion of the image covered by the Kernel.

Max Pooling also performs as a Noise Suppressant. It discards the noisy activations altogether and performs de-noising along with dimensionality reduction. On the other hand, Average Pooling simply performs dimensionality reduction as a noise-suppressing mechanism. Hence, we can say that Max Pooling performs a lot better than Average Pooling.

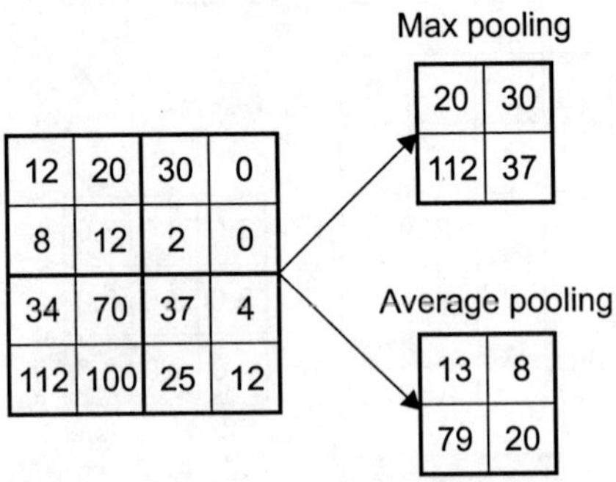

Types of Pooling

The Convolutional Layer and the Pooling Layer, together form the i-th layer of a Convolutional Neural Network. Depending on the complexities in the images, the number of such layers may be increased for capturing low-level details even further, but at the cost of more computational power.

After going through the above process, we have successfully enabled the model to understand the features. Moving on, we are going to flatten the final output and feed it to a regular Neural Network for classification purposes.

Classification — Fully Connected Layer (FC Layer)

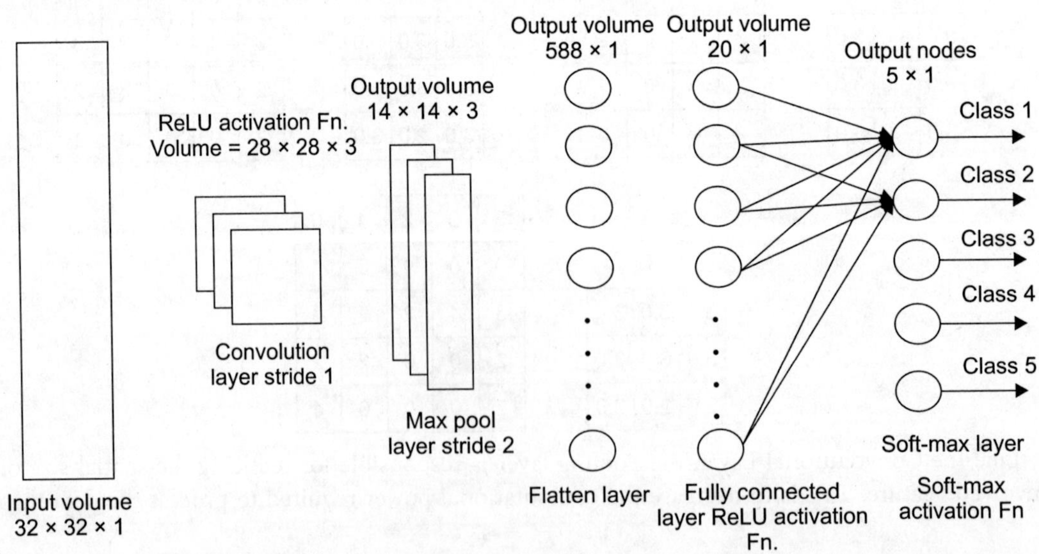

Adding a Fully-Connected layer is a (usually) cheap way of learning non-linear combinations of the high-level features as represented by the output of the convolutional layer. The Fully-Connected layer is learning a possibly non-linear function in that space.

Now that we have converted our input image into a suitable form for our Multi-Level Perceptron, we shall flatten the image into a column vector. The flattened output is fed to a feed-forward neural network and backpropagation is applied to every iteration of training. Over a series of epochs, the model can distinguish between dominating and certain low-level features in images and classify them using the Softmax Classification technique.

3.8 SIMILARITIES AND DIFFERENCES OF ANN VS. CNN

ANN uses weights and an activation function for the bulk of its method. The best way to describe how ANN works is that it artificially reconstructs how a brain's neural network works. After it gets something wrong, it goes back and "changes" the way it thinks, as a human would. The "layers" in ANN are rows of data points hosted through neurons that all use the same neural network. ANN uses weights to learn. Weights get changed after each iteration through the neuron in ANN. ANN goes back and changes the weights depending on the accuracy calculated by a "cost function". Comparatively, there is no neuron or weights in CNN. CNN instead casts multiple layers on images and uses filtration to analyze image inputs. These layers are the math layer, rectified linear unit layer, and fully connected layer. The purpose of these layers is to understand patterns that the network can "see", process output of data, and provide an n-dimensional vector output. That n-dimensional output is used to observe distinct features and connect them with the image input provided. It can then give the classification output to the user. Despite their differences, both methods use measures of the error to improve learning and produce epochs to analyze the effectiveness of models generated.

Input Processing Differences

ANN processes inputs in a different way than CNN. As a result, ANN is sometimes referred to as a Feed-Forward Neural Network because inputs are processed only in a forward-facing direction.

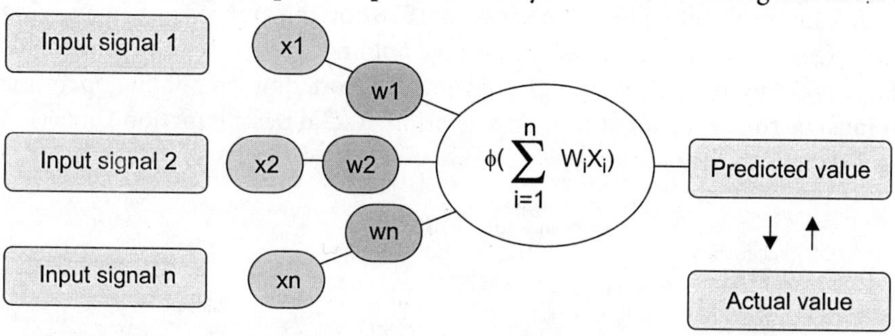

Because of the reliance on valid data inputs, ANN tends to be a less popular choice when analysing images. Meanwhile, CNN works in a compatible way with images as input data. Using filters on image results in feature maps. CNN does not process data in a forward-facing way but rather refers to the same data multiple times when creating maps.

ANN and CNN for Image Classification

With ANN, concrete data points must be provided. For example, in a model where we are trying to distinguish between dogs and cats, the width of the noses and length of the ears must be explicitly provided as data points. When using CNN, these spatial features are extracted from image input. This makes CNN ideal when thousands of features need to be extracted. Instead of having to measure each individual feature, CNN gathers these features on its own. Using ANN, image classification problems become difficult because 2-dimensional images need to be converted to 1-dimensional vectors. This increases the number of trainable parameters exponentially. Increasing trainable parameters takes storage and processing capability. In other words, it would be expensive. Compared to its predecessors, the main advantage of CNN is that it automatically detects the important features without any human supervision. This is why CNN would be an ideal solution to computer vision and image classification problems.

ANN vs. CNN for Data Classification

ANN is ideal for solving problems regarding data. Forward-facing algorithms can easily be used to process image data, text data, and tabular data. CNN requires many more data inputs to achieve its novel high accuracy rate. In many cases, to get the same accuracy as ANN for data processing, you have to use multiple data augmentation methods to widen the reaches of your data. In addition, ANN has the ability to implicitly detect complex nonlinear relationships between dependent and independent variables. It would also get you virtually the same accuracy rate as using CNN for data classification problems. This makes CNN an overkill solution for a data classification problem since you would have to augment your data to artificially inflate the dataset and deal with the storage and hardware dependencies of CNN. ANN is a comparatively lightweight way of solving data classification problems.

There are specific instances in which ANN could be preferred over CNN and vice versa. They are both unique in how they work mathematically, and this causes them to be better at solving specific problems. In general, CNN tends to be a more powerful and accurate way of solving classification problems. ANN is still dominant for problems where datasets are limited, and image inputs are not necessary. However, because of CNN's ability to view images as data, it's the most prevalent solution for computer vision and image-dependent machine learning problems.

3.9 DIFFERENT KINDS OF MODELS OF CNN

(a) **LeNet-5:** LeCun et al. introduced LeNet-5 in 1998 for the purpose of identifying handwritten numbers. Three convolutional layers, two average pooling layers, one fully connected layer, and one output layer make up the foundation of this model. Before doing a pooling operation, the sigmoid function must be run as the identification operation. Radial Basis Function Units (RBF) are used to categorise 10 digits in the output.

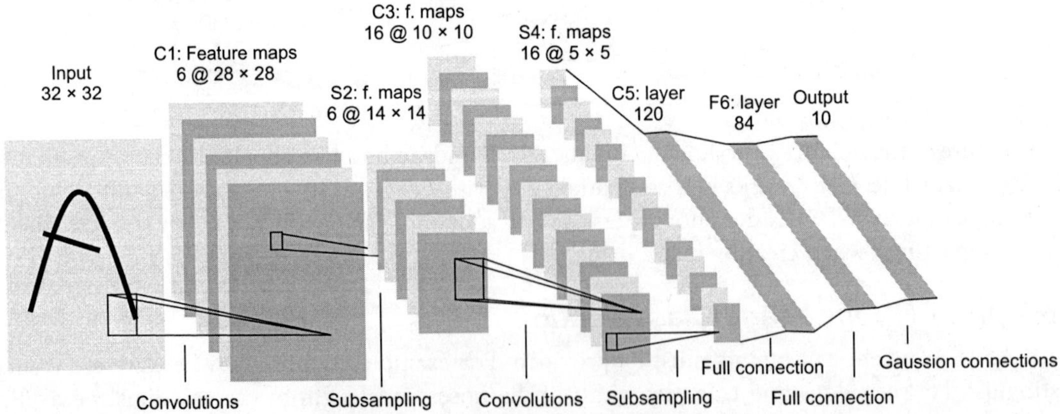

Fig. 5. Architecture of LeNet-5 [8]

LeNet-5 will have variable filter(kernel) sizes, filters, output sizes, and parameters for different layers.

Table 1. Architecture of LeNet-5

Layer	Filter size/stride	# filter	Output size	#Parameters
Convolution (C1)	5 × 5/1	6	28 × 28 × 6	156
Sub-sampling (S2)	2 × 2/2		14 × 14 × 6	12
Convolution (C3)	5 × 5/1	16	10 × 10 × 16	1516
Sub-sampling (S4)	2 × 2/2		5 × 5 × 16	32
Convolution (C5)	5 × 5	120	1 × 1 × 120	48120
Fully Connected (F6)	2 × 2		14 × 14 × 6	10164
Output				84

LeCun et al. introduced the dataset for the test of LeNet-5, which is composed of 60k training and 10k test input data for the recognition of handwritten digits. The dataset's larger character size is 20*20, while the employed normal picture size is 32*32; as a result, it will be normalised to create a 28*28 field.

(b) AlexNet: In 2012, Krizhevky et al. proposed the AlexNet, a brand-new and sophisticated idea of CNN (Convolutional Neural Network) for the categorization of ImageNet data. This model's features are nearly identical to those of LeNet-5, although it is somewhat larger.

This model has eight layers. 5 convolutional layers and 3 fully connected layers are included.

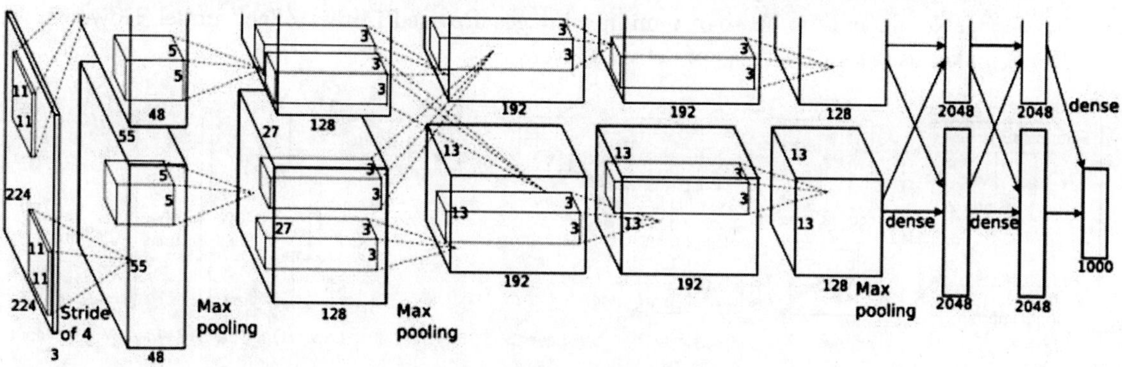

Fig. 6. Architecture of AlexNet [12]

In this approach, each LRN (Local Response Normalisation), also known as brightness normalisation, is followed by a max pooling layer.

For the classification of more than 1 million images among 999+ classes between ILSVRC (In 2010) and ILSVRC (In 2012), Krizhevsky et al. developed the AlexNet model. Most often, consumers will receive the top1 and top5 error rates. Different layers in AlexNet, like those in LeNet-5, have different filter sizes, padding, filters, output sizes, and parameters.

Table 2. Details of different layers of AlexNet

Layer	Filter size/stride	padding	# filter	Output size	#Parameters
Conv-1	11 × 11/4	0	96	55 × 55 × 96	34848
pool-1	3 × 3/2			27 × 27 × 96	
Conv-2	5 × 5/1	2	256	27 × 27 × 256	614400
pool-2	3 × 3/2			13 × 13 × 256	
Conv-3	3 × 3/1	1	384	13 × 13 × 384	981504
Conv-4	3 × 3/1	1	384	13 × 13 × 384	1327104
Conv-5	3 × 3/1	1	256	13 × 13 × 256	884736
pool3	3 × 3/2			6 × 6 × 256	
FC6				1 × 1 × 4096	37748736
FC7				1 × 1 × 4096	16777216
FC8				1 × 1 × 1000	4096000

(c) **ZFNet:** A new modified CNN (Convolutional Neural Network) named ZFnet was introduced in 2014 by Zeiler and Fergus. It is virtually identical to AlexNet in that it employs convolutional layers in the first and second layers of the picture. Zfnet has a sizable deep CNN (Convolutional Neural Network) network that applies the Novel Visualisation Technique for classifying several layers in multiple networks. This method uses a deconvolutional network, or "Deconvnet," which has numerous layers. Convnet is in opposition to Deconvnet now. This model accepts a feature map as an input, processes it using a variety of operations, and then outputs the results using a switch.

The ImageNet dataset's more than 1 million images are used in this ZFnet model. However, the ZFnet makes use of AlexNet's set of network layers.

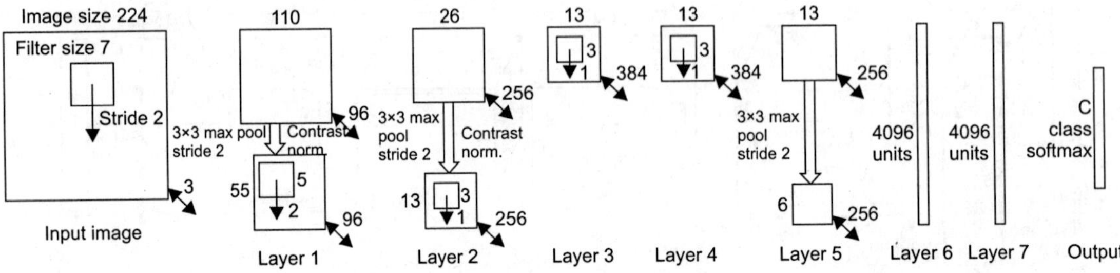

Fig. 7. Architecture of ZFNet [14]

(d) **VGGNet:** Simonyan and Zisserman introduced a new, deeper, and improved configuration of AlexNet in 2014, calling it VGGNet. This kind of model keeps the number of parameters and the size of the filters constant. In the VGGnet model, networks' filter size is 3 * 3. There are six possible network configurations used in this architecture.

Although VGGnet uses nearly identical training procedures to Alexnet, there is no image cropping and no scaling.

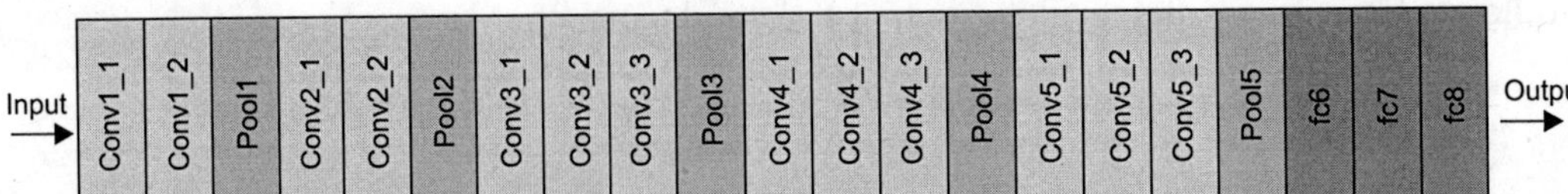

Fig. 8. Architecture of VGGNet (configuration D, VGG16)

(e) GoogleLeNet: Szegdy et al. released GoogleLeNet in 2014. Compared to other Convolutional CNNs (Convolutional Neural Networks), this model is unique.In this model, the number of layers in the network of images has risen, bringing the total to 22.

This CNN (Convolutional Neural Network) model has a low bidget, making it simple to utilise in embedded and mobile devices.

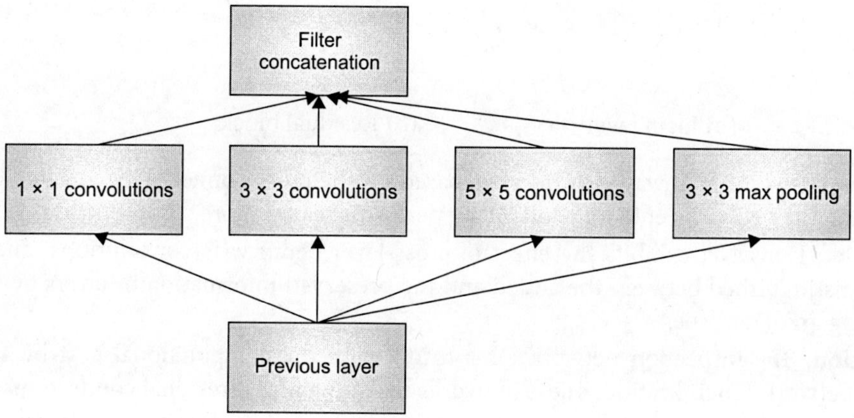

(a)

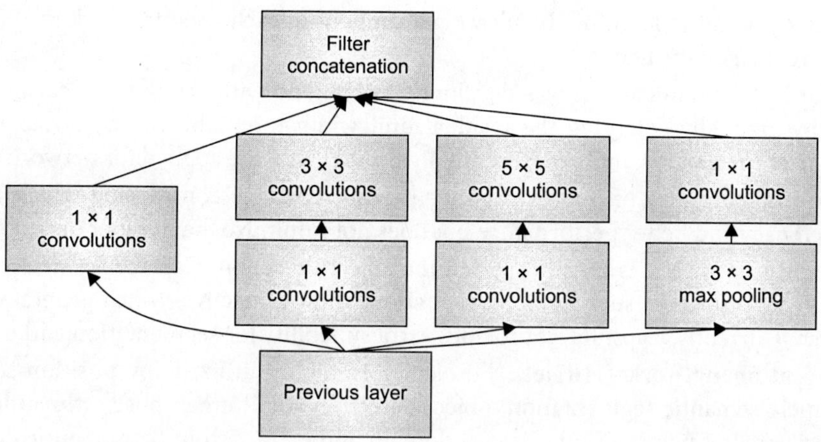

(b)

Fig. 9. (a) Naive version inception module, (b) Dimensionality reduction version [16]

(f) ResNet: He and his colleagues introduced a new CNN to address the performance issue because the deeper CNN occasionally performed worse. This is because the deeper the network, the more layers form, which causes performance to drop and error rates to rise. This makes performing some operations in the deeper network challenging and necessitates a different approach to optimisation. He then suggested a framework to address this issue. Additionally, residual mapping (H(x) = F(x) + x) is involved.

3*3 convolutional layer blocks, two filters, and a stride of two make up the ResNet model. This model made use of a batch of size of 128 layers with a 0.9 momentum.

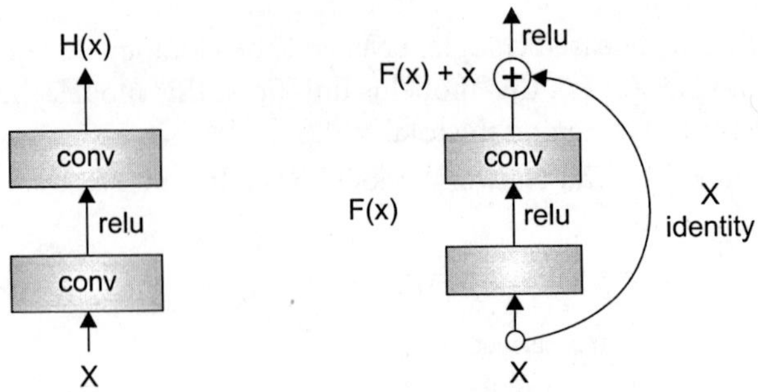

(*a*) Plain layer (*b*) Residual block

(g) **Highway network:** Highway networks are based on the cross-connectivity concept, conducive to increasing the network depth and enhancing performance for more complex tasks.

(h) **DenseNet:** DenseNet exhibits the effect of cross-layer depth wise-convolutions. These networks can be distinguished between the added and the preserved information in layers by resolving the vanishing gradient issue.

(i) **Inspection:** The inspection network aims to decrease the computational cost by annulling the deeper network generalization. These networks recently utilized residual connections to accelerate the Inception network training. Another enhanced version of the Inception Network is ResNext.

(j) **WideResNet:** WideResNet aims to solve feature reuse problems with transformations that impart a very small amount to learning. Inculcating a dropout in each residual block in WideResNet will efficiently regularize the network.

(k) **Pyramidal Net:** Pyramidal Net was developed to contend with the ResNet learning interference problem by gradually enlarging the residual unit width to enfold the most viable places to the appearance of the down-sampling. Recently Pyramidal Nets are applied for network widening.

(l) **Xception:** The core idea of Xception is depth-wise separable convolution which achieves extra learning efficacy and better performance but does not minimize the number of parameters.

(m) **CapsuleNet:** CapsuleNet is greatly applied for object detection. CapsuleNet detects the face and several feature properties such as size, orientation, and perspective, which general CNN does not accomplish. Currently, CapsuleNet provides extra suitability for segmentation and detection.

(n) **High-resolution network (HRNet):** HRNetare is highly utilized for position-sensitive vision tasks, namely semantic segmentation, object detection, and human pose estimation via getting a more precise representation in the spatial domain and extra-rich in the semantic domain. HRNet resembles a more vigorous backbone in many computer vision tasks.

(o) **Deep CNN:** Deep Convolutional Neural Network (Deep CNN) is a special neural network that has shown superior performance in computer vision and image processing applications. Deep CNN utilizes multiple feature extraction stages for automatic representation learning. Due to the representational capacity of the deep CNN reaches architectural innovations based on spatial exploitation, depth, multi-path, width, feature-map exploitation, channel boosting, and attention.

(p) **ID CNN:** 1D CNNs are the latest variants of conventional (2D) CNN and possess significant advances such as scarce training data handling and a low-cost and real-time implementation. Some of the emerging applications of 1D CNN are personalized biomedical data classification and early diagnosis, structural health monitoring, anomaly detection in power electronics, and electrical motor fault detection.

To summarize the different types of CNN architectures described above in an easy to remember form, you can use the following:

Architecture	Year	Key Features	Use Case
LeNet	1998	First successful applications of CNNs, 5 layers (alternating between convolutional and pooling), Used tanh/sigmoid activation functions	Recognizing handwritten and machine-printed characters
AlexNet	2012	Deeper and wider than LeNet, Used ReLU activation function, Implemented dropout layers, Used GPUs for training	Large-scale image recognition tasks
ZFNet	2013	Similar architecture to AlexNet, but with different filter sizes and numbers of filters, Visualization techniques for understanding the network	ImageNet classification
VGGNet	2014	Deeper networks with smaller filters (3×3), All convolutional layers have the same depth, Multiple configurations (VGG16, VGG19)	Large-scale image recognition
ResNet	2015	Introduced "skip connections" or "shortcuts" to enable training of deeper networks, Multiple configurations (ResNet-50, ResNet-101, ResNet-152)	Large-scale image recognition, won 1st place in the ILSVRC 2015
GoogleLeNet	2014	Introduced Inception module, which allows for more efficient computation and deeper networks, multiple versions (Inception v1, v2, v3, v4)	Large-scale image recognition, won 1st place in the ILSVRC 2014
MobileNets	2017	Designed for mobile and embedded vision applications, Uses depthwise separable convolutions to reduce the model size and complexity	Mobile and embedded vision applications, real-time object detection

3.10 PRACTICAL IMPLEMENTATION

Steps for Implementation of CNN using Python.

1. **Here we are going to import the necessary libraries which are required for performing CNN tasks.**

   import NumPy as np

   %matplotlib inline

   import matplotlib.image as mpimg

   import matplotlib.pyplot as plt

   import TensorFlow as tf

   tf.compat.v1.set_random_seed(2019)

2. **Below is the code to form the CNN model**

   model = tf.keras.models.Sequential([

   tf.keras.layers.Conv2D(16,(3,3),activation = "relu" , input_shape = (180,180,3)) ,

   tf.keras.layers.MaxPooling2D(2,2),

```
    tf.keras.layers.Conv2D(32,(3,3),activation = "relu"),
    tf.keras.layers.MaxPooling2D(2,2),
    tf.keras.layers.Conv2D(64,(3,3),activation = "relu"),
    tf.keras.layers.MaxPooling2D(2,2),
    tf.keras.layers.Conv2D(128,(3,3),activation = "relu"),
    tf.keras.layers.MaxPooling2D(2,2),
tf.keras.layers.Flatten(),
tf.keras.layers.Dense(550,activation="relu"),     #Adding the Hidden layer
tf.keras.layers.Dropout(0.1,seed = 2019),
tf.keras.layers.Dense(400,activation ="relu"),
tf.keras.layers.Dropout(0.3,seed = 2019),
tf.keras.layers.Dense(300,activation="relu"),
tf.keras.layers.Dropout(0.4,seed = 2019),
tf.keras.layers.Dense(200,activation ="relu"),
tf.keras.layers.Dropout(0.2,seed = 2019),
tf.keras.layers.Dense(5,activation = "softmax")  #Adding the Output Layer
])
```

A convoluted image can be too large and so it is reduced without losing features or patterns, so pooling is done.

Here Creating a Neural network is to initialize the network using the Sequential model from Keras.

Flatten()- Flattening transforms a two-dimensional matrix of features into a vector of features.

3. **To see summary of the CNN model**

model.summary()

It will print the following output

Model: "sequential"

Layer (type)	Output Shape	Param #
conv2d (Conv2D)	(None, 178, 178, 16)	448
max_pooling2d (MaxPooling2D)	(None, 89, 89, 16)	0
conv2d_1 (Conv2D)	(None, 87, 87, 32)	4640
max_pooling2d_1 (MaxPooling2	(None, 43, 43, 32)	0
conv2d_2 (Conv2D)	(None, 41, 41, 64)	18496
max_pooling2d_2 (MaxPooling2	(None, 20, 20, 64)	0
conv2d_3 (Conv2D)	(None, 18, 18, 128)	73856
max_pooling2d_3 (MaxPooling2	(None, 9, 9, 128)	0
flatten (Flatten)	(None, 10368)	0
dense (Dense)	(None, 550)	5702950
dropout (Dropout)	(None, 550)	0
dense_1 (Dense)	(None, 400)	220400
dropout_1 (Dropout)	(None, 400)	0
dense_2 (Dense)	(None, 300)	120300

dropout_2 (Dropout)	(None, 300)	0
dense_3 (Dense)	(None, 200)	60200
dropout_3 (Dropout)	(None, 200)	0
dense_4 (Dense)	(None, 5)	1005

Total params: 6,202,295
Trainable params: 6,202,295
Non-trainable params: 0

4. **To specify optimizers.**

```
from tensorflow.keras.optimizers import RMSprop,SGD,Adam
adam=Adam(lr=0.001)
model.compile(optimizer='adam', loss='categorical_crossentropy', metrics = ['acc'])
```

Optimizer is used to reduce the cost calculated by cross-entropy
The loss function is used to calculate the error
The metrics term is used to represent the efficiency of the model.

5. **Step to set the data directory and generate image data.**

```
bs=30     #Setting batch size
train_dir = "D:/Data Science/Image Datasets/FastFood/train/"  #Setting training directory
validation_dir = "D:/Data Science/Image Datasets/FastFood/test/"  #Setting testing directory
from tensorflow.keras.preprocessing.image import ImageDataGenerator
# All images will be rescaled by 1./255.
train_datagen = ImageDataGenerator( rescale = 1.0/255. )
test_datagen  = ImageDataGenerator( rescale = 1.0/255. )
# Flow training images in batches of 20 using train_datagen generator
#Flow_from_directory function lets the classifier directly identify the labels from the name of the directories the image lies in
train_generator=train_datagen.flow_from_directory(train_dir,batch_size=bs,class_
mode='categorical',target_size=(180,180))
# Flow validation images in batches of 20 using test_datagen generator
validation_generator = test_datagen.flow_from_directory(validation_dir,
batch_size=bs,
class_mode  = 'categorical',
target_size=(180,180))
```

The output will be:

Found 1465 images belonging to 5 classes.
Found 893 images belonging to 5 classes.

6. **Final step for fitting the model.**

```
history = model.fit(train_generator,
validation_data=validation_generator,
steps_per_epoch=150 // bs,
            epochs=30,
```

```
validation_steps=50 // bs,
        verbose=2)
```

The output will be:

```
Epoch 1/30
5/5 - 4s - loss: 0.8625 - acc: 0.6933 - val_loss: 1.1741 - val_acc: 0.5000
Epoch 2/30
5/5 - 3s - loss: 0.7539 - acc: 0.7467 - val_loss: 1.2036 - val_acc: 0.5333
Epoch 3/30
5/5 - 3s - loss: 0.7829 - acc: 0.7400 - val_loss: 1.2483 - val_acc: 0.5667
Epoch 4/30
5/5 - 3s - loss: 0.6823 - acc: 0.7867 - val_loss: 1.3290 - val_acc: 0.4333
Epoch 5/30
5/5 - 3s - loss: 0.6892 - acc: 0.7800 - val_loss: 1.6482 - val_acc: 0.4333
Epoch 6/30
5/5 - 3s - loss: 0.7903 - acc: 0.7467 - val_loss: 1.0440 - val_acc: 0.6333
Epoch 7/30
5/5 - 3s - loss: 0.5731 - acc: 0.8267 - val_loss: 1.5226 - val_acc: 0.5000
Epoch 8/30
5/5 - 3s - loss: 0.5949 - acc: 0.8333 - val_loss: 0.9984 - val_acc: 0.6667
Epoch 9/30
5/5 - 3s - loss: 0.6162 - acc: 0.8069 - val_loss: 1.1490 - val_acc: 0.5667
Epoch 10/30
5/5 - 3s - loss: 0.7509 - acc: 0.7600 - val_loss: 1.3168 - val_acc: 0.5000
Epoch 11/30
5/5 - 4s - loss: 0.6180 - acc: 0.7862 - val_loss: 1.1918 - val_acc: 0.7000
Epoch 12/30
5/5 - 3s - loss: 0.4936 - acc: 0.8467 - val_loss: 1.0488 - val_acc: 0.6333
Epoch 13/30
5/5 - 3s - loss: 0.4290 - acc: 0.8400 - val_loss: 0.9400 - val_acc: 0.6667
Epoch 14/30
5/5 - 3s - loss: 0.4205 - acc: 0.8533 - val_loss: 1.0716 - val_acc: 0.7000
Epoch 15/30
5/5 - 4s - loss: 0.5750 - acc: 0.8067 - val_loss: 1.2055 - val_acc: 0.6000
Epoch 16/30
5/5 - 4s - loss: 0.4080 - acc: 0.8533 - val_loss: 1.5014 - val_acc: 0.6667
Epoch 17/30
5/5 - 3s - loss: 0.3686 - acc: 0.8467 - val_loss: 1.0441 - val_acc: 0.5667
Epoch 18/30
5/5 - 3s - loss: 0.5474 - acc: 0.8067 - val_loss: 0.9662 - val_acc: 0.7333
```

```
Epoch 19/30
5/5 - 3s - loss: 0.5646 - acc: 0.8138 - val_loss: 0.9151 - val_acc: 0.7000
Epoch 20/30
5/5 - 4s - loss: 0.3579 - acc: 0.8800 - val_loss: 1.4184 - val_acc: 0.5667
Epoch 21/30
5/5 - 3s - loss: 0.3714 - acc: 0.8800 - val_loss: 2.0762 - val_acc: 0.6333
Epoch 22/30
5/5 - 3s - loss: 0.3654 - acc: 0.8933 - val_loss: 1.8273 - val_acc: 0.5667
Epoch 23/30
5/5 - 3s - loss: 0.3845 - acc: 0.8933 - val_loss: 1.0199 - val_acc: 0.7333
Epoch 24/30
5/5 - 3s - loss: 0.3356 - acc: 0.9000 - val_loss: 0.5168 - val_acc: 0.8333
Epoch 25/30
5/5 - 3s - loss: 0.3612 - acc: 0.8667 - val_loss: 1.7924 - val_acc: 0.5667
Epoch 26/30
5/5 - 3s - loss: 0.3075 - acc: 0.8867 - val_loss: 1.0720 - val_acc: 0.6667
Epoch 27/30
5/5 - 3s - loss: 0.2820 - acc: 0.9400 - val_loss: 2.2798 - val_acc: 0.5667
Epoch 28/30
5/5 - 3s - loss: 0.3606 - acc: 0.8621 - val_loss: 1.2423 - val_acc: 0.8000
Epoch 29/30
5/5 - 3s - loss: 0.2630 - acc: 0.9000 - val_loss: 1.4235 - val_acc: 0.6333
Epoch 30/30
5/5 - 3s - loss: 0.3790 - acc: 0.9000 - val_loss: 0.6173 - val_acc: 0.8000
```

The above function trains the neural network using the training set and evaluates its performance on the test set. The functions return two metrics for each epoch 'acc' and 'val_acc' which are the accuracy of predictions obtained in the training set and accuracy attained in the test set respectively.

3.11 APPLICATIONS OF CNN

CNNs provide an optimal architecture for uncovering and learning key features in image and time-series data. CNNs are a key technology in applications such as:

Medical Imaging: CNNs can examine thousands of pathology reports to visually detect the presence or absence of cancer cells in images.

Audio Processing: Keyword detection can be used in any device with a microphone to detect when a certain word or phrase is spoken ("Hey Siri!"). CNNs can accurately learn and detect the keyword while ignoring all other phrases regardless of the environment.

Object Detection: Automated driving relies on CNNs to accurately detect the presence of a sign or other object and make decisions based on the output.

Synthetic Data Generation: Using Generative Adversarial Networks (GANs), new images can be produced for use in deep learning applications including face recognition and automated driving.

Pose Estimation: Most of the recent works attracts more attention towards learning multiple levels of representations and abstractions for human-body pose estimation task by utilizing CNNs. DeepPose, multi-resolution CNNa, and dual-source CNN are the current CNN variants used for pose estimation.

Text Detection and Recognition: In recent times, due to the increasing trend of high-level visual understanding in computer vision research, text recognition of on-scene images is a major focus. Implementing CNN for text recognition of on-scene images captures many appearance variations in unconstrained environments with stronger and richer feature representations. Recent works include text detection and localization without recognition, text recognition on cropped text images, and end-to-end text spotting.

Action Recognition: Action Recognition based on their visual appearance and motion dynamics is one of the challenging problems in computer vision. Recently, CNN efficaciously utilized for action analysis in still images and videos sequences. A pre-trained CNN is used to represent full images of actions and achieve a high level of performance in action analysis. 3D convolutional layers are applied to video sequences for action recognition with increased performance and effectiveness.

Speech Processing: For Automatic Speech Recognition (ASR), CNNs and deep CNNs provide impressive performance via the local connectivity and frequency shift capturing in human speech signals. Additionally, the effect of CNNs for Statistical Parametric Speech Synthesis (SPSS) with the help of a generative model constitutes the conditional distribution of the acoustic features from the linguistic features.

Natural Language Processing: In recent years, CNN has been administered quickly in designing and executing natural language processing tasks (NLP) such as text categorization, semantic parsing, search query retrieval, sentence modelling and classification, and prediction. Statistical language modelling is one of the applications of CNN in NLP, and this combines recurrent highway networks for better modelling. Text classification CNN and deep CNN are applied to obtain high impactful performance. Through these two NLP tasks, CNN demands more improvement to achieve e state-of-the-art outcome.

3.12 RECENT RESEARCH RELATED TO CNN

A very high concentration of research is done in the area of image classification. It is a part of the deep learning and pattern recognition fields. It helps human computer interaction gain significant interest in various research fields. Midlevel learning techniques are frequently employed in image classification to concentrate on the coding or pooling process, but they are also willing to highlight the mechanism of image composition, which has a significant impact on the extraction of features.

Effective picture content exploration is achieved using a hierarchical image decomposition technique. The semantic breakdown of the image's content is just as important to understanding the image as its structure and texture. The semantic content of one image can be compared to the semantic content of other photos with the aid of several types of features extraction methods.

Many deep learning techniques are being produced nowadays, particularly for images from remote sensing. These techniques use an examination of the properties of images to capture scenes from the environment. The approach of remote sensing image recognition was initially presented by Zhang et al. Multilayer stacked autoencoder was used in an architecture to obtain the high features of the remote sensing images, and it was operated in an unsupervised manner.

In this research, deep CNN was used to describe and suggest a new groundbreaking classification strategy to get pixel pair characteristics. This method takes input from samples of photos and pairs them with two additional samples after adhering to the condition that samples taken from separate images are marked as 0.

The CNN feature that learns image features directly from a set of raw hyperspectral data is employed for the categorization of the samples.

Data is required for training in order to change numerous parameters, and the pipeline in CNN's deep model architecture uses this data.

Following is an explanation of the structure needed for the training and classification of purposed images. (Proposed Framework for Classification). There are three steps in a framework of this kind:

1. Samples' pixel-pair model
2. Building its CNN
3. A method of voting to verify a sample's label

B. **Using CNN (Convolution Neural Network) Architecture to Extract a Feature**

The PPF in image classification is obtained using the CNN architecture. As the CNN includes a convolution layer, a max pooling layer, and a fully connected layer, it will release correlation by establishing local connections between neurons in various image-layering levels. Ten convolution layers, three pooling layers, and a ReLU (rectified linear unit) will be present in the image classification algorithm.

Pooling layers come after convolution layers, therefore if there are more convolution layers, there will also be more pooling layers.

Consider the following scenario: Assuming d=200 layers and a 1*3 convolution layer, there will be 2*200*1 convolution layers present in the layer with the 1*9*1 kernel in the first convolution layer and 2*192*10 tensors produced by it. The second convolution layer will be similar, but it will produce a single 1*192*10 tensor in the layer of image classification.

In classifying low-resolution images, this will be quite helpful.

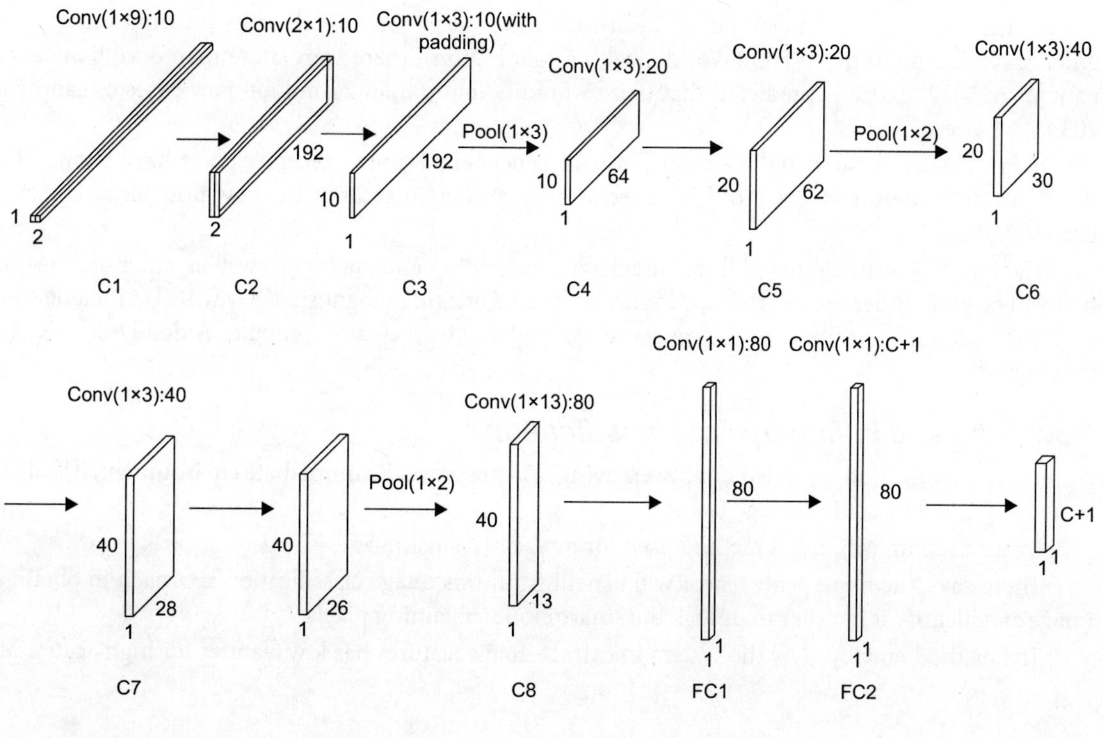

C. **Joint Classification with voting strategy**

In this CNN architecture voting strategy classification, pixels with the same features will be placed in the same class as a combined classification with voting strategy during testing of the picture, and pixels will be compared with the aid of neighbouring region sample.

Lets take an example of 3*3 pixel of image sample

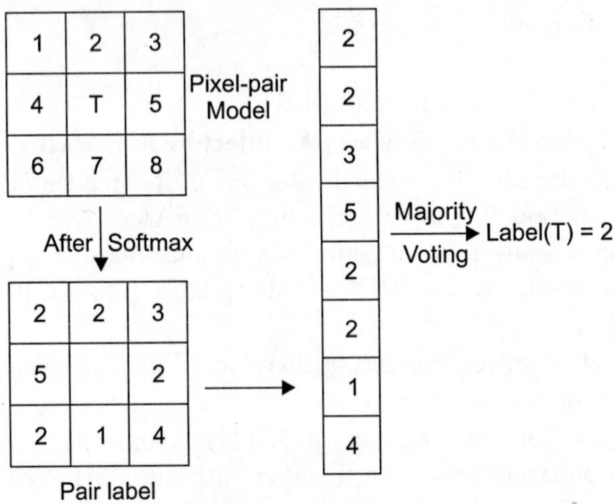

Example of joint classification with a 3 × 3 window.

How is it being related to cancer?

Cancer has emerged as a major public health issue in recent years, with cases growing increasingly quickly. According to the WHO (World Health Organisation), there were more than 8 million cancer patients in 2012, and it is predicted that there would be more than 20 million new cases of cancer by 2030.

Breast cancer is currently the most frequent cancer in women. Recent studies have shown that, thanks to the widespread usage of image technology and architecture, it is now possible to diagnose breast cancer.

The imaging technologies will include diagnosis grading and staging as well as other architecture that will be used under the microscope for breast cancer imaging diagnosis. They will also include some machine learning algorithms for the cancer image that will help create Computer Aided Design (CAD) for diagnosis.

How is it used in fingerprint classification?

As picture classification is carried out by removing features from the immediate environment, it will also be accomplished by coding image features.

Image decomposition is a method used for image investigation.

These days, the fingerprint sensor will benefit from this image classification approach to obtain an image and identify it in order to unlock the smartphone. obtaining pixels

The method employed by the system to extract image features has low features for high accuracy.

The purpose of fingerprint observation is to quickly identify persons in an image by using signals from the face, fingerprint, iris, voice, and written signature. And if we forget, it will keep our PIN, pattern, key, or card so we can still access the gadget.

SVM (Support Vector Machines) will be used to recognise bogus fingerprints so that the dataset containing the data of real fingerprints may be matched. The following tools are used to capture and identify fingerprints: FX2000, Digital 4000B, Italdata ET10.

3.13 RESEARCH CHALLENGES AND FUTURE IMPACTS ON CNN

- Although all CNNs have attained resounding success in several research studies, there are still many difficulties that procure further examination.
- Owing to the tendency of CNNs that become deeper and deeper, the requirement of dataset and computing power are abundant. Exploring supervised learning in CNN architectures will support overcoming the labelled dataset collection problem.
- It is necessary to investigate developing CNN models with reduced complexity and fast execution without loss of accuracy.
- Another challenge is considerable skill and experience for suitable hyperparameters selection. The enhancement in current optimization techniques for learning deep CNN architectures is to be addressed.
- Ensemble learning is one of the future prospective research areas in CNNs to improve generalization and robustness on diverse categories of image processing applications to extract different levels of semantic representations.
- In image processing applications, ID CNN is encouraged for sequential data owing to its better feature extraction ability and effective computations with a limited number of parameters.
- The research work on CNN with attention mechanism may be carried out as future scope to preserve the spatial relevance of objects and their distinguishing features at succeeding stages of learning.
- Cloud-based platforms will be utilized to develop computationally intensive CNN applications as another future research work.

3.14 CONCLUSION

Convolutional neural network has evolved from their inception with LeNet to the streamlined efficiency of MobileNets. Each architecture, from AlexNet to ResNet and beyond, has brought unique enhancements that have deepened our understanding and usage of CNNs. They have pushed the boundaries of what's possible in image recognition and classification tasks, and have had widespread applications in various domains. The future of CNNs holds exciting opportunities and challenges, promising to further transform our digital lands.

Review Questions

Solved Examples

Q.1. What does 1 × 1 convolution mean in a neural network?

Ans. A 1 × 1 convolution simply means an input pixel with all its channels to an output pixel, not looking at anything around itself. It is often used to reduce the number of depth channels since it is often very slow to multiply volumes with extremely large depths.

```
input (256 depth) -> 1 × 1 convolution (64 depth) -> 4 × 4 convolution (256 depth)
input (256 depth) -> 4 × 4 convolution (256 depth)
```

Q.2. How artificial neurons learns?

Ans. This is a two-paradigm process:

Associative Mapping: Here the network produces a pattern output by working in a pattern on the given input.

Regularity Detection: In this, units learn to respond to properties of the input patterns. Whereas in associative mapping the network stores the relationships among patterns, in regularity detection the response of each unit has a particular 'meaning.' This type of learning mechanism is essential for feature discovery and knowledge representation.

Q.3. Why so many convolutional layers are added to CNN?

Ans. It is like having detectives at different levels of expertise. The first detective (first layer) knows about basic stuff like edges. The next detective (second layer) combines what the first one found and looks for more complex patterns. As you add more detectives (more layers), they work together to understand the entire picture, from small details to big scenes.

So, why so many layers? It is like having a team of detectives, each specializing in different aspects, working together to solve the mystery of the picture. They help the computer see not just the pieces but also how they fit together, making it good at recognizing things in pictures.

Q.4. Explain the use of the pooling layer in CNN.

Ans. The main purpose of the pooling layer is to progressively reduce the spatial size of the input image, so that number of computations in the network is reduced. Pooling performs down sampling by reducing the size and sending only the important data to the next layers in CNN.

Q.5. How would you visualize features of CNN in an image classification task?

Ans. Convolutional neural networks, have internal structures that are designed to operate upon two-dimensional image data, and as such preserve the spatial relationships for what was learned by the model. Specifically, the two-dimensional filters learned by the model can be inspected and visualized to discover the types of features that the model will detect, and the activation map's output by convolutional layers can be inspected to understand exactly what features were detected for a given input image.

Q.6. Why is CNN preferred over ANN for image data?

Ans. Feedforward neural networks can learn a single feature representation of the image but in the case of complex images, ANN will fail to give better predictions, this is because it cannot learn pixel dependencies present in the images. CNN can learn multiple layers of feature representations of an image by applying filters, or transformations Similar to this you can give your statement with other comparisons.

Unsolved Questions

1. What do you understand by Leaky ReLU activation function?
2. Which strategy does not prevent a model from over-fitting to the training data?
3. Evaluate the size of a feature map, given that the image size is 32x32, filter size is 5x5, stride is 1, and no padding.
4. What is a flattening layer in CNN architecture?
5. Discuss the applications of CNN.

Multiple Choice Questions

Q.1. What is the primary purpose of pooling layers in CNNs?

(*a*) Reducing overfitting
(*b*) Increasing model complexity
(*c*) Enhancing image resolution
(*d*) Applying non-linear activations.

Q.2. Which activation function is commonly used in CNNs?

(*a*) Sigmoid
(*b*) ReLU
(*c*) Tanh
(*d*) Leaky ReLU

Q.3. In CNNs, what is the role of the "padding" in the input image?

(*a*) Enhance image contrast
(*b*) Reduce the image size
(*c*) Prevent spatial down sampling
(*d*) Improve color saturation

Q.4. What layer connects the output of one neuron to the input of another?

(*a*) Recurrent layer
(*b*) Pooling layer
(*c*) Fully connected layer
(*d*) Dropout layer

Q.5. Which CNN architecture won the ImageNet Large Scale Visual Recognition Challenge in 2012?

(*a*) AlexNet
(*b*) VGGNet
(*c*) ResNet
(*d*) Inception

Answer Key

1. (*a*) 2. (*b*) 3. (*c*) 4. (*c*) 5. (*a*)

Fill in the Blanks

1. A CNN typically has three layers: a convolutional layer, a pooling layer, and a ________ layer.
2. ________ is the purpose of data augmentation in CNN training.
3. ________ technique allows CNNs to process images of varying sizes.
4. Convolutional layer ________ patterns and features in a CNN.
5. Dropout "turns off" a random preset fraction of the units in a layer, by setting their values to ________ during training.

Answer Key

1. Fully connected
2. Prevent overfitting
3. Transfer learning.
4. Detects
5. zero

❑❑❑

4 RNN and LSTMs, Applications of RNNs in Real World

4.1 INTRODUCTION TO RECURRENT NEURAL NETWORKS

A recurrent neural network (RNN) is a variation of a basic neural network. RNNs are good for processing sequential data such as natural language processing and audio recognition. They had, until recently, suffered from short-term-memory problems. Here we will focus on RNN, the vanishing gradient problem and the solutions to this problem known as long-short-term-memory (LSTM)and gated recurrent units(GRU).

4.2 RECURRENT NEURAL NETWORKS

Recurrent Neural Network is a generalization of feedforward neural network that has an internal memory. RNN is recurrent in nature as it performs the same function for every input of data while the output of the current input depends on the past one computation. After producing the output, it is copied and sent back into the recurrent network. For deciding, it considers the current input and the output that it has learned from the previous input.

Unlike feedforward neural networks, RNNs can use their internal state (memory) to process sequences of inputs. This makes them applicable to tasks such as unsegmented, connected handwriting recognition or speech recognition. In other neural networks, all the inputs are independent of each other. But in RNN, all the inputs are related to each other.

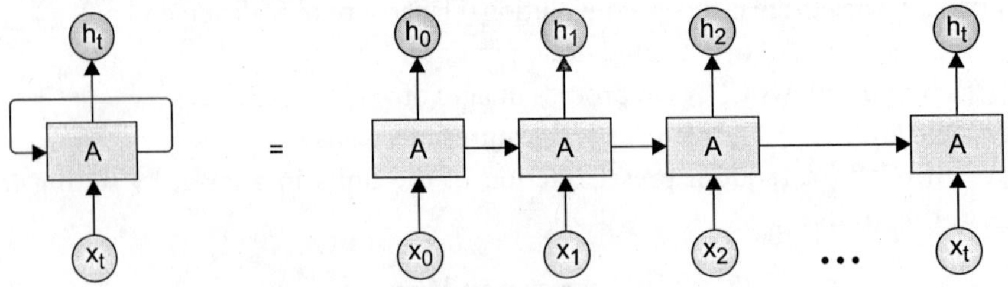

Fig. 1. An unrolled recurrent neural network.

First, it takes the X(0) from the sequence of input and then it outputs h(0) which together with X(1) is the input for the next step. So, the h(0) and X(1) is the input for the next step. Similarly, h(1) from the next is the input with X(2) for the next step and so on. This way, it keeps remembering the context while training.

The formula for the current state is

$$h_t = f(h_{t-1}, x_t)$$

Applying Activation Function:

$$h_1 = \tan h(W_{hh}h_1 + W_{xh}x_1)$$

where, W is weight, h is the single hidden vector, W_{hh} is the weight at previous hidden state, W_{hx} is the weight at current input state, tan h is the Activation function, that implements a Non-linearity that squashes the activations to the range$[-1.1]$

Output:

$$y_t = W_{hy}h_t$$

where, Y_t is the output state. W_{hy} is the weight at the output state.

First, let's cover the basic neural network architecture, neural nets are trained with 3 basic steps:

1. A forward pass that makes a prediction.
2. A comparison of the prediction to the ground truth using a loss function. The loss function outputs an error value.
3. Using that error value, perform back propagation which calculates the gradients for each node in the network.

In contrast, an RNN contains a hidden state that is feeding it information from previous states:

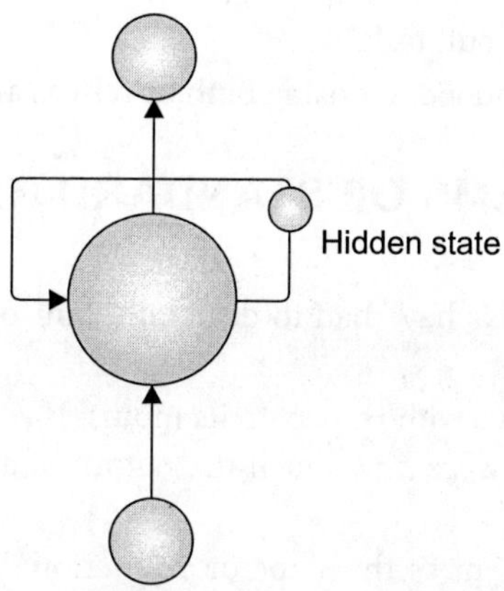

The concept of a hidden state is analogous to integrating sequential data in order to make a more accurate prediction. Consider how much easier it is to predict the motion of a ball if your data is still shots of the ball in motion:

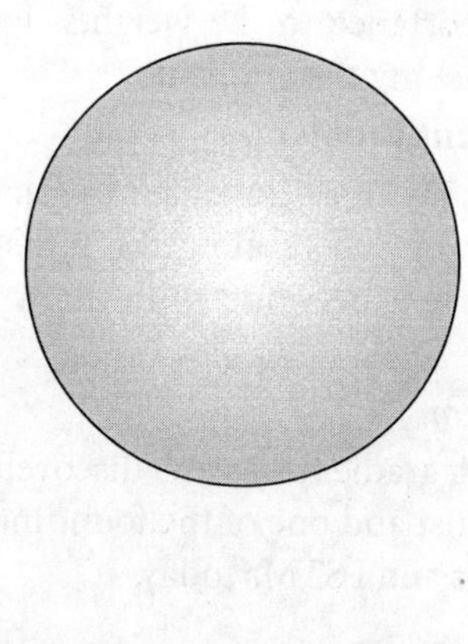

With no sequence information, it is impossible to predict where it is moving, in contrast, if you know the previous locations:

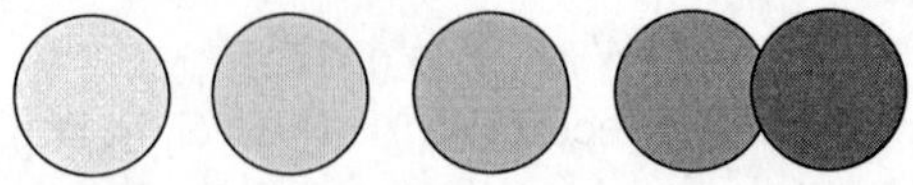

Predictions will be more accurate. The same logic is applicable to estimating the next word in a sentence, or the next piece of audio in a song. This information is the hidden state, which is a representation of previous inputs.

4.3 ADVANTAGES OF RECURRENT NEURAL NETWORK

1. RNN can model sequence of data so that each sample can be assumed to be dependent on previous ones
2. Recurrent neural network are even used with convolutional layers to extend the effective pixel neighbourhood.

4.4 DISADVANTAGES OF RECURRENT NEURAL NETWORK

1. Gradient vanishing and exploding problems.
2. Training an RNN is a very difficult task.
3. It cannot process very long sequences if using tanh or relu as an activation function.

4.5 COMMON PROBLEMS OF STANDARD RECURRENT NEURAL NETWORKS

There are two major obstacles RNNs have had to deal with, but to understand them, you first need to know what a gradient is.

A gradient is a partial derivative with respect to its inputs. If you do not know what that means, just think of it like this: a gradient measure how much the output of a function changes if you change the inputs a little bit.

You can also think of a gradient as the slope of a function. The higher the gradient, the steeper the slope and the faster a model can learn. But if the slope is zero, the model stops learning. A gradient simply measures the change in all weights about the change in error.

(a) **Exploding gradient:** Exploding gradients are when the algorithm, without much reason, assigns a stupidly high importance to the weights. Fortunately, this problem can be easily solved by truncating or squashing the gradients.

Avoiding Exploding Gradient Problem

In general, exploding gradients can be avoided by carefully configuring the network model, such as using a small learning rate, scaling the target variables, and using a standard loss function. However, in recurrent networks with many input time steps, exploding gradients may still be an issue.

(b) **Vanishing Gradient Problem**

The problem of the vanishing gradient was first discovered by Sepp (Joseph) Hochreiter back in 1991. Sepp is a genius scientist and one of the founding people, who contributed significantly to the way that we use RNNs and LSTMs today.

The second person is YoshuaBengio, a professor at the University of Montreal. He also discovered the vanishing descent problem but a bit later – he wrote about it in 1994. Yoshua is another person pushing the envelope in the space of deep learning and RNNs.

To train an RNN, we use an application of back-propagation called back-propagation through time (BPTT). Since the weights at each layer are tuned via the Chain Rule, their gradient values will exponentially shrink as it propagates through each time step, eventually "vanishing".

The vanishing gradient problem causes the gradients to shrink. But, if a gradient is small, it will not be possible to effectively update the weights and biases of the initial layers with each training session.

These initial layers are vital for recognizing the core elements of the input data, so, if their weights and biases are not properly updated, it is possible that the entire network could be inaccurate.

Impact of Vanishing Gradient Problem

1. Limited learning capacity
2. Difficulty in capturing the long-term dependencies
3. Slow convergence & training instability
4. Preferential learning in shallow layers
5. Architectural design considerations

Methods proposed to overcome the vanishing gradient problem:

1. **Residual neural networks (ResNets):** One of the newest and most effective ways to resolve the vanishing gradient problem is with residual neural networks, or ResNets (not to be confused with recurrent neural networks). It was noted before ResNets that a deeper network would have higher training error than the shallow network.

   The weights of a neural network are updated using the backpropagation algorithm. The backpropagation algorithm makes a small change to each weight in such a way that the loss of the model decreases. How does this happen? It updates each weight such that it takes a step in the direction along which the loss decreases. This direction is nothing but the gradient of this weight (concerning the loss).

   Using the chain rule, we can find this gradient for each weight. It is equal to (local gradient) x (gradient flowing from ahead),

   Here comes the problem. As this gradient keeps flowing backwards to the initial layers, this value keeps getting multiplied by each local gradient. Hence, the gradient becomes smaller and smaller, making the updates to the initial layers very small, increasing the training time considerably. We can solve our problem if the local gradient somehow became 1.

2. **Multi-level hierarchy:** It is one of the most basic and older solutions for a multilayer neural network model facing the vanishing gradient problem. It is simply a method that follows the procedure of training one level at a time and fine-tuning the level by backpropagation. So that every layer learns a compressed observation which goes ahead for the next level.

3. **Long short term memory (LSTM):** A simple LSTM helps the gradient size to remain constant. The activation function we use in the LSTM often works as an identity function which is a derivative of 1. So in gradient backpropagation, the size of the gradient does not vanish

4. ReLU
5. Batch normalization
6. Weight initialization
7. Gradient clipping
8. Skip connections
9. Gated architectures
10. Reduced network depth
11. Faster hardware

LSTM and GRU as solutions

LSTMs and GRUs were created as a solution to the vanishing gradient problem. They have internal mechanisms called gates that can regulate the flow of information.

4.6 TYPES OF RNN

RNNs are categorized based on the four network sequences, namely,

1. One to One Network
2. One to Many Network
3. Many to One Network
4. Many to Many Network
5. **RNN:** One to One Model

RNN: One to One Model

The one-to-one RNN is a typical sequence in neural networks, with only one input and one output. Application – Image classification

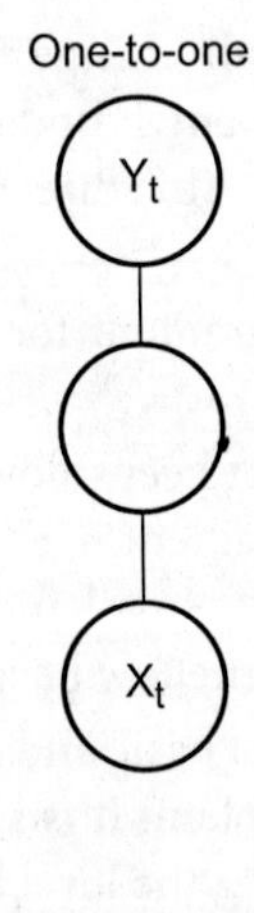

RNN: One to Many Model

One to Many network has a single input feed into the node, producing multiple outputs. Application – Music generation, image captioning, etc.

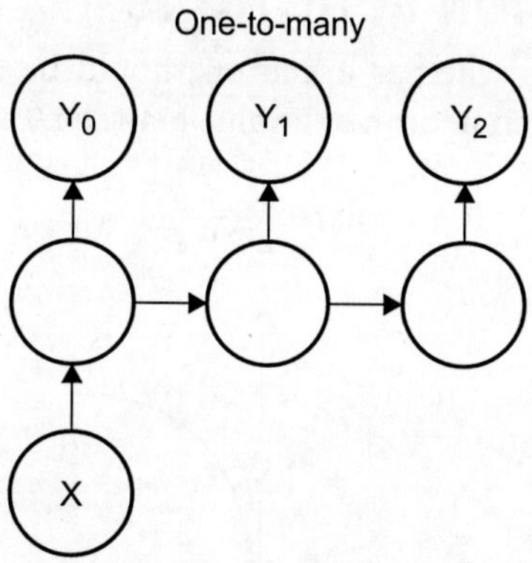

RNN: Many to One Model

Many to One architecture of RNN is utilized when there are several inputs for generating a single output. Application – Sentiment analysis, rating model, etc.

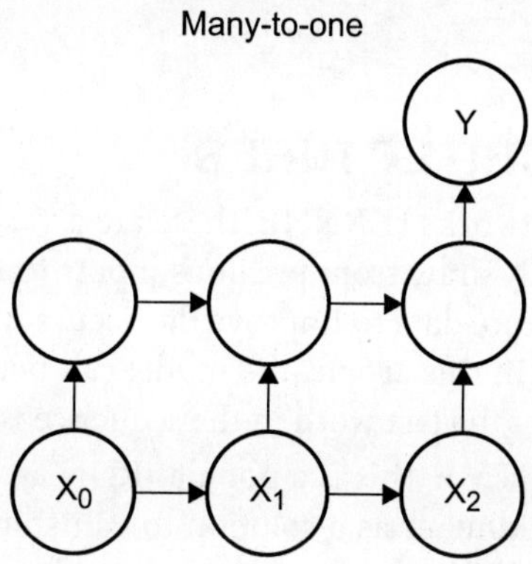

RNN: Many to Many Model

Many to Many RNN models, as the name implies, have multiple inputs, and produce multiple outputs. This model is also incorporated where input and output layer sizes are different. Application – Machine translation.

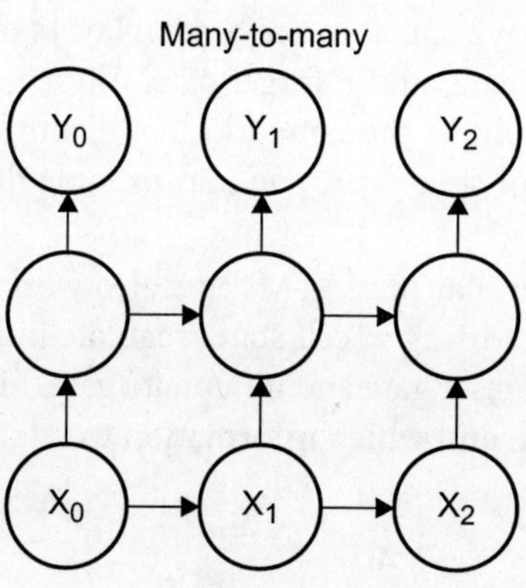

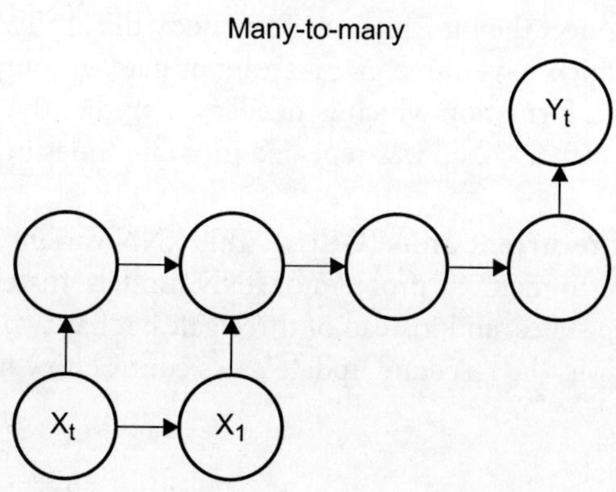

4.7 COMMON ACTIVATION FUNCTIONS

An activation function determines whether a neuron should be activated. The nonlinear functions typically convert the output of a given neuron to a value between 0 and 1 or –1 and 1.

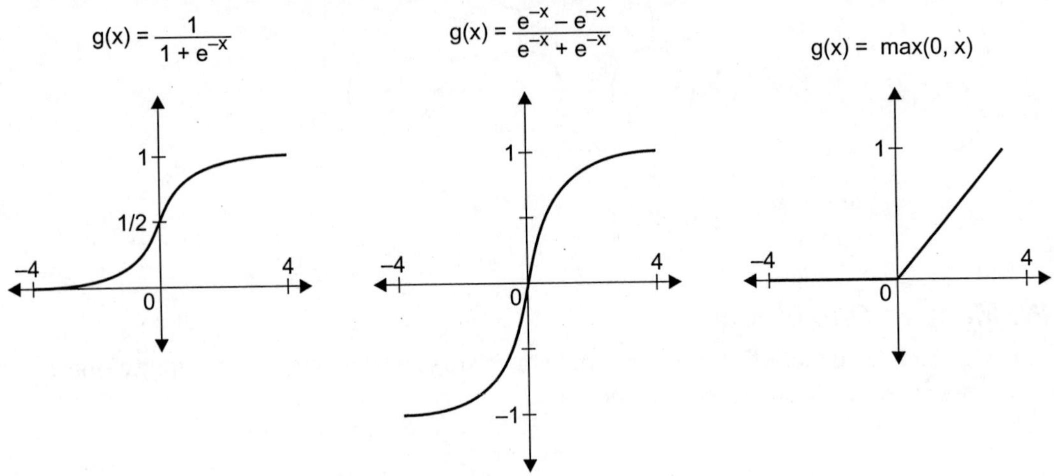

4.8 VARIANT RNN ARCHITECTURES

Bidirectional recurrent neural networks (BRNN): These are a variant network architecture of RNNs. While unidirectional RNNs can only draw from previous inputs to make predictions about the current state, bidirectional RNNs pull in future data to improve the accuracy of it. If we return to the example of "feeling under the weather" earlier in this article, the model can better predict that the second word in that phrase is "under" if it knew that the last word in the sequence is "weather."

Long short-term memory (LSTM): This is a popular RNN architecture, which was introduced by Sepp Hochreiter and JuergenSchmidhuber as a solution to vanishing gradient problem. In their paper (PDF, 388 KB) (link resides outside IBM), they work to address the problem of long-term dependencies. That is, if the previous state that is influencing the current prediction is not in the recent past, the RNN model may not be able to accurately predict the current state. As an example, let us say we wanted to predict the italicized words in following, "Alice is allergic to nuts. She cannot eat peanut butter." The context of a nut allergy can help us anticipate that the food that cannot be eaten contains nuts. However, if that context was a few sentences prior, then it would make it difficult, or even impossible, for the RNN to connect the information. To remedy this, LSTMs have "cells" in the hidden layers of the neural network, which have three gates–an input gate, an output gate, and a forget gate. These gates control the flow of information which is needed to predict the output in the network. For example, if gender pronouns, such as "she," was repeated multiple times in prior sentences, you may exclude that from the cell state.

Gated recurrent units (GRUs): This RNN variant is similar the LSTMs as it also works to address the short-term memory problem of RNN models. Instead of using a "cell state" regulate information, it uses hidden states, and instead of three gates, it has two—a reset gate and an update gate. Like the gates within LSTMs, the reset and update gates control how much and which information to retain.

4.9 REAL WORLD APPLICATIONS OF RNN

1. **Business Applications of Recurrent Neural Networks**

   RNN Text Generation - Text Summarization, Report Generation, Conversational UI

   Generating text with recurrent neural networks is probably the most straightforward way of applying RNN in the context of the business operation.

   From a business standpoint, text generation is valuable as a means for streamlining the workflow and minimizing the routine.

   Natural language generation relies on Recurrent Neural Networks predictive algorithms. Since the language is sequentially organized with grammar and bound into cohesion with semantics - it is relatively easy to train a model to produce generic text documents for multiple purposes.

   Let us look at the most common:

   (a) **Text summarization** - the process involves condensing the original text into a distillation of critical points and its subsequent reiteration into a cohesive summary. Summarization is used in project management to quickly onboard new members and keep an eye on the progress in general. This approach is also used to create news digests and streamline the news article production pipeline.

   (b) **Document generation** - commonly used in banking and insurance to create custom forms based upon templates adapted for the specific client with relevant information.

   (c) **Report Generation** - in this case, text generation serves as a form of data visualization. Except, instead of turning data into bars and charts, and graphs, the text is transformed into a formatted document with template sentences covering key points. Here is an example of this kind of report: "There were 100 visitors on-site during 24-hour period, which is two visitors more compared with the previous 24-hour period. Twenty-five visitors came from Facebook, 10 of which bounced off instantly, while the other 15 made from 5 to 20 clicks on the following page".

   (d) **Conversational Interfaces and chatbots** are amongst the most prominent casual uses of text generation. In this case, the algorithm is trained on the knowledge base combined with the behavioural intent scenarios. For example, a lead generation scenario is designed to gather information about the potential client, while a customer support scenario is designed to assist customers with product use. In addition to text generation, Conversational UI also requires a sentiment analysis component to correctly dissect the input message.

2. **RNN Application in Machine Translation - Content Localization**

   Machine translation is another field where RNN is widely applied due to its capability to determine the context of the message.

   Here is why - high-quality translation can be a bridge towards the expansion of the foreign language market. In a way, translated content can be considered as a broad form of service personalization.

   From a technical standpoint, it seems like machine translation operation is a mere substitution of words representing certain concepts with the equivalent terms in the other language.

   These days, the most prominent machine translation application is Google Translate. Also, there are numerous custom recurrent neural network applications used to localize content by various platforms. Just look at eCommerce platforms like Amazon, AliExpress, and eBay. They all use machine translation to adapt content like product cards and helps with the efficiency of the search results.

3. **Visual Search, Face detection, OCR Applications - Image Recognition**

   Humans tend to think visually and have an extensive visual shorthand reference board that helps them to navigate in the world. Until recently, this peculiar feature of the human mind was not taken into consideration when it comes to customer services. Now it is a full-fledged feature commonly used in a variety of fields, such as search engines, eCommerce stores, and OCR apps.

   Image recognition is one of the major points of computer vision. It is also the most accessible form of RNN to explain.

   At its core, the algorithm is designed to recognize one unit of input (the image) into multiple groups of output (the description of the image).

   The image recognition framework includes

   (a) A convolutional neural network that processes the image and recognizes the features of the pictures,

   (b) Recurrent neural networks that use the known features to make sense of the image and put together a cohesive description.

   The benefits of image recognition for business are obvious - it is a streamlining tool that makes it easier for the customer to operate with the service, find relevant images, navigate through information, and make purchases.

   The most prominent industries for image recognition are Search engines, eCommerce, social media.

   (a) **Search engines** are the basic application of visual search. Google, Bing, and DuckDuckGo are the most prominent examples of recurrent neural network image recognition. The goal is to images that fit the input query or find images that look like an input image. To do that, the image is recognized and described. The resulting information is then used to find relevant search matches.

   (b) In the case of **eCommerce**, image recognition is used for object detection and visual search purposes. The goal is to improve the product database and make it easier to navigate. In addition to that, visual search contributes to the product recommendation and consequently to the service personalization. The way Amazon and AliExpress use visual search results in vast streamlining of the user journey and better engagement with more possibilities of further purchases.

   (c) In the cases of **social media** like Facebook or Instagram, the primary use case of image recognition is face recognition. The difference between face recognition and basic image recognition is an additional layer of processing. There is a general recognition of the shape of the face, and then there is the matching of the unique credentials of the individual face based on available samples. The same principle is also used for transformative filters in photoediting applications.

4. **RNN Text Classification - Semantic Search**

   Navigating in the vast spaces of information is one of the major requirements in the data-driven world. As one of the premier recurrent neural network examples, semantic search is one of the tools that make it easier and much more productive. In addition to that, semantic search simplifies the continuous updates and revisions of the knowledge base.

   These days, semantic search is widely used in a variety of fields that: involve high turnaround of sensitive information or vast knowledge bases; require accessibility and speed to provide a decent level of workflow efficiency.

Here's how semantic search RNN application works:

- The input message is analysed for context. The process involves - feature extraction and context recognition.
- The result is a deconstruction of the input message to its moving parts. In addition to that, the algorithm looks for the related queries and checks them for relevance to the current query.
- Then, the processed input is checked and matched with the available knowledge base.
- The matches are presented as output results.

Semantic Search is commonly used in the following fields:

(a) **Customer support** - semantic search is to navigate the product/service knowledge base and customer cards. You can also read our case study for the project that involves the usage of a semantic search for customer support.

(b) **Banking** - in this case, semantic search is used to navigate through customer documents and double-check the validity of the proceedings at each step. It is also one of the tools for fraud detection when it comes to document or handwriting fraud.

(c) **Project documentation** - SS is used to navigate through documents and simplify access to the information. In addition to that, the Semantic search is often used to implement changes or corrections into a large amount of documentation quickly.

(d) **Employee Onboarding and general Q&A** - in this case, semantic search makes it easier to understand the ins and outs of the organization for the newbies and turns the knowledge base into an easily accessible reference tool.

(e) Search engines like Google and Amazon are amongst the most progressive types of semantic search. In this case, SS also involves a web scraper that looks for the relevant results. The input query is processed as usual, but it is also matched with the standard search patterns and more specific criteria such as corresponding region, language, or type of content (depending on the query). In addition to that, the resulting information contributes to further service personalization.

5. **RNN Text Classification - Sentiment Analysis**

Natural Language Processing is one of the core fields for Recurrent Neural Network applications due to its sheer practicality. A large chunk of business intelligence from the internet is presented in natural language form and because of that RNN are widely used in various text analytics applications. The most prominent field of recurrent neural network natural language processing is sentiment analysis. Sentiment analysis is one of the most exciting applications of recurrent neural networks. The reason for that is simple - versatility.

There are five major use cases for recurrent neural network sentiment analysis. Let us take a closer look:

(a) **Brand Management** - sentiment analysis is used to track the perception of the general perception of the brand by customers from different audience segments. Subsequently, it is used to analyse the specific aspects of the perception - find patterns of interest and use it for the benefit of the business operation.

(b) **Market Research** - in this case, sentiment analysis is used to collect information regarding specific aspects of the market (use of technology, audience reaction, and involvements) across various platforms.

(c) **Product Analytics** - in this case, sentiment analysis is used to manage and analyse all sorts of customer feedback regarding the product or its specific aspects to plan further improvements. In the case of customer Support, sentiment analysis is used to analyse the feedback and manage the support operation. You get an intent analysis of the customer (i.e., what kind of help he needs), and then you get an insight into the customer's opinion.

(d) Voice of the customer analysis uses SA to define and specify target audience segments - this includes customer's wants and needs, expectations from theproduct, and so on.

6. **Ad Fraud, Spam Detection, Bot Detection - Anomaly Detection**

   The lion's share of fraudulent activities on the internet is performed via automated algorithms with clearly distinguishable patterns. In addition to that, traditional fraud like handwriting faking is widespread when it comes to document fraud.

   In both cases, the recurrent neural network framework can be a powerful weapon against fraud of all walks, which is good in terms of effective budget spending and money-making.

7. **Stock Price Forecasting - Predictive Analytics**

   In a way, recurrent neural network stock prediction is one of the purest representations of RNN applications. It is all tweaking numbers to understand what the next figure might be.

   The critical term is time series prediction, which is a representation of the number figure fluctuation or transformation over time. Apps like Stock Market Sensei use this approach.

   The transformation includes a specific criterion that affected the changes (for example, the connection of the special price to the other expenses). The combination of the elements above is then taken into consideration upon calculation of the predictions.

   The predictions themselves range by probability from the most to the least possible from the available data. As a result, the stock market trader gets more solid grounds for decision making and reduces most risks.

Difference between ANN, CNN and RNN

	ANN	CNN	RNN
Type of Data	Tabular Data, Text Data	Image Data	Sequence data
Parameter Sharing	No	Yes	Yes
Fixed Length input	Yes	Yes	No
Recurrent Connections	No	No	Yes
Vanishing and Exploding Gradient	Yes	Yes	Yes
Spatial Relationship	No	Yes	No
Performance	ANN is considered to be less powerful than CNN, RNN.	CNN is considered to be more powerful than ANN, RNN.	RNN includes less feature compatibility when compared to CNN.
Application	Facial recognition and Computer vision.	Facial recognition, text digitization and Natural language processing.	Text-to-speech conversions.

Main advantages	Having fault tolerance, Ability to work with incomplete knowledge.	High accuracy in image recognition problems, Weight sharing.	Remembers each and every information, Time series prediction.
Disadvantages	Hardware dependence, Unexplained behavior of the network.	Large training data needed, don't encode the position and orientation of object.	Gradient vanishing, exploding gradient.

4.10 LONG SHORT-TERM MEMORY (LSTM) NETWORKS

Long Short-Term Memory (LSTM) networks are a modified version of recurrent neural networks, which makes it easier to remember past data in memory. The vanishing gradient problem of RNN is resolved here. LSTM is well-suited to classify, process and predict time series given time lags of unknown duration. It trains the model by using back-propagation. In an LSTM network, three gates are present:

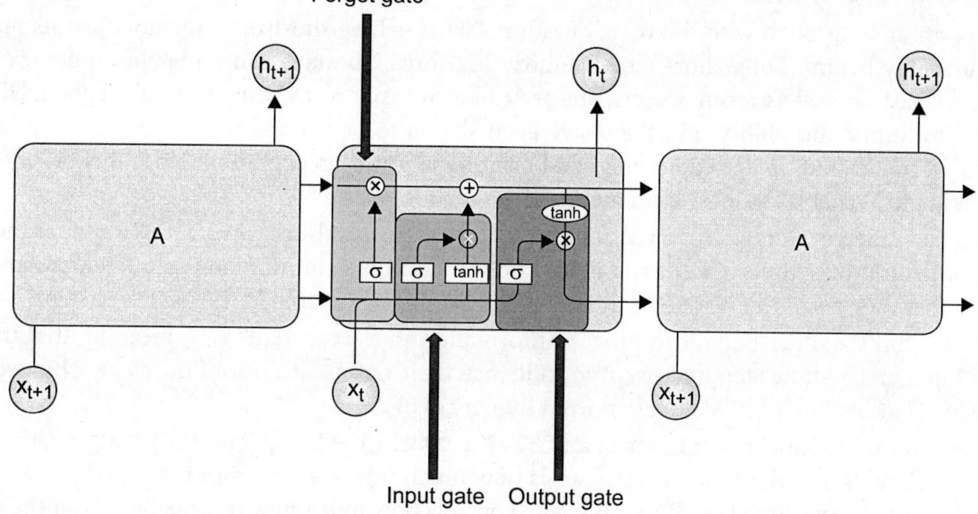

LSTM gates

1. **Input gate** — discover which value from input should be used to modify the memory. Sigmoid function decides which values to let through 0, 1. and tanh function gives weightage to the values which are passed deciding their level of importance ranging from –1 to 1.

$$i_t = \sigma(W_i \cdot [h_{t-1}, x_t] + b_i)$$

$$\tilde{C}_t = \tan\text{h}\,(W_C \cdot [h_{t-1}, x_t] + b_C)$$

2. **Forget gate** — discover what details to be discarded from the block. It is decided by the sigmoid function. it looks at the previous state(h_{t-1}) and the content input (X_t) and outputs a number between 0(omit this) and 1(keep this) for each number in the cell state C_{t-1}.

$$f_t = \sigma(W_i \cdot [h_{t-1}, x_t] + b_f)$$

3. **Output gate** — the input and the memory of the block is used to decide the output. Sigmoid function decides which values to let through 0, 1. and tanh function gives weightage to the values which are passed deciding their level of importance ranging from –1 to 1 and multiplied with output of Sigmoid.

$$o_t = \sigma(W_o\,[h_{t-1}, x_t] + b_o)$$
$$h_t = o_t * \tanh\,(C_t)$$

The gates in an LSTM perform a 3-step process:

(1) Decide what to forget (state)
(2) Decide what to remember (state)
(3) The actual "forgetting" and update of the state
(4) Production of the output

To wrap up, in an LSTM, the forget gate decides what is relevant to keep from prior steps. The input gate decides what information is relevant to add from the current step. The output gate determines what the next hidden state should be.

For the GRU, which is the newer generation of RNNs, it is quite like the LSTM, except that GRUs got rid of the cell state and used the hidden state to transfer information.

4.11 HOW LSTMS WORK?

So, as we are now through with the basic question, "what is long short-term memory" let us move on to the ideology behind Long short term memory networks. Humans can remember memories from the distant past, as well as recent events, and we can also easily recall sequences of events. LSTMs are designed to mimic this ability, and they have been shown to be successful in a variety of tasks, such as machine translation, image captioning, and even handwriting recognition. Does this bring an easy undertaking to "What is the long-term memory"?

The key difference between LSTMs and other types of neural networks is the way that they deal with information over time. Traditional neural networks process information in a "feedforward" way, meaning that they take in input at one-time step and produce an output at the next time step.

LSTMs, on the other hand, can process information in a "recurrent" way, meaning that they can take in input at one-time step and use it to influence their output at future time steps. This recurrent processing is what allows LSTMs to learn from sequences of data.

There are four main components to an LSTM network: The forget gate, the input gate, the output gate, and the cell state. The forget gate controls how much information from the previous time step is retained in the current time step. The input gate controls how much new information from the current time step is added to the cell state. The output gate controls how much information from the cell state is used to produce an output at the current time step. And finally, the cell state is a vector that represents the "memory" of the LSTM network; it contains information from both the previous time step and the current time step.

4.12 LSTM VS. RNN

Long Short-Term Memory neural networks are types of recurrent neural networks (RNN) that are well-suited for modelling sequence data. In contrast to RNNs, which tend to struggle with long-term dependencies, LSTMs can remember information for extended periods of time. This makes them ideal for tasks such as language modeling, where it is important to be able to capture the context of a sentence to predict the next word. LSTMs are also commonly used in machine translation and speech recognition applications.

Difference Between RNN and LSTM

Recurrent Neural Networks RNNs	Long Short-Term Memory LSTM
Recurrent layer feedback loops are a feature of RNNs. They are able to keep information in "memory" as a result.	A form of RNN called LSTM networks employs special units in addition to conventional units.
Standard RNNs might be difficult to train to address issues that call for learning long-term temporal dependencies.	A "memory cell" found in LSTM units is capable of storing data in memory for extended periods of time. They can learn longer-term dependencies thanks to this memory cell.
This is due to the loss function's gradient's exponential decrease over time (called the vanishing gradient problem).	By adding new gates, such as input and forget gates, which improve control over the gradient flow and better preserve "long-range dependencies," LSTMs address the disappearing and expanding gradient difficulties.
Information isn't kept in the memory of an RNN for very long.	Information is kept in the memory for a very long time by LSTM.

There are several advantages that LSTMs have over traditional RNNs.

First, they are much better at handling long-term dependencies. This is due to their ability to remember information for extended periods of time.

Second, LSTMs are much less susceptible to the vanishing gradient problem. This is because they use a different kind of activation function, known as an LSTM cell, which helps to preserve information over long sequences.

Finally, LSTMs are very efficient at modeling complex sequential data. This is because they can learn high-level representations that capture the structure of the data.

Despite these advantages, LSTMs do have some drawbacks.

First, they are more complicated than traditional RNNs and require more training data in order to learn effectively.

Second, they are not well-suited for online learning tasks, such as prediction or classification tasks where the input data is not a sequence. Third, LSTMs can be slow to train on large datasets. This is due to the fact that they must learn the parameters of the LSTM cells, which can be computationally intensive.

Finally, LSTMs may not be appropriate for all types of data. For example, they may not work well with highly nonlinear data or data with a lot of noise.

4.13 WHAT ARE BIDIRECTIONAL LSTMS?

Bidirectional LSTMs are a type of recurrent neural network that is often used for natural language processing tasks. Unlike traditional LSTMs, which read input sequentially from left to right, bidirectional LSTMs can read input in both directions, allowing them to capture context from both the past and the future.

This makes them well-suited for tasks such as named entity recognition, where it is important to be able to identify entities based on their surrounding context. Bidirectional LSTMs are also sometimes used for machine translation, where they can help to improve the accuracy of the translation by taking into account words that appear later in the sentence.

4.14 LSTM APPLICATIONS

LSTM has been used to achieve state-of-the-art results in a wide range of tasks such as language modelling, machine translation, image captioning, and more.

1. **Language Modelling:** One of the most common applications of LSTM is language modeling. Language modeling is the task of assigning a probability to a sequence of words. In order to do this, LSTM must learn the statistical properties of language so that it can predict the next word in a sentence.
2. **Machine Translation:** Another common application of LSTM is a machine translation. Machine translation is the process of translating one natural language into another. LSTM has been shown to be effective for this task because it can learn the long-term dependencies that are required for accurate translations.
3. **Handwriting Recognition:** Handwriting recognition is the task of automatically recognizing handwritten text from images or scanned documents. This is a difficult task because handwritten text can vary greatly in terms of style and quality, and there are often multiple ways to write the same word. However, because LSTMs can remember long-term dependencies between strokes, they have been shown to be effective for handwriting recognition tasks.
4. **Image Captioning:** LSTM can also be used for image captioning. Image captioning is the task of generating a textual description of an image. This is a difficult task because it requires understanding both the visual content of an image and the linguistic rules for describing images. However, LSTM works well at image captioning by learning how to interpret images and generate appropriate descriptions.
5. **Image Generation using Attention Models:** Attention models are a type of neural network that can learn to focus on relevant parts of an input when generating an output. This is especially useful for tasks like image generation, where the model needs to focus on different parts of the image at different times. LSTMs can be used together with attention models to generate images from textual descriptions.
6. **Question Answering:** LSTMs can also be used for question-answering tasks. Given a question and a set of documents, an LSTM can learn to select passages from the documents that are relevant to the question and use them to generate an answer. This task is known as reading comprehension and is an important testbed for artificial intelligence systems.

   Recently, Google released the SQuAD dataset, which contains 100,000+ questions answered by crowd workers on a set of Wikipedia articles. Several different neural networks have been proposed for tackling this challenge, and many of them use LSTMs in some way or another.
7. **Video-to-Text Conversion:** Video-to-text conversion is the task of converting videos into transcripts or summaries in natural language text. This is a difficult task because it requires understanding both the audio and visual components of the video in order to generate accurate text descriptions. LSTMs have been used to develop successful video-to-text conversion systems.
8. **Polymorphic Music Modelling:** Polyphonic music presents a particular challenge for music generation systems because each note must be generated independently while still sounding harmonious with all the other notes being played simultaneously. One way to tackle this problem is to use an LSTM network trained on polyphonic music data. This approach has been shown to generate convincing polyphonic music samples that sound like human performances.

9. **Speech Synthesis:** Speech synthesis systems typically use some form of acoustic modeling in order to generate speech waveforms from text input. Recurrent neural networks are well suited for this task due to their ability to model sequential data such as speech signals effectively.
10. **Protein Secondary Structure Prediction:** Protein secondary structure prediction is another important application of machine learning in biology. Proteins are often described by their primary structure (the sequence of amino acids) and their secondary structure (the three-dimensional shape).

    Secondary structure prediction can be viewed as a sequence labeling task, where each residue in the protein sequence is assigned one of three labels (helix, strand, or coil). Long Short-Term Memory networks have been shown to be effective at protein secondary structure prediction, both when used alone and when used in combination with other methods such as support vector machines.

4.15 LIMITATIONS OF LSTM

LSTMs are not perfect, however, and there are certain limitations to their abilities. Here, we will explore some of those limitations and what they mean for the future of artificial intelligence.

1. **Temporal Dependencies:** One of the biggest limitations of LSTMs is their inability to handle temporal dependencies that are longer than a few steps. This was demonstrated in a paper published by Google Brain researchers in 2016. The researchers found that when they trained an LSTM on a dataset with long-term dependencies (e.g., 100 steps), the network struggled to learn the task and generalize to new examples.

   This limitation arises because LSTMs use a forget gate to control what information is kept in the cell state and what is forgotten. However, this gate can only forget information that is a few steps back; anything further back is forgotten completely. As a result, LSTMs struggle to remember dependencies that are many steps removed from the current input.

   There are two possible ways to address this limitation: either train a larger LSTM with more cells (which requires more data) or use a different type of neural network altogether. Researchers from DeepMind recently proposed a new type of recurrent neural network called the Neural Stack Machine, which they claim can learn temporal dependencies of arbitrary length.

   However, it remains to be seen whether this model will be able to scale to large datasets and complex tasks like machine translation and automatic question answering.
2. **Limited Context Window Size:** Another limitation of LSTMs is their limited context window size. A context window is the set of inputs that the network uses to predict the next output; for instance, in a language model, an input might be a sequence of words while the output is the next word in the sentence. The size of the context window is determined by the number of recurrent units in the LSTM; typically, this number is between 2 and 4.

   This means that an LSTM can only consider a limited number of inputs when making predictions; anything outside of the context window is ignored completely. This can be problematic for tasks like machine translation, where it's important to consider the entire input sentence (not just the last few words) in order to produce an accurate translation.

   There are two possible ways to address this limitation as well: either train a larger LSTM with more cells (which requires more data) or use Attention-based models instead, which have been shown to be better at handling long input sequences. However, both methods come with their own trade-offs and challenges (e.g., Attention models usually require more training data).

4.16 GATED RECURRENT UNIT NETWORKS

Gated Recurrent Unit (GRU) is a type of recurrent neural network (RNN) that was introduced by Cho et al. in 2014 as a simpler alternative to Long Short-Term Memory (LSTM) networks. Like LSTM, GRU can process sequential data such as text, speech, and time-series data.

The basic idea behind GRU is to use gating mechanisms to selectively update the hidden state of the network at each time step. The gating mechanisms are used to control the flow of information in and out of the network. The GRU has two gating mechanisms, called the reset gate and the update gate.

The reset gate determines how much of the previous hidden state should be forgotten, while the update gate determines how much of the new input should be used to update the hidden state. The output of the GRU is calculated based on the updated hidden state.

The equations used to calculate the reset gate, update gate, and hidden state of a GRU are as follows:

Reset gate: r_t = sigmoid(W_r * [h_{t – 1}, x_t])
Update gate: z_t = sigmoid(W_z * [h_{t – 1}, x_t])
Candidate hidden state: h_t′ = tanh(W_h * [r_t * h_{t – 1}, x_t])
Hidden state: h_t = (1 – z_t) * h_{t – 1} + z_t * h_t′
where W_r, W_z, and W_h are learnable weight matrices, x_t is the input at time step t, h_{t – 1} is the previous hidden state, and h_t is the current hidden state.

In summary, GRU networks are a type of RNN that use gating mechanisms to selectively update the hidden state at each time step, allowing them to effectively model sequential data. They have been shown to be effective in various natural language processing tasks, such as language modelling, machine translation, and speech recognition

Prerequisites: Recurrent Neural Networks, Long Short-Term Memory Networks

To solve the Vanishing-Exploding gradients problem often encountered during the operation of a basic Recurrent Neural Network, many variations were developed. One of the most famous variations is the **Long Short Term Memory Network (LSTM)**. One of the lesser-known but equally effective variations is the **Gated Recurrent Unit Network (GRU)**.

Unlike LSTM, it consists of only three gates and does not maintain an Internal Cell State. The information which is stored in the Internal Cell State in an LSTM recurrent unit is incorporated into the hidden state of the Gated Recurrent Unit. This collective information is passed onto the next Gated Recurrent Unit. The different gates of a GRU are as described below:

1. **Update Gate(z):** It determines how much of the past knowledge needs to be passed along into the future. It is analogous to the Output Gate in an LSTM recurrent unit.
2. **Reset Gate(r):** It determines how much of the past knowledge to forget. It is analogous to the combination of the Input Gate and the Forget Gate in an LSTM recurrent unit.
3. **Current Memory Gate ():** It is often overlooked during a typical discussion on Gated Recurrent Unit Network. It is incorporated into the Reset Gate just like the Input Modulation Gate is a sub-part of the Input Gate and is used to introduce some non-linearity into the input and to also make the input Zero-mean. Another reason to make it a sub-part of the Reset gate is to reduce the effect that previous information has on the current information that is being passed into the future.

The basic work-flow of a Gated Recurrent Unit Network is similar to that of a basic Recurrent Neural Network when illustrated, the main difference between the two is in the internal working within each recurrent unit as Gated Recurrent Unit networks consist of gates which modulate the current input and the previous hidden state.

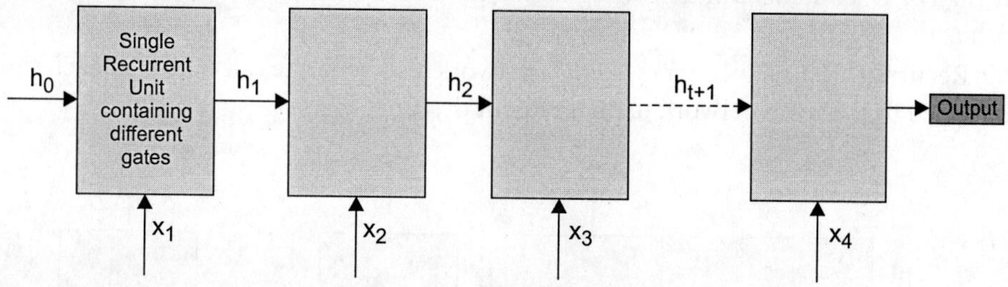

4.17 WORKING OF A GATED RECURRENT UNIT

- Take input the current input and the previous hidden state as vectors.
- Calculate the values of the three different gates by following the steps given below:-
  1. For each gate, calculate the parameterized current input and previously hidden state vectors by performing element-wise multiplication (Hadamard Product) between the concerned vector and the respective weights for each gate.
  2. Apply the respective activation function for each gate element-wise on the parameterized vectors. Below given is the list of the gates with the activation function to be applied for the gate.

Update Gate: Sigmoid Function
Reset Gate: Sigmoid Function

- The process of calculating the Current Memory Gate is a little different. First, the Hadamard product of the Reset Gate and the previously hidden state vector is calculated. Then this vector is parameterized and then added to the parameterized current input vector.

$$\bar{h}_t = \tanh(W \odot x_i + W \odot (r_i \odot h_{t-1}))$$

- To calculate the current hidden state, first, a vector of ones and the same dimensions as that of the input is defined. This vector will be called ones and mathematically be denoted by 1. First, calculate the Hadamard Product of the update gate and the previously hidden state vector. Then generate a new vector by subtracting the update gate from ones and then calculate the Hadamard Product of the newly generated vector with the current memory gate. Finally, add the two vectors to get the currently hidden state vector.

$$h_t = z_t \odot h_{t-1} + (1 - z_t) \odot \bar{h}_t$$

The above-stated working is stated as below:

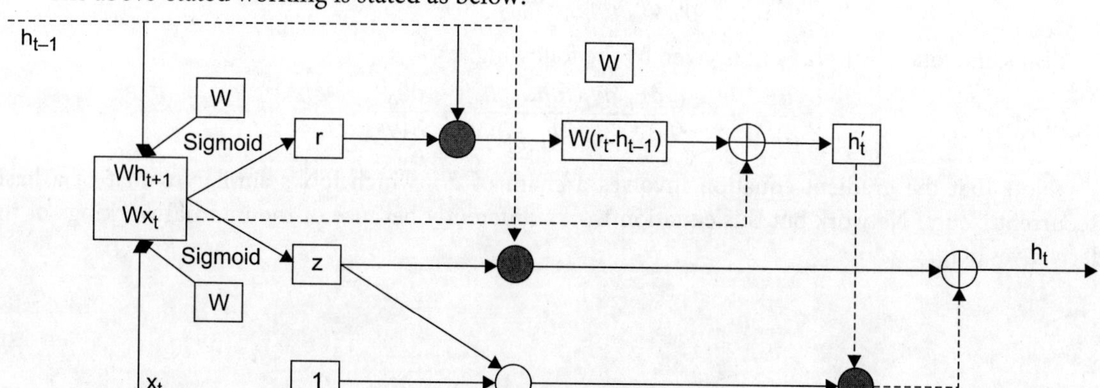

Note that the blue circles denote element-wise multiplication. The positive sign in the circle denotes vector addition while the negative sign denotes vector subtraction(vector addition with negative value). The weight matrix W contains different weights for the current input vector and the previous hidden state for each gate.

Just like Recurrent Neural Networks, a GRU network also generates an output at each time step and this output is used to train the network using gradient descent.

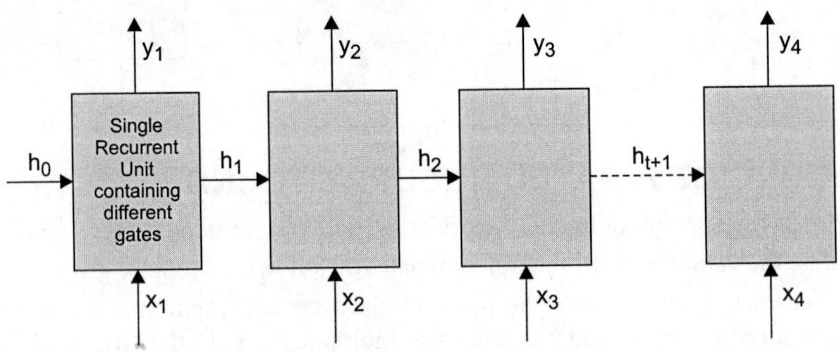

Note that just like the workflow, the training process for a GRU network is also diagrammatically similar to that of a basic Recurrent Neural Network and differs only in the internal working of each recurrent unit.

The Back-Propagation Through Time Algorithm for a Gated Recurrent Unit Network is similar to that of a Long Short Term Memory Network and differs only in the differential chain formation.

Let y'_t be the predicted output at each time step and y_t be the actual output at each time step. Then the error at each time step is given by:-

$$E_t = -y_t \log (\bar{y}_t)$$

The total error is thus given by the summation of errors at all time steps.

$$E = \bullet_t E_t \quad \Rightarrow \quad E = \sum_t -y_t \log(\bar{y}_t)$$

Similarly, the valued E/dW can be calculated as the summation of the gradients at each time step.

$$\frac{\partial E}{\partial W} = \sum_t \frac{\partial E_t}{\partial W}$$

Using the chain rule and using the fact that y'_t is a function of h_t and which indeed is a function of h'_t, the following expression arises:

$$\frac{\partial E_t}{\partial W} = \frac{\partial E_t}{\partial \bar{y}_t}\frac{\partial \bar{y}_t}{\partial h_t}\frac{\partial h_t}{\partial h_{t-1}}\frac{\partial h_{t-1}}{\partial h_{t-2}}\cdots\frac{\partial h_0}{\partial W}$$

Thus, the total error gradient is given by the following:

$$\frac{\partial E}{\partial W} = \sum_t \frac{\partial E_t}{\partial \bar{y}_t}\frac{\partial \bar{y}_t}{\partial h_t}\frac{\partial h_t}{\partial h_{t-1}}\frac{\partial h_{t-1}}{\partial h_{t-2}}\cdots\frac{\partial h_0}{\partial W}$$

Note that the gradient equation involves a chain of dh_t which looks similar to that of a basic Recurrent Neural Network but this equation works differently because of the internal workings of the derivatives of h_t.

How do Gated Recurrent Units solve the problem of vanishing gradients?

The value of the gradients is controlled by the chain of derivatives starting from $\frac{\partial h_t}{\partial h_{t-1}}$. Recall the expression for h_t:

$$h_t = z_t \odot h_{t-1} + (1 - z_t) \odot \bar{h}_t$$

Using the above expression, the value for $\frac{\partial h_t}{\partial h_{t-1}}$ is

- $$\frac{\partial h_t}{\partial h_{t-1}} = z + (1-z)\frac{\partial \bar{h}_t}{\partial h_{t-1}}$$

Recall the expression for $\bar{h}_t$:

$$\bar{h}_t = \tanh(W \odot x_t + W \odot (r_t \odot h_{t-1}))$$

Using the above expression to calculate the value of $\frac{\partial \bar{h}_t}{\partial h_{t-1}}$:

$$\frac{\partial \bar{h}_t}{\partial h_{t-1}} = \frac{\partial(\tanh(W \odot x_t + W \odot (r_t \odot h_{t-1})))}{\partial h_{t-1}} \Rightarrow \frac{\partial \bar{h}_t}{\partial h_{t-1}} = (1-\bar{h}_t^2)(W \odot r)$$

Since both the update and reset gate use the sigmoid function as their activation function, both can take values either 0 or 1.

Case 1($z = 1$): In this case, irrespective of the value of r, the term $\frac{\partial \bar{h}_t}{\partial h_{t-1}}$ is equal to z which in turn is equal to 1.

Case 2A($z = 0$ and $r = 0$): In this case, the term $\frac{\partial \bar{h}_t}{\partial h_{t-1}}$ is equal to 0.

Case 2B($z = 0$ and $r = 1$): In this case, the term $\frac{\partial \bar{h}_t}{\partial h_{t-1}}$ is equal to $(1-\bar{h}_t^2)(W)$. This value is controlled by the weight matrix which is trainable and thus the network learns to adjust the weights in such a way that the term $\frac{\partial \bar{h}_t}{\partial h_{t-1}}$ comes closer to 1.

Thus the back-propagation through time algorithm adjusts the respective weights in such a manner that the value of the chain of derivatives is as close to 1 as possible.

4.18 ADVANCED DEEP LEARNING MODELS USED IN RESEARCH

Bilateral-Long Short- Term Memory (Bi-LSTM)

The optimal feature vectors selected by the optimization models are subjected to the Bi-LSTM-CNN model. Here, the fully connected layer of CNN is replaced by the bilateral working of LSTM. The CNN model used here has nine convolutional layers. Each and every feature vectors are the individual input to the neural network. The Bi-LSTM has an input layer, a bilateral layer and the output layer in which the bilateral layer has backward and forward pass. The working of both the pass will change based on the weight updation process.

The input features are represented as $Q = (q_1, q_2, \dots q_d)$ at which there are d number of features. The hidden layer sequence is given as,

$$h_g = \sigma(W_{ih}q_g + W_{hh}h_{g-1} - b_h)$$

where, b_h is the hidden layer bias, W_{ih} is the weight between input layer and hidden layer, σ is the sigmoid function and h_{g-1} is the value of previous hidden layer. The output of bilateral layer is given as,

$$y_g = W_{hy} + b_y$$

where, b_y is the bias at output of backward and forward pass, which has the weight of W_{hy} between the hidden layer and output of both hidden layers. The relation between these gating signals is expressed in the following equations,

$$I_g = \sigma(W_{mI}q_g + W_{hI}h_{g-1} + W_{CI}C_{g-1} + bias_I)$$
$$F_g = \sigma(W_{mF}q_g + W_{hF}h_{g-1} + W_{CF}C_{g-1} + bias_F)$$
$$C_g = \sigma(F_gC_{g-1} + I_g \tanh(W_{mC}q_g + W_{hC}h_{g-1} + bias_C)$$
$$O_g = \sigma(W_{mO}q_g + W_{hO}h_{g-1} + W_{CO}C_{g-1} + bias_O)$$

where, I_g is the input gate, F_g is the forget gate at which the cell activation can be performed by previous cell vector, O_g is the output gate and C_g is the cell activation, which is generated by both input and output gates. W and *bias* indicates the weight and bias term for corresponding gates. C_{g-1} is the peephole, a decision taken by the cell activation to get the input, delete the stored memory and set the output gate. The network diagram of Bi-LSTM is below.

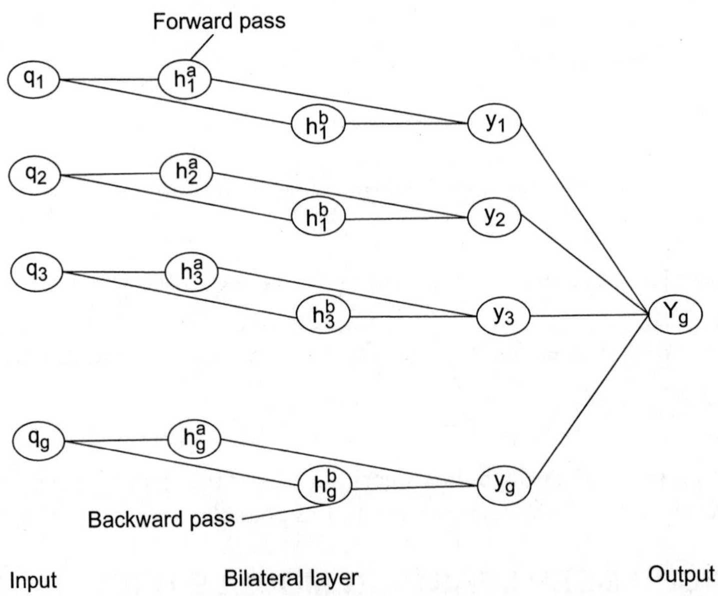

BiLSTM Layering

The forward pass is denoted by h^a and backward pass as h^b, which differ by the weight updation mechanism. In forward pass the weight is updated from first to last whereas in backward pass the weight is updated from last to first. The two factor of weight updation will enhance the accuracy model for the segmentation.

$$h_g^a = \sigma(W_{mh^a} g_g + W_{h^a h^a} h^a_{g-1} + bias_{h^a})$$

$$h_g^b = \sigma(W_{mh^b} g_g + W_{h^b h^b} h_{g-1}^b + bias_{h^b})$$

$$y_g = W_{h^a y} h_g^a + W_{h^b y} h_g^b + bias_y$$

The above equation is the output equation that follows the hidden layer validation. Then similar to the CNN the output is subjected to the softmax function. The overall loss of the system can be given as follows:

$$L^* = \arg\min_L \frac{1}{N} \sum_i \sum_{\kappa=1}^{3} \| \hat{p}_k - p_k \|_2^2 + w \| \hat{v}_k + v_k \|_2^2$$

where, the output translation, output rotation, quality of feature based on translation and rotation and weight for it is denoted by p_κ, v_κ, κ and w respectively. The gradient descent algorithm is utilized to reduce the subjected loss function.

Deep Neural Network

The deep neural network is nothing but the general neural network model that is used with other conventional type of neural networks like recurrent neural network, conventional neural network and artificial neural network. But the difference is in the hidden layering. The deep neural network has input layer, output layer and *n* number of hidden layers (similar neurons on each layer), which depends upon the use or applications. The increase in hidden layers improves the learning process of the model. The figure below shows the structure of deep neural network.

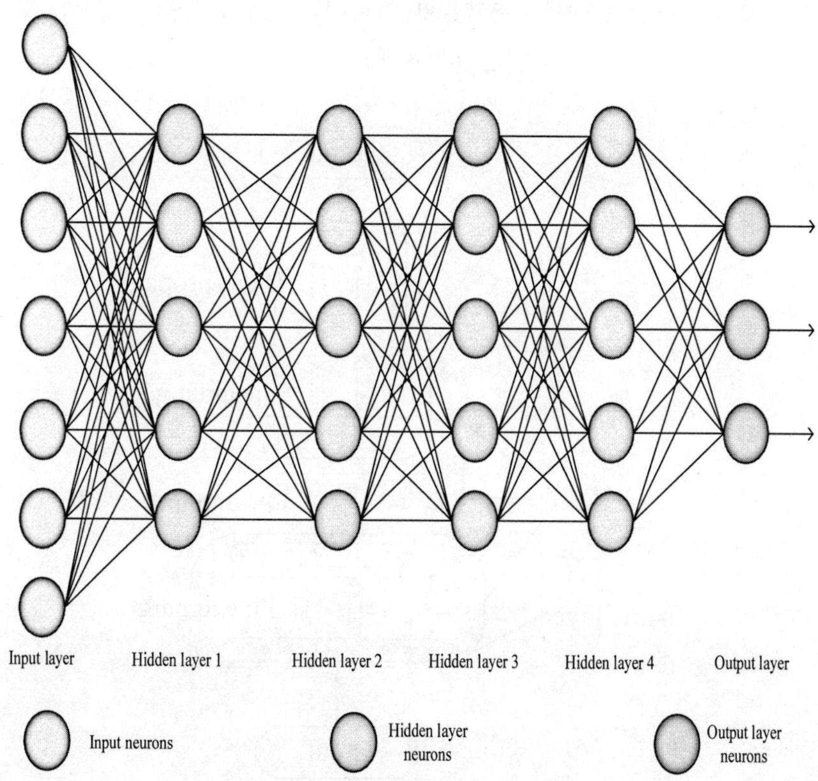

Structure of deep neural network

Deep Belief Network

DBN is also an artificial intelligence, which inhibits several other models within it like back propagation algorithm and restricted Boltzman machine (RBM). The method has input layer as visible layer, and multiple number of hidden layers that will serve one another and finally the output layer. The layer that serves to other layer without connecting themselves is named as RBM while the propagation of data in output layer to other layer is named as back propagation. All the neurons are connected by the energy functions that is there is no connection between the layers. The probability function of the RBM is given as,

$$P(h_i = 1/v) = f(b_i + W_i v)$$
$$P(v_i = 1/h) = f(a_i + W_i h)$$

where, v and h indicates the visible layer and hidden layer with the biases b and h respectively for i^{th} layer. The weight of the layers is denoted as W for i^{th} layer. The functions in the above equation are noted as,

$$f(x) = \frac{1}{(1+e^{-x})}$$

Then the energy function and the probability distribution for visible and hidden layer is given as,

$$E(v, h) = \sum_{i \in v} a_i v_i - \sum_{j \in h} h_i b_i - \sum_{i,j} h_i v_i W_{ij}$$

$$p(v, h) = \frac{1}{z} \exp(-E(v, h)$$

The marginal distribution of visible layer is given as,

$$p(v) = \frac{1}{z} \sum_{h} \exp(-E(v, h)$$

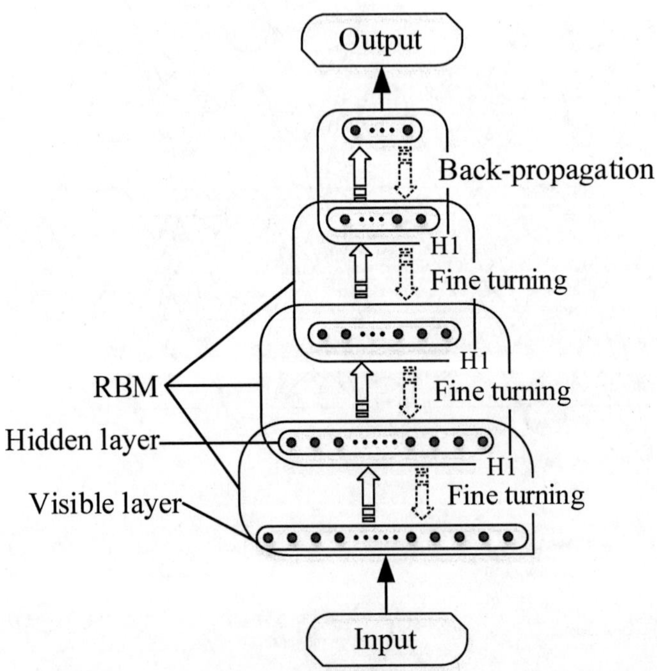

Structure of DBN

The probability function is considered as a likelihood function with the parameter $\phi \in \{W, a, b\}$ with the input vector is v. If the input sample is given then the parameter ϕ will be reconsidered so as to increase $p(v, \phi)$. For efficient analysis of probability function the gradient method is used. The structure of DBN is given in figure.

On gradient method the likelihood function is denoted as $\log p(v, \phi)$ at which the monotonicity of the function is not changed. The neuron processing steps on DBN is represented in Fig. To reconsidering the values in gradient with greater learning efficiency,

$$\phi(u+1) = \phi(u) + r * \left(-\frac{\partial \log p(v, \phi)}{\partial \phi}\right)$$

where, $\phi \in \{W, A, B\}$, the parameter inside the set is represented below:

$$-\frac{\partial \log p(v, W_{ij})}{\partial W_{ij}} = E_v[p(h_i \mid v) * v_j] - v_j^{(i)} * f(W_i * v^{(i)} + b_i)$$

$$-\frac{\partial \log p(v, b_i)}{\partial b_i} = E_v[p(h_i \mid v) * v_j] - v_j^{(i)} * f(W_i * v^{(i)})$$

$$-\frac{\partial \log p(v, a_i)}{\partial a_i} = E_v[p(h_i \mid v) * v_j] - v_j^{(i)}$$

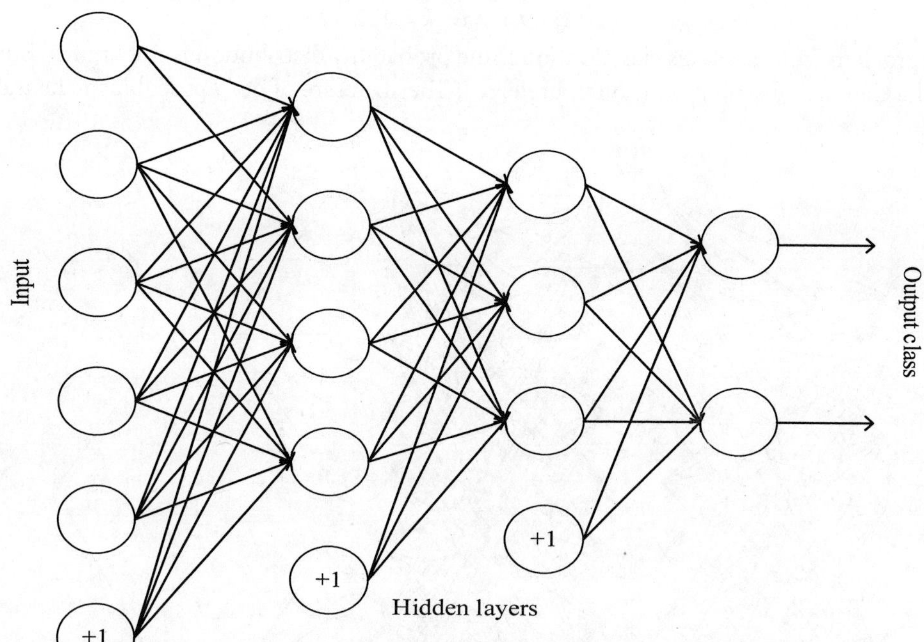

Neuron processing in DBN

Training of DBN

The DBN can be trained by layer-wise unsupervised learning and fine turning method. At layer-wise method, the Boltzmann machine is trained by original data and fix the parameters of RBM. This process is continued for all Boltzmann layers. At the DBN layer the suitable results are found. While in Fine tuning the back propagation network is used also to revise the weight the gradient descent algorithm is utilized in whole network.

Deep Probabilistic Neural Network

Probabilistic neural network is a feed forward network used for recognition and classification. The network is based on Bayes-Parzen model, since the probability density function is calculated by the Parzen window while, the Bayes function will estimate the allocated class with highest probability for the input data. A class will be set only for the input data that have high probability density function. Thereby reducing the probability of misclassification.

The statistical model for the neural network concerning bayes network is called Kernel Fisher discriminant analysis. It is based on multi-layered network with four layers, such as:

1. Input layer
2. Pattern layer
3. Summation layer
4. Output layer

To define the probability density function by Bayes theorem, initially consider the sample (data) $s = [s_1, s_2, \ldots s_n]$, where n is the total number of data on the dataset with the prior probability sample belongs to p^{th} host system is l_p and cost for misclassification is c_p then the distribution function for host $f_1(s), f_2(s), \ldots f_p(s), \ldots f_F(s)$, then the Bayes function is given as,

$$l_i c_i f_i(s) > l_k c_k f_k(s) \; \forall \; k \neq i \quad k = 1, 2, \ldots P$$

The problem with the Bayes classification is the probability distribution is not known. But on other models the Gaussian distribution is often preferred. The structure of deep probabilistic neural network is given in figure below.

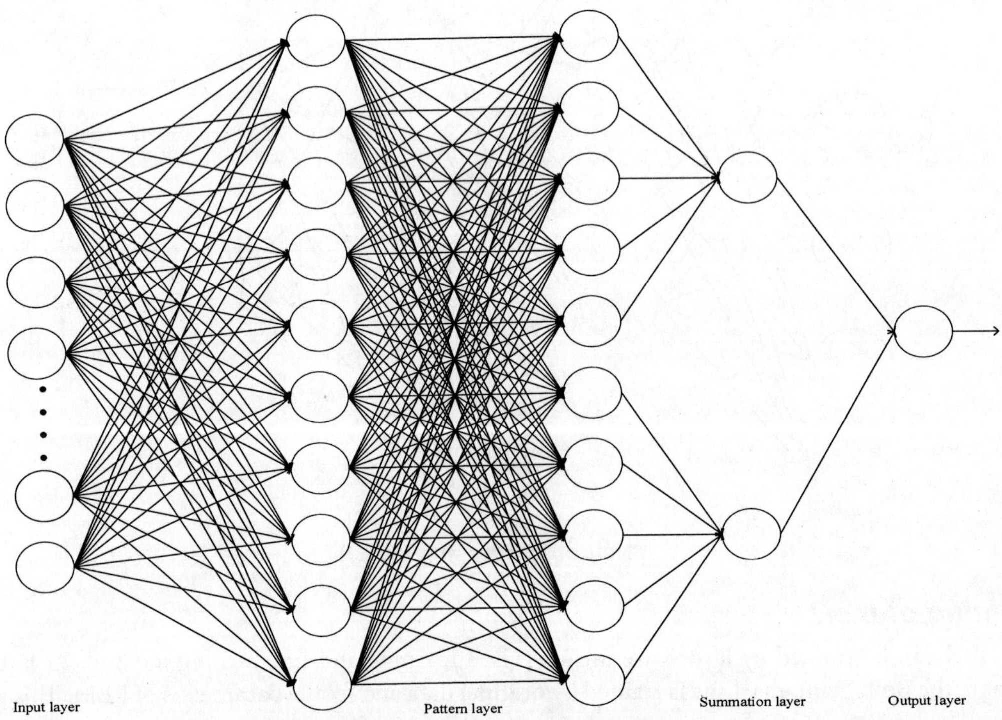

Structure of deep probabilistic neural network

In case of unknown distribution function, the statistical methods are used which has the problem of high misclassification problem. Thus, here a multivariate density function is derived as,

$$q(s_1, s_2, \dots s_n) = \frac{1}{T(\sigma_1, \sigma_2, \sigma_n)} \sum_{i=1}^{T} G\left(\frac{s_1 - s_{1-i}}{\sigma_i}, \frac{s_2 - s_{2-i}}{\sigma_2}, \dots \frac{s_n - s_{n-i}}{\sigma_n}\right)$$

where, $\sigma_1, \sigma_2, \dots \sigma_n$ is the kernel width, G is the weighting function and T is total number of training samples. The gaussian function is obtained as follows:

$$q(s) = \frac{1}{(2\pi)^{\pi/2}\sigma^n} \times \frac{1}{T} \sum_{i=1}^{T} \exp - \frac{||s - s_i||^2}{2\sigma^2}$$

where, s_i indicates the ith training vector, s is random variable vector, T and ω indicates the total training samples and smoothing parameter.

Deep Recurrent Neural Network

The recurrent neural network [203-205] is also an artificial neural network that has the feed forward mechanism with the connections in hidden layer. The artificial intelligence-based method has input layer, hidden layer and output layer. Here on hidden layer, the recurrent state information is fed back on the previous stage with the activation function thereby, exhibiting temporal behaviour. Let the input feature is indicated as, $Q = (q_1, q_2, \dots q_d)$ where, q_i is the data at i^{th} time step. Then the recurrent state on hidden layer is,

where, ϕ is a nonlinear function such as hyperbolic tangent function. The recurrent state execution is given in Fig.

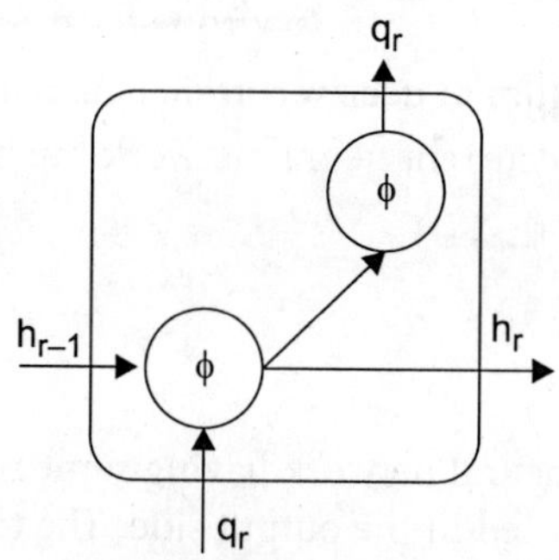

Recurrent state processing

The output of recurrent network is $G = g_1, g_2, \dots g_d$. The rule to update the recurrent hidden state is given as,

$$h_r = \phi(Wq_r + Uh_{r-1})$$

where, W and U are the coefficient matrix and activation for recurrent hidden units. Let the probability distribution be $p(q_1, q_2, \dots q_d)$, which is decomposed to,

$$p(q_1, q_2, \dots q_d) = p(q_1) \dots p(q_d | q_1, \dots, q_{d-1})$$

The conditional probability distribution is modelled with a recurrent network, at which $p(q_r | q_1, \dots q_{r-1}) = \phi(h_r)$. The Figure gives the structure of deep recurrent neural network.

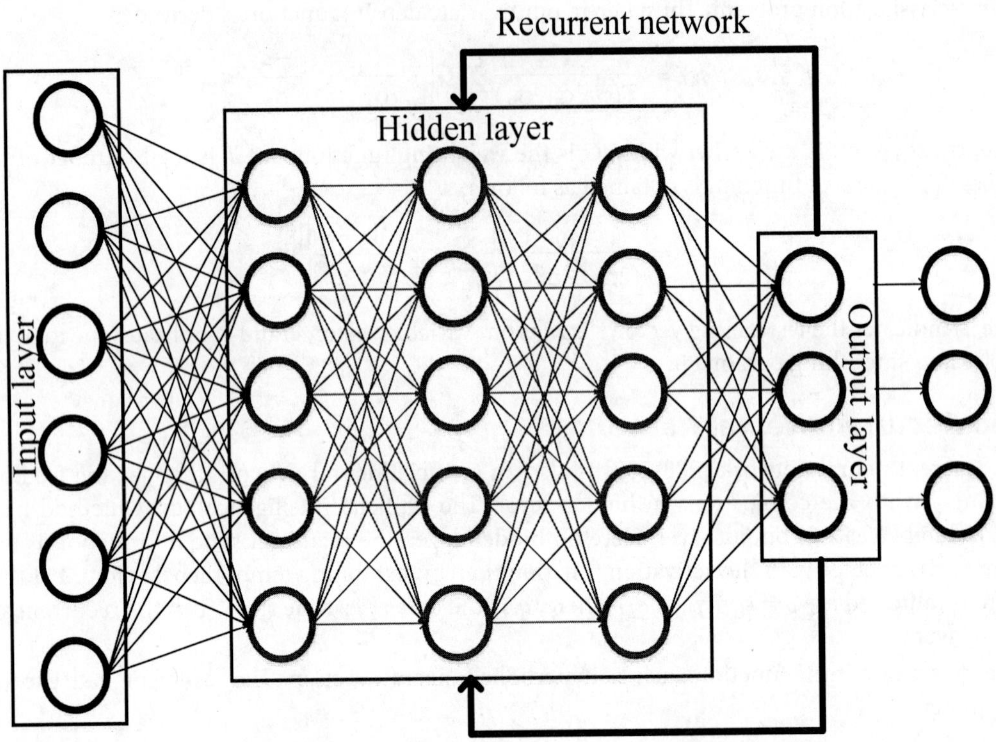

Structure of deep recurrent neural network

The overall output of the deep recurrent neural network can be computed as follows:

$$Q_{r-1} = \phi_{2r-1} h_{2r} + b^O$$

where, b^O is the bias at output layer.

Adaptive Auto-Encoder

The auto-encoder is a symmetrical neural network having same network at the input side for encoding and the reverse of same network is used in the output side. The training data is fed at the intermediate processing stage between the encoder and decoder. Those huge amount of data can able to learn from the specified features. This type of neural network is used to reconstruct data using the input feature and training data. In traditional encoder, the input feature is copied at the hidden layer while processing; hence the details of the features at this layer is not obtained or else false result may generate. Due to this here an adaptive auto encoder is designed which comprises deep neural network and auto-encoder.

Auto-Encoder

The layers involved in auto-encoder are input layer, encoding layer, decoding layer, latent representation and output layer. The auto-encoder is a feed forward network with single layer perceptron and without the non-recurrent network. Here the output layer and input layer have equal number of neurons that can define two transitions of encoding and decoding. Figure gives the structure of auto-encoder.

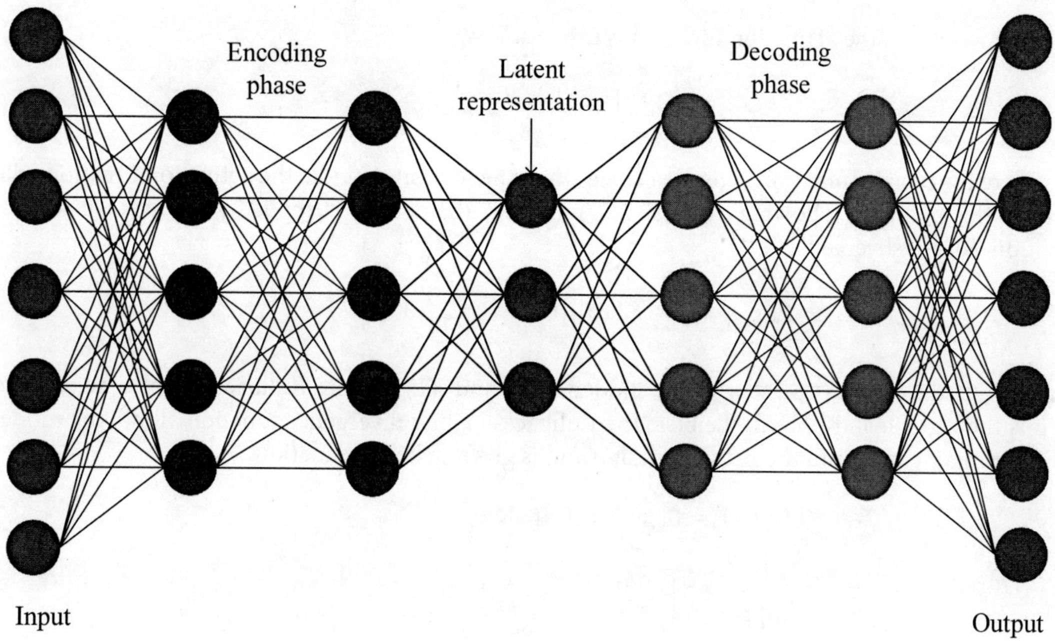

Structure of auto-encoder

The auto-encoders are classified as,

- Sparse auto-encoder
  - Regularized auto-encoder
  - Denoising auto-encoder
  - Contractive auto-encoder
- Concrete auto-encoder
- Variational auto-encoder

The input to the neural network is the features, which are represented as $Q = (q_1, q_2, \dots q_d)$ with d as the total number of features extracted. The selection of activation function in the model is a major step encountered in the processing. Here the sigmoid function is used for the activation function. Then the processing at the hidden layer is given as,

$$h(q_m, W, b) = \sigma(Wq_m + b); \qquad m = 1, 2, \dots d$$

where, σ is the sigmoid function, W is the weight and b is bias at the hidden layer. Then the output layer function is given as,

$$O = \sigma(Wh(q_m, W, b) + c)$$

where, c is the parameter that elate the involvement of feature to reach the objective. Then the term is given to the hidden layer, where the operating neurons are controlled during present iteration. Let $a_r(q)$ represents the activation function for r^{th} hidden layer. The back propagation is performed to send the weights to update on hidden layers thereby improving the learning rate and reducing the learning error on the gradients. This propagation is performed for reduction of learning error which is obtained during the computation of network weights gradient. The activation function is given as,

$$a = \text{sigmoid}\,(Wq + b)$$

The weight on the activation function is expressed as,

$$A_r = \frac{1}{d}\sum_{m=1}^{d}[a_r q_d]$$

Here the penalty function is needed since when the neurons are idle the activation function will be zero. At this point the following expression is followed. The penalty is applied when average activation function value is diverged.

$$P_{\text{penalty}} = \sum_{n=1}^{h_r} KL(\rho||\rho_r)$$

where, h_r is the neurons present at the hidden layer and $KL(.)$ is the Kullback–Leibler divergence at $\rho \cdot \rho$ is the variable in Kullback–Leibler. The Kullback–Leibler divergence function allows the model to exhibit proper entropy on the network design and is given in below equation:

$$KL(\rho||\rho_r) = \rho_{\log}\frac{\rho}{\rho_r} + (1-\rho)\log\frac{1-\rho}{1-\rho_r}$$

$$KL(\rho||\rho_r) = \begin{cases} 0; & \rho_r = \rho \\ C_{\text{adaptive}}; & \text{else} \end{cases}$$

The adaptive constant is obtained by applying the cost function. The expression for adaptive constant is given as,

$$C_{\text{adaptive}}(W,b) = C(W,b) + \alpha \sum_{r=1}^{h_r} KL(\rho||\rho_r)$$

where, α is the penality weight of the Kullback–Leibler divergence. The optimization issue found at this network is the need of minimizing the adaptive constant $C_{\text{adaptive}}(W, b)$, which is effectively solved by the SFLO algorithm. The algorithm iteratively updates the bias and weight using the learning rate η, which is indicated in following equation:

$$b_m(d) = b_m(d) - \eta\frac{\partial}{\partial b_m(d)}C_{\text{adaptive}}(W,b)$$

$$W_{mr}(d) = W_{mr}(d) - \eta\frac{\partial}{\partial W_{mr}(d)}C_{\text{adaptive}}(W,b)$$

Generative Adversarial Networks (GANs)

GANs is an approach for generative modelling using deep learning methods such as CNN (Convolutional Neural Network). Generative modelling is an unsupervised learning approach that involves automatically discovering and learning patterns in input data such that the model can be used to generate new examples from the original dataset.

GANs is a way of training a generative model by framing problem as a supervised learning problem with two sub-models. There are two components of GANs:

Generator: It is trained to generate new dataset, for example in computer vision it generates new images from existing real-world images.

Discriminator: It compares those images with some real-world examples and classify real and fake images.

Example: The Generator generates some random images (eg. tables) and then the discriminator compares those images with some real-world table images and sends the feedback to itself and Generator. Look at GAN structure in figure:

Applications of GAN:

1. Generating Images
2. Super Resolution
3. Image Modification
4. Photo realistic images
5. Face Ageing

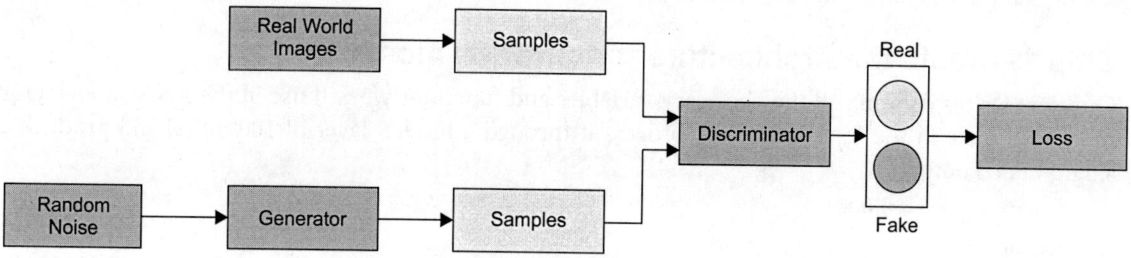

4.19 PRACTICAL IMPLEMENTATION

Build a Recurrent Neural Network from Scratch in Python

Coding RNN using Python

Step 0: Data Preparation

This is an inevitable first step in any data science project – preparing the data before we do anything else.

What does our network model expect the data to be like? It would accept a single sequence of length 50 as input. So the shape of the input data will be:

(number_of_records × length_of_sequence × types_of_sequences)

Here, types_of_sequences are 1, because we have only one type of sequence – the sine wave.

On the other hand, the output would have only one value for each record. This will of course be the 51st value in the input sequence. So it's shape would be:

(number_of_records × types_of_sequences) #where types_of_sequences is 1

Let us dive into the code. First, import the necessary libraries:

```
%pylab inline
import math
```

To create a sine wave like data, we will use the sine function from Python's math library:

```
sin_wave = np.array([math.sin(x) for x in np.arange(200)])
```

Visualizing the sine wave we've just generated:

```
plt.plot(sin_wave[:50])
```

Note that we looped for (num_records – 50) because we want to set aside 50 records as our validation data. We can create this validation data now:

```
X_val = []
Y_val = []
for i in range(num_records - 50, num_records):
X_val.append(sin_wave[i:i+seq_len])
Y_val.append(sin_wave[i+seq_len])
X_val = np.array(X_val)
X_val = np.expand_dims(X_val, axis=2)
Y_val = np.array(Y_val)
Y_val = np.expand_dims(Y_val, axis=1)
```

Step 1: Create the Architecture for our RNN model

Our next task is defining all the necessary variables and functions we will use in the RNN model. Our model will take in the input sequence, process it through a hidden layer of 100 units, and produce a single valued output:

```
learning_rate = 0.0001
nepoch = 25
T = 50              # length of sequence
hidden_dim = 100
output_dim = 1
bptt_truncate = 5
min_clip_value = -10
max_clip_value = 10
```

We will then define the weights of the network:

```
U = np.random.uniform(0, 1, (hidden_dim, T))
W = np.random.uniform(0, 1, (hidden_dim, hidden_dim))
V = np.random.uniform(0, 1, (output_dim, hidden_dim))
```

Here,

U is the weight matrix for weights between input and hidden layers

V is the weight matrix for weights between hidden and output layers

W is the weight matrix for shared weights in the RNN layer (hidden layer)

Finally, we will define the activation function, sigmoid, to be used in the hidden layer:

```
def sigmoid(x):
    return 1 / (1 + np.exp(-x))
```

Step 2: Train the Model

Now that we have defined our model, we can finally move on with training it on our sequence data. We can subdivide the training process into smaller steps, namely:

Step 2.1: Check the loss on training data

Step 2.1.1: Forward Pass

Step 2.1.2: Calculate Error

Step 2.2: Check the loss on validation data

Step 2.2.1: Forward Pass

Step 2.2.2: Calculate Error

Step 2.3: Start actual training

Step 2.3.1: Forward Pass

Step 2.3.2: Backpropagate Error

Step 2.3.3: Update weights

We need to repeat these steps until convergence. If the model starts to overfit, stop! Or simply predefine the number of epochs.

Step 2.1: Check the loss on training data

We will do a forward pass through our RNN model and calculate the squared error for the predictions for all records in order to get the loss value.

```
for epoch in range(nepoch):
  # check loss on train
  loss = 0.0
  # do a forward pass to get prediction
  for i in range(Y.shape[0]):
    x, y = X[i], Y[i]                # get input, output values of each record
  prev_s = np.zeros((hidden_dim, 1))  # here, prev-s is the value of the previous activation of hidden layer; which is initialized as all zeroes
    for t in range(T):
  new_input = np.zeros(x.shape)   # we then do a forward pass for every timestep in the sequence
  new_input[t] = x[t]            # for this, we define a single input for that timestep
  mulu = np.dot(U, new_input)
  mulw = np.dot(W, prev_s)
      add = mulw + mulu
      s = sigmoid(add)
  mulv = np.dot(V, s)
  prev_s = s
   # calculate error
  loss_per_record = (y - mulv)**2 / 2
     loss += loss_per_record
   loss = loss / float(y.shape[0])
```

Step 2.2: Check the loss on validation data

We will do the same thing for calculating the loss on validation data (in the same loop):

```
   # check loss on val
  val_loss = 0.0
   for i in range(Y_val.shape[0]):
     x, y = X_val[i], Y_val[i]
```

```
prev_s = np.zeros((hidden_dim, 1))
    for t in range(T):
new_input = np.zeros(x.shape)
new_input[t] = x[t]
mulu = np.dot(U, new_input)
mulw = np.dot(W, prev_s)
        add = mulw + mulu
        s = sigmoid(add)
mulv = np.dot(V, s)
prev_s = s
loss_per_record = (y - mulv)**2 / 2
val_loss += loss_per_record
val_loss = val_loss / float(y.shape[0])
  print('Epoch: ', epoch + 1, ', Loss: ', loss, ', Val Loss: ', val_loss)
```

You should get the below output:

```
Epoch: 1 , Loss: [[101185.61756671]] , Val Loss: [[50591.0340148]]
...
...
```

Step 2.3: Start actual training

We will now start with the actual training of the network. In this, we will first do a forward pass to calculate the errors and a backward pass to calculate the gradients and update them. Let me show you these step-by-step so you can visualize how it works in your mind.

Step 2.3.1: Forward Pass

In the forward pass:

We first multiply the input with the weights between input and hidden layers

Add this with the multiplication of weights in the RNN layer. This is because we want to capture the knowledge of the previous timestep

Pass it through a sigmoid activation function

Multiply this with the weights between hidden and output layers

At the output layer, we have a linear activation of the values so we do not explicitly pass the value through an activation layer

Save the state at the current layer and also the state at the previous timestep in a dictionary

Here is the code for doing a forward pass (note that it is in continuation of the above loop):

```
  # train model
  for i in range(Y.shape[0]):
    x, y = X[i], Y[i]
    layers = []
prev_s = np.zeros((hidden_dim, 1))
dU = np.zeros(U.shape)
     dV = np.zeros(V.shape)
```

```
dW = np.zeros(W.shape)
dU_t = np.zeros(U.shape)
dV_t = np.zeros(V.shape)
dW_t = np.zeros(W.shape)
dU_i = np.zeros(U.shape)
dW_i = np.zeros(W.shape)
    # forward pass
    for t in range(T):
new_input = np.zeros(x.shape)
new_input[t] = x[t]
mulu = np.dot(U, new_input)
mulw = np.dot(W, prev_s)
        add = mulw + mulu
        s = sigmoid(add)
mulv = np.dot(V, s)
layers.append({'s':s, 'prev_s':prev_s})
prev_s = s
```

Step 2.3.2: Backpropagate Error

After the forward propagation step, we calculate the gradients at each layer, and backpropagate the errors. We will use truncated back propagation through time (TBPTT), instead of vanilla backprop. It may sound complex but its straight forward.

The core difference in BPTT versus backprop is that the backpropagation step is done for all the time steps in the RNN layer. So, if our sequence length is 50, we will backpropagate for all the timesteps before the current timestep.

If you have guessed correctly, BPTT seems very computationally expensive. So instead of backpropagating through all previous timestep, we backpropagate till x timesteps to save computational power. Consider this ideologically similar to stochastic gradient descent, where we include a batch of data points instead of all the data points.

Here is the code for backpropagating the errors:

```
    # derivative of pred
dmulv = (mulv - y)
    # backward pass
    for t in range(T):
dV_t = np.dot(dmulv, np.transpose(layers[t]['s']))
dsv = np.dot(np.transpose(V), dmulv)
        ds = dsv
dadd = add * (1 - add) * ds
dmulw = dadd * np.ones_like(mulw)
dprev_s = np.dot(np.transpose(W), dmulw)
        for i in range(t-1, max(-1, t-bptt_truncate-1), -1):
            ds = dsv + dprev_s
```

```
dadd = add * (1 - add) * ds
dmulw = dadd * np.ones_like(mulw)
dmulu = dadd * np.ones_like(mulu)
dW_i = np.dot(W, layers[t]['prev_s'])
dprev_s = np.dot(np.transpose(W), dmulw)
new_input = np.zeros(x.shape)
new_input[t] = x[t]
dU_i = np.dot(U, new_input)
        dx = np.dot(np.transpose(U), dmulu)
dU_t += dU_i
dW_t += dW_i
      dV += dV_t
dU += dU_t
dW += dW_t
```

Step 2.3.3: Update weights

Lastly, we update the weights with the gradients of weights calculated. One thing we must keep in mind that the gradients tend to explode if you do not keep them in check. This is a fundamental issue in training neural networks, called the exploding gradient problem. So, we must clamp them in a range so that they do not explode. We can do it like this

```
      if dU.max() >max_clip_value:
dU[dU>max_clip_value] = max_clip_value
      if dV.max() >max_clip_value:
        dV[dV >max_clip_value] = max_clip_value
      if dW.max() >max_clip_value:
dW[dW>max_clip_value] = max_clip_value
      if dU.min() <min_clip_value:
dU[dU<min_clip_value] = min_clip_value
      if dV.min() <min_clip_value:
        dV[dV <min_clip_value] = min_clip_value
      if dW.min() <min_clip_value:
dW[dW<min_clip_value] = min_clip_value
    # update
    U -= learning_rate * dU
    V -= learning_rate * dV
    W -= learning_rate * dW
```

On training the above model, we get this output:

Epoch: 1 , Loss: [[101185.61756671]] , Val Loss: [[50591.0340148]]

Epoch: 2 , Loss: [[61205.46869629]] , Val Loss: [[30601.34535365]]

```
Epoch: 3 , Loss: [[31225.3198258]] , Val Loss: [[15611.65669247]]
Epoch: 4 , Loss: [[11245.17049551]] , Val Loss: [[5621.96780111]]
Epoch: 5 , Loss: [[1264.5157739]] , Val Loss: [[632.02563908]]
Epoch: 6 , Loss: [[20.15654115]] , Val Loss: [[10.05477285]]
Epoch: 7 , Loss: [[17.13622839]] , Val Loss: [[8.55190426]]
Epoch: 8 , Loss: [[17.38870495]] , Val Loss: [[8.68196484]]
Epoch: 9 , Loss: [[17.181681]] , Val Loss: [[8.57837827]]
Epoch: 10 , Loss: [[17.31275313]] , Val Loss: [[8.64199652]]
Epoch: 11 , Loss: [[17.12960034]] , Val Loss: [[8.54768294]]
Epoch: 12 , Loss: [[17.09020065]] , Val Loss: [[8.52993502]]
Epoch: 13 , Loss: [[17.17370113]] , Val Loss: [[8.57517454]]
Epoch: 14 , Loss: [[17.04906914]] , Val Loss: [[8.50658127]]
Epoch: 15 , Loss: [[16.96420184]] , Val Loss: [[8.46794248]]
Epoch: 16 , Loss: [[17.017519]] , Val Loss: [[8.49241316]]
Epoch: 17 , Loss: [[16.94199493]] , Val Loss: [[8.45748739]]
Epoch: 18 , Loss: [[16.99796892]] , Val Loss: [[8.48242177]]
Epoch: 19 , Loss: [[17.24817035]] , Val Loss: [[8.6126231]]
Epoch: 20 , Loss: [[17.00844599]] , Val Loss: [[8.48682234]]
Epoch: 21 , Loss: [[17.03943262]] , Val Loss: [[8.50437328]]
Epoch: 22 , Loss: [[17.01417255]] , Val Loss: [[8.49409597]]
Epoch: 23 , Loss: [[17.20918888]] , Val Loss: [[8.5854792]]
Epoch: 24 , Loss: [[16.92068017]] , Val Loss: [[8.44794633]]
Epoch: 25 , Loss: [[16.76856238]] , Val Loss: [[8.37295808]]
```

Time to get the predictions and plot them to get a visual sense of what we have designed.

Step 3: Get predictions

We will do a forward pass through the trained weights to get our predictions:

```
preds = []
for i in range(Y.shape[0]):
  x, y = X[i], Y[i]
prev_s = np.zeros((hidden_dim, 1))
  # Forward pass
  for t in range(T):
mulu = np.dot(U, x)
mulw = np.dot(W, prev_s)
    add = mulw + mulu
    s = sigmoid(add)
mulv = np.dot(V, s)
prev_s = s
preds.append(mulv)
preds = np.array(preds)
```

Plotting these predictions alongside the actual values:

```
plt.plot(preds[:, 0, 0], 'g')
plt.plot(Y[:, 0], 'r')
plt.show()
```

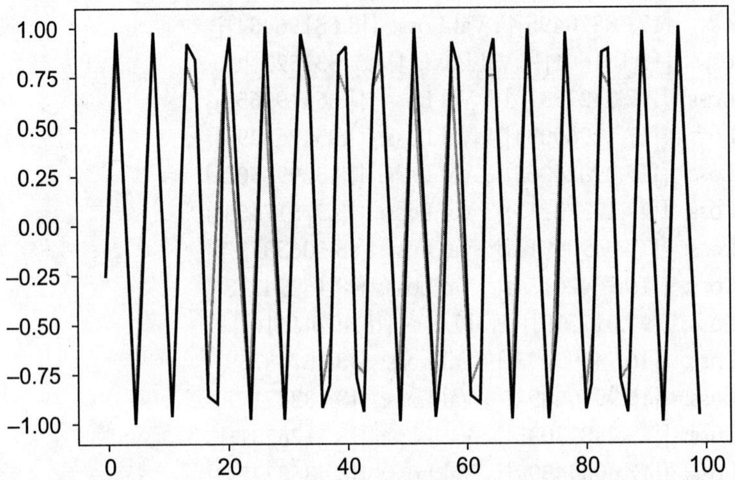

This was on the training data. How do we know if our model did not overfit? This is where the validation set, which we created earlier, comes into play:

```
preds = []
for i in range(Y_val.shape[0]):
    x, y = X_val[i], Y_val[i]
prev_s = np.zeros((hidden_dim, 1))
    # For each time step...
    for t in range(T):
mulu = np.dot(U, x)
mulw = np.dot(W, prev_s)
        add = mulw + mulu
        s = sigmoid(add)
mulv = np.dot(V, s)
prev_s = s
preds.append(mulv)
preds = np.array(preds)
plt.plot(preds[:, 0, 0], 'g')
plt.plot(Y_val[:, 0], 'r')
plt.show()
```

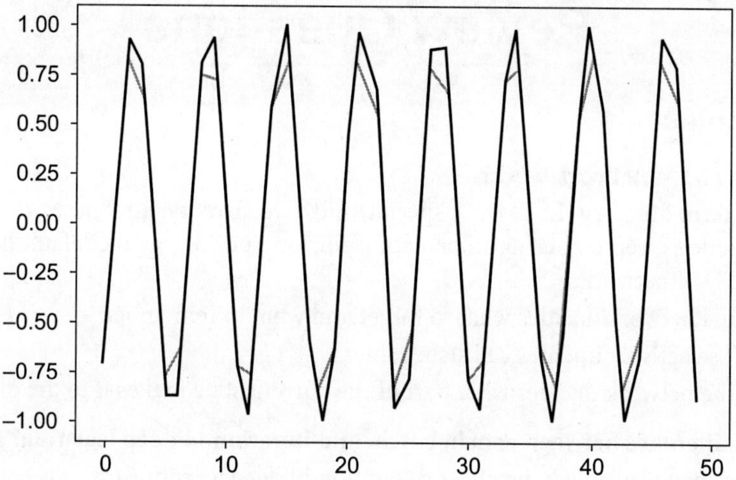

Not bad. The predictions are looking impressive. The RMSE score on the validation data is respectable as well:

```
from sklearn.metrics import mean_squared_error
math.sqrt(mean_squared_error(Y_val[:, 0] * max_val, preds[:, 0, 0] * max_val))
0.127191931509431
```

4.20 CONCLUSION

RNN extensions that essentially expand the memory are known as long short-term memory networks (LSTMs). As a result, it is adapted to learning from significant experiences with very lengthy time gaps between them. LSTM networks differ from RNN because they have a forget gate. This gate enables the network to discard data that is no longer necessary. As a result, LSTM networks are better at discovering long-term dependencies. The input sequences for these neural networks can be of any length. The vanishing gradient problem is more likely to affect RNN than LSTM networks, which are unable to experience it.

Review Questions

Solved Examples

Q.1. How does an LSTM network work?

Ans. Long-Short-Term Memory (LSTM) is a special kind of recurrent neural network capable of learning long-term dependencies, remembering information for long periods as its default behavior. There are three steps in an LSTM network:

- **Step 1:** The network decides what to forget and what to remember.
- **Step 2:** It selectively updates cell state values.
- **Step 3:** The network decides what part of the current state makes it to the output.

Q.2. What is the difference between epoch, batch, and iteration in deep learning?

Ans. The difference between epoch, batch, and iteration in deep learning are

- **Epoch:** Represents one iteration over the entire dataset (everything put into the training model).
- **Batch:** Refers to when we cannot pass the entire dataset into the neural network at once, so we divide the dataset into several batches.
- **Iteration:** If we have 10,000 images as data and a batch size of 200. then an epoch should run 50 iterations (10,000 divided by 50).

Q.3. Why is a deep neural network better than a shallow neural network?

Ans. Both deep and shallow neural networks can approximate the values of a function. But the deep neural network is more efficient as it learns something new in every layer. A shallow neural network has only one hidden layer. But a deep neural network has several hidden layers that create a deeper representation and computation capability.

Q.4. How can you train hyperparameters in a neural network?

Ans. Hyperparameters in a neural network can be trained using four components:

Batch size: Indicates the size of the input data.

Epochs: Denotes the number of times the training data is visible to the neural network to train.

Momentum: Used to get an idea of the next steps that occur with the data being executed.

Learning rate: Represents the time required for the network to update the parameters and learn.

Q.5. What are the reasons for mini-batch gradient being so useful?

Ans. The reasons for mini-batch gradient being so useful are

- Mini-batch gradient is highly efficient compared to stochastic gradient descent.
- It lets you attain generalization by finding the flat minima.
- Mini-batch gradient helps avoid local minima to allow gradient approximation for the whole dataset.

Unsolved Questions

1. Explain generative adversarial network.
2. What are some of the uses of autoencoders in deep learning?
3. What are the reasons for mini-batch gradient being so useful?
4. What do you mean by Boltzmann machine?
5. Why are deep neural networks preferred over shallow neural networks?

Multiple Choice Questions

Q.1. Is it possible to capture implicit reasoning process by patten classification network?

(*a*) yes (*b*) maybe
(*c*) no (*d*) cannot be determined.

Q.2. Associative memory, if used in feedback structure of hopfield type can function as?

(*a*) data memory (*b*) cluster
(*c*) content addressable memory (*d*) none of the mentioned.

Q.3. In feedforward network, the associations corresponding to input – output patterns are stored in?

(*a*) activation state (*b*) output layer
(*c*) hidden layer (*d*) none of the mentioned

Q.4. Neuro – Fuzzy systems can lead to more powerful neural network?

(*a*) yes (*b*) no
(*c*) may be (*d*) cannot be determined

Q.5. What is the objective of associative memories?

(*a*) to store patters (*b*) to recall patterns
(*c*) to store association between patterns (*d*) none of the mentioned

Answer Key

1. (*a*) 2. (*c*) 3. (*d*) 4. (*a*) 5. (*c*)

Fill in the Blanks

1. The perceptron convergence theorem is applicable for both _______ and bipolar data.
2. In GRNN and _______ networks training is completely avoided.
3. Pattern storage task generally accomplished by a feedback network consisting of processing units with _______ output functions.
4. The nature of mapping problem decides overall number of _______ in hidden layers.
5. The objective of perceptron learning is to adjust _______ along with class identification.

Answer Key

1. Binary 2. PNN 3. Non-linear 4. Units 5. Weight

❑❑❑

5 Creating and Deploying Networks using TensorFlow and Keras

5.1 INTRODUCTION TO TENSORFLOW

TensorFlow is an open-source machine learning framework for all developers. It is used for implementing machine learning and deep learning applications. To develop and research on fascinating ideas on artificial intelligence, Google team created TensorFlow. TensorFlow is designed in Python programming language, hence it is considered an easy-to-understand framework.TensorFlow is basically a software library for numerical computation using data flow graphs where:

- nodes in the graph represent mathematical operations.
- edges in the graph represent the multidimensional data arrays (called tensors) communicated between them. (Please note that tensor is the central unit of data in TensorFlow).

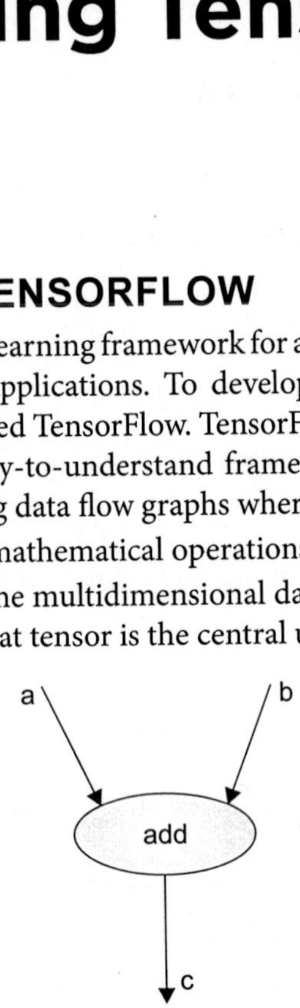

Consider the diagram above

Here, add is a node which represents addition operation. a and b are input tensors and c is the resultant tensor. This flexible architecture allows you to deploy computation to one or more CPUs or GPUs in a desktop, server, or mobile device with a single API!

Let us now consider the following important features of TensorFlow:

- It includes a feature of that defines, optimizes, and calculates mathematical expressions easily with the help of multi-dimensional arrays called tensors.
- It includes a programming support of deep neural networks and machine learning techniques.
- It includes a high scalable feature of computation with various data sets.
- TensorFlow uses GPU computing, automating management. It also includes a unique feature of optimization of same memory and the data used.

5.2 HISTORY OF TENSORFLOW

Many years ago, deep learning started to exceed all other machine learning algorithms when giving extensive data. Google has seen it could use these deep neural networks to upgrade its services:

- Google search engine
- Gmail
- Photo

They build a framework called TensorFlow to permit researchers and developers to work together in an AI model. Once it approved and scaled, it allows lots of people to use it.

It was first released in 2015, while the first stable version was coming in 2017. It is an open- source platform under Apache Open-Source License. We can use it, modify it, and reorganize the revised version for free without paying anything to Google.

5.3 WHY IS TENSORFLOW SO POPULAR?

TensorFlow is well-documented and includes plenty of machine learning libraries. It offers a few important functionalities and methods for the same.

TensorFlow is also called a "Google" product. It includes a variety of machine learning and deep learning algorithms. TensorFlow can train and run deep neural networks for handwritten digit classification, image recognition, word embedding and creation of various sequence models.

- **Models can be developed easily**: TensorFlow supports high-level APIs, through which Machine Learning models can be built easily using Neural Networks.
- **Complex Numeric Computations can be done:** As the input dataset is huge, the mathematical computations/calculations can be done easily.
- **Consists of Machine Learning APIs**: TensorFlow is rich in Machine Learning APIs that are of both low-level and high-level. Stable APIs are available in Python and C. Presently, working on APIs for Java, JavaScript, Julia, Matlab, R, etc.
- **Easy deployment and computation using CPU, GPU:**TensorFlow supports training and building models on CPU and GPU. Computations can be done on both CPU and GPU and can be compared too.
- **Contains pre-trained models and datasets**: Google has included many datasets and pre-trained models in TensorFlow. Datasets include mnist, vgg_face2, ImageNet, coco etc.
- **Pre-trained models for mobiles, embedded devices, and production:** The Machine Learning models can be deployed on mobile and embedded devices using TensorFlow. Pre-trained models can be directly used for production.
- **Tensorboard, a kit using TensorFlow's visualization toolkit made ML easy through model graphs:**Tensorboard is TensorFlow's visualization toolkit used to display images, graphs, etc.
- **Supporting Keras:**Keras is a high-level API of TensorFlow that is built on top of TensorFlow and Theano. Nowadays, Keras has become popular as a widely used TensorFlow API.
- **Open Source:**TensorFlow is an open-source platform, free to use and allows developers and researchers to build and deploy Machine Learning models.

Use Cases/Applications of TensorFlow

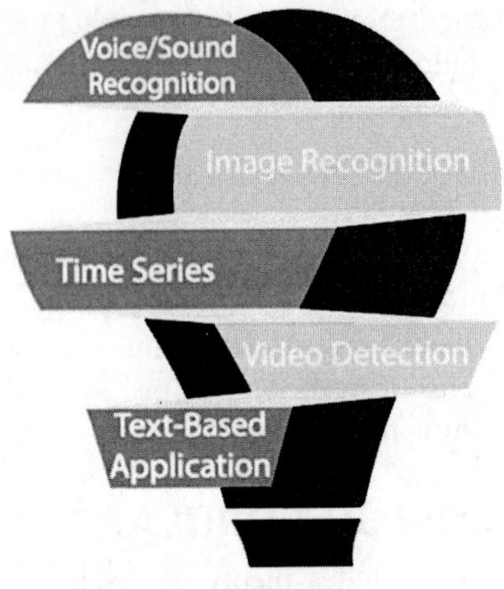

5.4 ARCHITECTURE OF TENSORFLOW

The TensorFlow runtime is a cross-platform library. The system architecture which makes this combination of scale flexible. We have basic familiarity with TensorFlow programming concepts such as the computation graph, operations, and sessions.

Some terms need to be understood first to understand TensorFlow architecture. The terms are TensorFlow Servable, servable Streams, TensorFlow Models, Loaders, Sources, Manager, and Core. The term and their functionality in the architecture of TensorFlow are described below.

TensorFlow architecture is appropriate to read and modify the core TensorFlow code.

1. **TensorFlow Servable:** These are the central uncompleted units in TensorFlow serving. Servables are the objects that the clients use to perform the computation.

   The size of a servable is flexible. A single servable may consist of anything from a lookup table to a unique model in a tuple of interface models. Servable should be of any type and interface, which enabling flexibility and future improvements such as:

   - Streaming results
   - Asynchronous modes of operation.
   - Experimental APIs
2. **Servable Versions:** TensorFlow server can handle one or more versions of the servables, over the lifetime of any single server instance. It opens the door for new algorithm configurations, weights, and other data can be loaded over time. They also can enable more than one version of a servable to be charged at a time. They also allow more than one version of a servable to be loaded concurrently, supporting roll-out and experimentation gradually.
3. **Servable Streams:** A sequence of versions of any servable sorted by increasing version of numbers.
4. **TensorFlow Models:** A serving represents a model in one or more servables. A machine-learned model includes one or more algorithm and lookup the embedding tables. A servable can also serve like a fraction of a model; for example, an example, a large lookup table be served as many instances.

5. **TensorFlow Loaders:** Loaders manage a servable's life cycle. The loader API enables common infrastructure which is independent of the specific learning algorithm, data, or product use-cases involved.
6. **Sources in TensorFlow Architecture:** In simple terms, sources are modules that find and provide servable. Each reference provides zero or more servable streams at a time. For each servable stream, a source supplies only one loader instance for every servable.

   Each source also provides zero or more servable streams. For each servable stream, a source supplies only one loader instance and makes available to be loaded.
7. **TensorFlow Managers:** TensorFlow managers handle the full lifecycle of a Servables, including:
   - Loading Servables
   - Serving Servables
   - Unloading Servables

   Manager observes to sources and tracks all versions. The Manager tries to fulfill causes, but it can refuse to load an Aspired version.

   Managers may also postpone an "**unload**." For example, a manager can wait to unload as far as a newer version completes loading, based on a policy to assure that at least one version is loaded all the times.

   For example, GetServableHandle (), for clients to access the loaded servable instances.
8. **TensorFlow Core:** This manages the below aspects of servables:

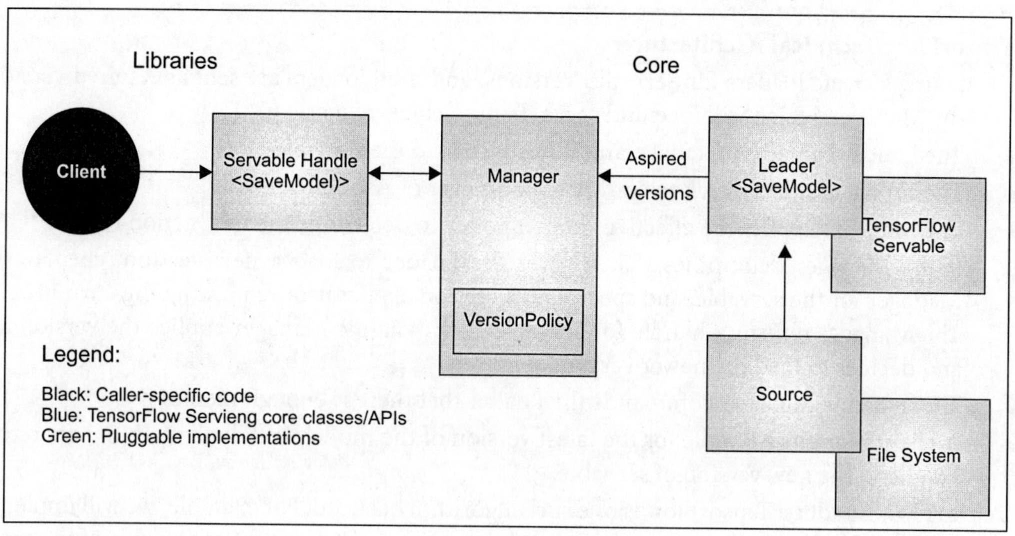

- Lifecycle
- Metrics
- TensorFlow serving core satisfaction servables and loaders as the opaque objects.

9. Life of a Servable:

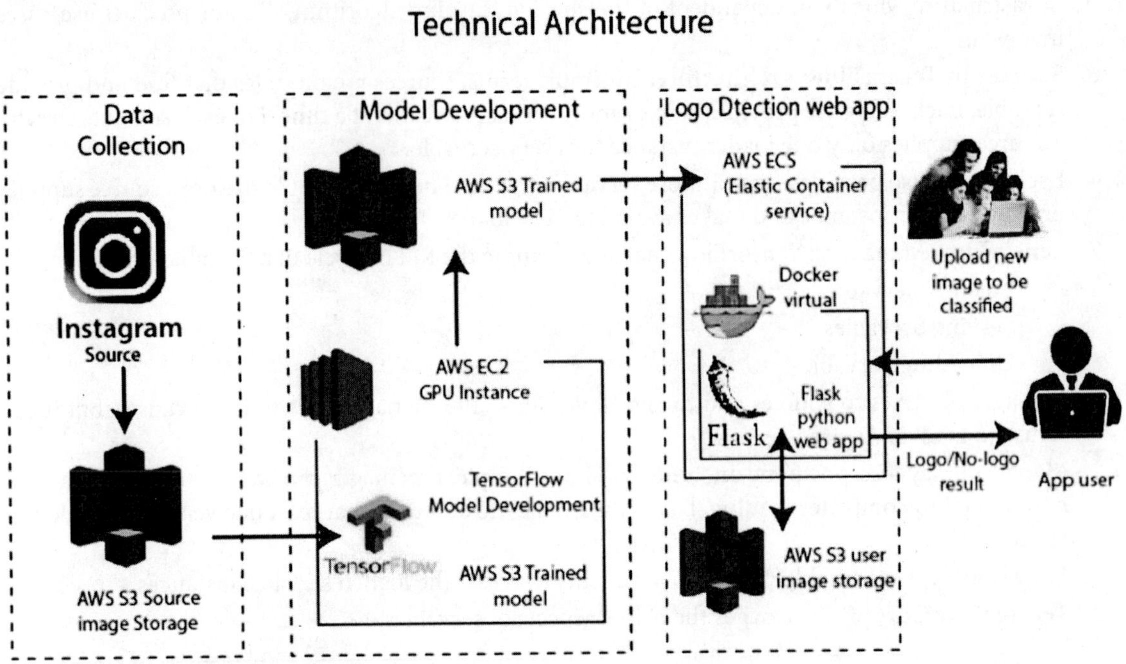

TensorFlow Technical Architecture:

- Sources create loaders for Servable Versions, and then loaders are sent as Aspired versions to the Manager, which will load and serve them to client requests.
- The Loader contains metadata, and it needs to load the servable.
- The source uses a callback to convey the Manager of Aspired version.
- The Manager applies the effective version policy to determine the next action to take.
- If the Manager determines that it gives the Loader to load a new version, clients ask the Manager for the servable, and specifying a version explicitly or requesting the current version. The Manager returns a handle for servable. The dynamic Manager applies the version action and decides to load the newer version of it.
- The dynamic Manager commands the Loader that there is enough memory.
- A client requests a handle for the latest version of the model, and dynamic Manager returns a handle to the new version of servable.

10. **TensorFlow Loaders:** TensorFlow is one such algorithm backend. For example, we will implement a new loader to load, provide access, and unload an instance of a new type of servable of the machine learning model.
11. **Batcher in TensorFlow Architecture:** Batching of TensorFlow requests into a single application can significantly reduce the cost f performing inference, especially in the presence of hardware accelerators and GPUs. TensorFlow serving has a claim batching device that approves clients to batch their type-specific assumption beyond request into batch quickly. And request that algorithm systems can process more efficiently.

5.5 TENSORFLOW BASICS

TensorFlow is a machine learning framework and developed by **Google Brain Team**. It is derived from its core framework: **Tensor**. In TensorFlow, all the computations involve tensors. A tensor is a vector or a matrix of n-dimensions which represents the types of data. All the values in a TensorFlow identify data type with a known shape. The shape of the data is the dimension of the matrix or array.

Representation of a Tensor

In **TensorFlow**, a tensor is the collection of feature vector (Like, array) of n-dimension. For instance, if we have any 2 × 3 matrix with values 1 to 6, we write:

$$\begin{bmatrix} 1 & 3 & 5 \\ 2 & 4 & 6 \end{bmatrix}$$

TensorFlow represents this matrix as:

[[1, 3, 5],
[2, 4, 6]]

If we create any three-dimensional matrix with values 1 to 8, we have:

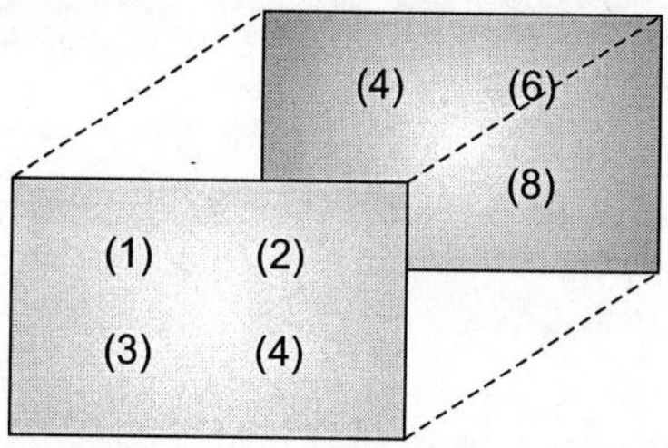

TensorFlow represents this matrix as:

[[[1, 2,],
[[3, 4],
[[5, 6],
[[7, 8]]

Note: A tensor is represented with a scalar or can have a shape of more than three dimensions. It is just difficult to anticipate high dimension.

5.6 TYPES OF TENSOR

All computations pass through one or more Tensors in TensorFlow. A tensor is an object which has three properties which are as follows:

- A unique label (name)
- A dimension (shape)
- A data type (dtype)

Each operation we will TensorFlow involves the manipulation of a tensor. There are four main tensors we can create:

- tf.Variable
- tf.constant

- tf.placeholder
- tf.SparseTensor

In the tutorial, we will learn how to create the **tf.constant** and a **tf. Variable.**

Make sure that we activate the conda environment with TensorFlow. We named this environment **hello-tf.**

For Windows user:

```
activate hello-tf
```

For macOS user:

```
source activate hello-tf
```

After we have done that, we are ready to import tensorflow

```
#Import tf
import tensorflow as tf
```

Create a tensor of n-dimension

We begin with the creation of a tensor with one dimension, namely a scalar.

To create a tensor, we can use tf.constant ()

```
tf.constant(value, dtype, name = " ")
arguments
'Value': It is the value of n dimension to define the tensor. And it is optional.
'dtype': Define the type of data:
'tf.string': String variable
'tf.float32': Float variable
'tf.int16': Integer variable
"name": Name of the tensor. Optional. By default, 'Const_1:0'
```

To create a tensor of dimension 0, We must run below code.

```
## rank 0
## Default name
r1=tf.constant (1, tf.int18)
print (r1)
```

Output:

```
Tensor ("Const: 0", shape (), dtype=int18
```

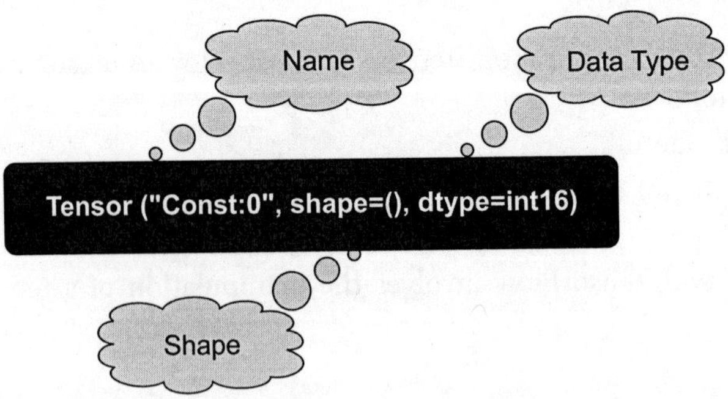

```
# Name my_scalar
r2 = tf.constant(1, tf.int18, name = "my_scalar")
print(r2)
```

Output:

```
Tensor ("my_scalar:0", shape=( ), dtype=int18
```

Each tensor is displayed by the name of tensor. Each tensor object is generated with
a unique label (name),
a dimension (shape)
a data type (dtype).
We can define a tensor with decimal values or with a string to change the type of the data.

```
#Decimal data
q1_decimal = tf.constant(1.12345, tf.float32)
print(q1_decimal)
#String data
q1_string = tf.constant('JavaTpoint", tf.string)
print(q1_string)
```

Output:

```
Tensor('Const_1:0", shape=( ), dtype=float32)
Tensor("Const_2:0", shape=( ), dtype=string)
```

A tensor of 1 dimension can be created as follows:

```
## Rank 1_vector = tf.constant([1, 3, 6], tf.int18)
print(q1_vector)
q2_boolean = tf.constant(True, True, False], tf.bool)
print(q2_boolean)
```

Output:

```
Tensor ("Const_5:0", shape=(4), dtype=int18)
Tensor("Const_4:0", shape=(4), dtype=bool)
```

We can notice the shape is only composed in 1 column.
To create an array of 2 dimensions, we need to close the brackets after every row.

Example:

```
## Rank 2
q2_matrix = tf.constant([[1, 2],
[3, 4]], tf.int18)
print(q2_matrix)
```

Output:

```
Tensor('Const_6:0", shape=(2, 2), dtype=int18)
```

The matrix possess 2 rows and 2 columns are filled with value 1, 2, 3, 4.
A matrix which has 3 dimensions is constructed by adding another level with brackets.

```
# Rank 3
q3_matrix = tf.constant([[[1, 2], [3, 4], [5, 6]]], tf.int18)
print(q3_matrix)
```

Output:

```
Tensor("Const_6:0", shape=(1, 3, 2), dtype=int18)
```

The matrix looks like the below given picture

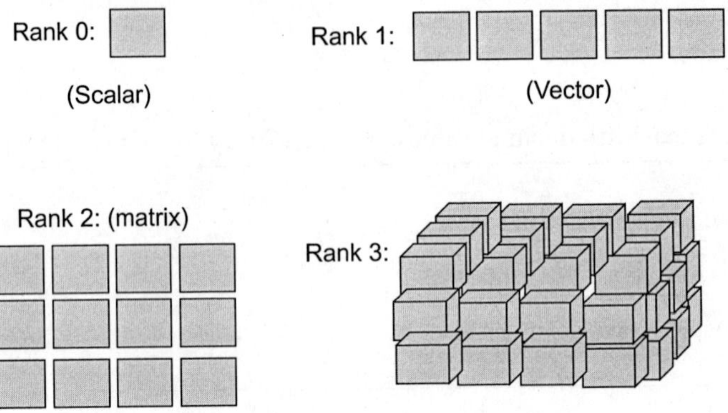

Shape of tensor

When we print the tensor, TensorFlow guesses the shape. However, we can get the shape property. Below, we construct a matrix filled with a number from 10 to 15 and we check the shape of m_shape

```
# Shape of a tensor
m_shape = tf.constant([[11, 10], [13, 12], [15, 14]])
m_shape = shape
```

Output:

```
TensorShape ([Dimension(2), Dimension(3)])
```

The matrix has 2 rows and 3 columns.

TensorFlow is some useful commands to create a vector or a matrix filled with 0 or 1. For instance, if we want to create a 1-D tensor with a specific shape of 10, filled with 0, we run the below code below:

```
# Create a vector of 0
print(tf.zeros(10))
```

Output:

```
Tensor("zeros:0", shape=(10,), dtype=float32)
```

The property works for matrix. Here, we create a 10 × 10 matrix filled with 1.

```
# Create a vector of 1
print(tf.ones([10, 10])
```

Output:

```
Tensor("ones:0", shape=(10, 10), dtype=float23)
```

We use the shape of a given matrix to make a vector 1. The matrix m_shape is 3x2 dimensions. We can create a tensor with 3 rows filled by one's with the given code:

```
# Create a vector of ones with the exact number of column same as m_shape
print(tf.ones(m_shape.shape[0]))
```

Output:

```
Tensor("ones_1:0", shape=(3), dtype=float42)
```

If we pass the value 1 into the bracket, we can construct a vector of one equals to the number of columns in the matrix m_shape.

```
# Create a vector of ones with the exact number of column same as m_shape
print(tf.ones(m_shape.shape[1]))
```

Output:

```
Tensor("ones_3:0", shape=(2, 3), dtype=float32)
```

Finally, we create a matrix 3 × 2 with one.

```
print(tf.ones(m_shape.shape))
```

Output:

```
Tensor('ones_3:0", shape=(2, 3), dtype=float32)
```

5.7 TYPES OF DATA

The second property of the tensor is the type of data. A tensor can only one type of data at one time. A tensor can have only one type of data. We can return the type with the property dtype.

```
print(m_shape.dtype)
```

Output:

```

```

In some conditions, we want to change the type of data. In TensorFlow, it is possible by tf.cast method.

Example

Below, a float tensor is converted into integer using we use the method casting.

```
# Change type of data
type_float = tf.constant[3.123456788, tf.float23)
type_int=tf.cast(type_float, dtype=tf.int23)
print(type_int.dtype)
print(type_float.dtype)
```

Output:

```
<dtype: 'float'>
<dtype: 'int23'>
```

TensorFlow chooses the type of data when the argument is not specified during the creation of tensor. TensorFlow will guess what the most likely types of data is. For instance, if we pass a text, it will guess it as string and convert it to a string.

Creating Operator

5.8 SOME USEFUL TENSORFLOW OPERATORS

We know how to create a tensor with TensorFlow. It is time to perform mathematical operations.

TensorFlow contains all the necessary operations. We can begin with a simple one. We will use TensorFlow method to compute the square of any number. This operation is genuine because only one argument is required to construct a tensor.

The square of a number is constructed by the function tf.sqrt(x) x as a floating number.

```
x=tf.constant[2.0], dtype=tf.float32)
print(tf.sqrt(x))
```

Output:

```
Tensor("Sqrt:0", shape=(1,), dtype=float32)
```

Note: The output returns a tensor object and not the result of the square of 2. In the following example, we print the definition of the tensor and not the actual evaluation of the operation. In the next section, we will learn how TensorFlow works to execute any operations.

Below is a list of commonly used operations. The idea is the same. Epoch operation requires one or many arguments.

- tf.exp(a)
- tf.sqrt(a)
- tf.add(a,b)
- tf.substract(a,b)
- tf.multiply(a,b)
- tf.div(a,b)
- tf.pow(a,b)

Example:

```
# Add
tensor_a=tf.constant([3, 4]], dtype=tf.int32)
tensor_b=tf.constant([[1, 2]], dtype=tf.int32)
tensor_add=tf.add(tensorflow_a, tensor_b)print(tensor_add)
```

Output:

```
Tensor("Add:0", shape=(3, 4), dtype=int32)
```

Explanation of code

Create any two tensors:

- One tensor with 1 and 2
- Second tensor with 3 and 4

We add both tensors.

Notice: That both needs to have the same shape. We can execute a multiplication of two tensors.

```
#Multiply
tensor_multiply=tf.multiply(tensor_x, tensor_y)
print9tensor_multiply)
```

Output:

```
Tensor("Mul:0", shape=(3, 4), dtype=int23)
```

Variable

We have only created constant tensors. Data always arrive with different values; we use the variable class. It will represent a node where the value will change.

To create a variable, we use tf.get_variable() method

```
tf.get_variable(name = " ", values, dtype, initializer)
argument
- 'name = " ": Name of the variable
- 'values': Dimension of the tensor
- 'dtype': Type of data. Optional
- 'initializer': How to initialize the tensor. Optional
If initializer is specified. Then here no need to include the "values" as the shape of "initializer" is used.
```

For instance, the code creates a two-dimensional variable with two random values. By default, TensorFlow returns a random value. We name the variable "var."

```
# Create a Variable
## Create 2 Randomized values
var = tf.get_variable("var", [1, 2])
print(var.shape)
```

Output:

```
(1, 2)
```

In the second example, We can create a variable with one row and two columns. We need to use [1,2] to create the dimension of the variable.

The initials values of the tensor are zero. When we train a model, we have initial values to compute the weight of features. We set the initial value to zero.

```
var_init_1 = tf.get_variable("var_init_2", [1, 2], dtype=tf.int23, initializer=tf.zeros_initializer)
print(var_init_1.shape)
```

Output:

```
(2, 1)
```

We can pass the value of a constant tensor in the variable. We create a constant tensor with the method tf.constant(). We use this tensor to initialize the variable.

The first value of the variable are 10, 20, 30, 40 and 50. The new tensors have a shape of 2 × 2.

```
# Create any 2 × 2 matrixtensor_const = tf.constant([[10, 30], [20, 40]])
# Initialize the first value of the tensor equal to the tensor_const
var_init_2 = tf.get_variable('var_init_2", dtype=tf.int23, initializer=tensor_const)
print(var_init_2.shape)
```

Output:

```
(2, 2)
```

Placeholder

Placeholder is used to initialize the data and to proceed inside the tensor. To supply a placeholder, we need to use the method feed_dict. The placeholder will fed only within a session.

In our next example, we see how we create a placeholder with the method tf.placeholder. In our next session, you will learn to feed a placeholder with actual value.

The syntax is:

```
tf.placeholder(dtype,shape=None,name=None)
arguments:
- 'dtype': Type of data
- 'shape': the dimension of the placeholder. Optional. By default, the shape of the data.
- "Name": Name the placeholder. Optional
data_placeholder_a = tf.placeholder(tf.float23, name = "data_placeholder_a")
print(data_placeholder_a)
```

Output:

```
Tensor("data_placeholder_a:0", dtype=float32)
```

TensorFlow works in 3 main components:

- Graph
- Tensor

Session

Graphs and sessions are independent. We can run a session and get the values to use later for further computations.

In the example below, we will:

- Create two tensors
- Create an operation
- Open a session
- Print the result

Step-1: We create two tensors x and y

```
## Create run and evaluate a session
X = tf.constant([2])
X = tf.constant([2])
```

Step-2: We create the operator by multiplying x and y

```
## Create a operator
multiply = tf.multiply(x, y)
```

Step-3: we open a session. All the computations will happen with the session. When we are done, we need to close the session.

```
## Create a session to run the given code
Sess = tf.Session()result_1=sess.run(multiply)
print(result_1)
sess.close()
```

Output:

```
[8]
```

Explanation of Code

- **tf.Session():** Open a session. All the operations will flow with the sessions
- **Run (Multiply):** Execute the operation which is created in step2.
- **print(result_1):** Finally, we can print the result
- **close():** Close the session

The result **"8"**, is the multiplication of var **x** and **y.**

Another way to create a session is to create inside a block. The advantage is it closes the session.

```
With tf.Session() as sess:
result_2 = multiply.eval()
print(result_2)
```

Output:

```
[8]
```

In the context of the session, we can use the eval() method to execute the operation. It is equivalent to run() function. It makes the code more reliable.

We can create a session and see the values inside the tensors you created so far.

```
## Check the tensors created before
sess = tf.Session()
print(sess.run(r1))
print(sess.run(r2_matrix))
print(sess.run(r3_matrix))
```

Output:

```
1
[[1  2]
  [3  4]
[[[1  2]
  [3  4]
  [5  6]]]
```

Variables are empty by default, even after we create a tensor. We need to initialize the variable if we want to use the variable. The object tf.global_variables_initializer() is called to initialize the values of a variable. This object will initialize all the variables. This is helpful before we train a model.

We can check the values of the variables we created before. Note that we need to use run to evaluate the tensor.

```
sess.run(tf.global_variables_intializer())
print(sess.run(var))
print(sess.run(var_initi_1))
print(sess.run(var_init_2))
```

Output:

```
[[-0.05356491  0.75867283]]
[[0  0]]
[[10  20]]
  [30  40]]
```

We can use the placeholder we created and feed it with the actual value. We need to pass the data in the method feed_dict.

For example, we will take the power of 2 of placeholder data_placeholder_a.

```
import numpy as np
power_a = tf.pow(data_placeholder_a, 3)
with tf.Session() as sess:
data = np.random.rand(1, 11)
print(sess.run(power_a, feed_dist=(data_placeholder_a:data)))
```

Explanation of Code

- import numpy as np:
- Import numpy library to create data
- tf.pow(data_placeholder_a, 3): Create the ops
- np.random.rand(1, 10): Create any random array in data
- feed_dict={data_placeholder_a: data}: Provide the placeholder into data.

Output:

```
[[0.05478135  0.27213147  0.8803037  0.0398424  0.21172127  0.01445725  0.02584014  0.37639
```

Graph

The graph shows a **node** and **edge.** The node is the representation of operation, i.e., the unit of computation. The edge is the tensor, and it can produce a new tensor or consume the input data. It depends on the dependencies between individual operations.

Tensor Flow depends on a brilliant approach to render the operation. All computations are represented with a dataflow schema. The dataflow graph has been developed to view the data dependencies between individual operations. Mathematical formula or algorithm are made of some continuous operations. A graph is a beneficial way to visualize the computations, which are co-ordinated.

The structure of the graph connects the operations (i.e., the nodes) and how those operations are feed. Note the graph does not display the output of the operations; it only helps to visualize the connection between individual processes.

Example: Imagine we want to evaluate the given function:

$$f(x, z) = xz + x^2 + z + 5$$

TensorFlow creates a graph to execute the service. The **graph** looks like this:

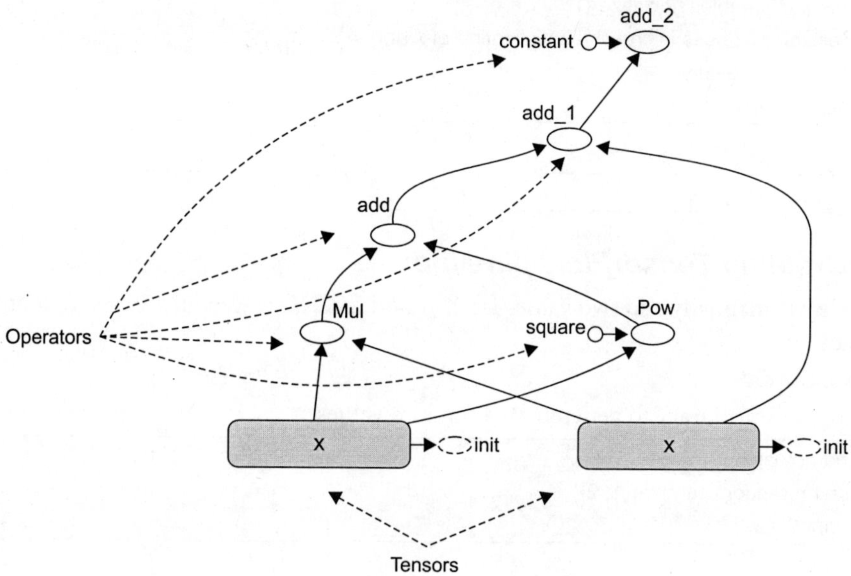

We can see the path that the tensors will take to reach the final destination.

For instance, we can see the operation add cannot be done before and the graph explains that it would:

- Compute and:
- Add 1) together
- Add to 2)
- Add 3) to

```
x = tf.get_variable("x", dtype=tf.int32, initializer=tf.constant([5]))
z = tf.get_variable("z", dtype=tf.int32, initializer=tf.constant([6]))
c = tf.constant([5], name = "constant")square = tf.constant([2], name = "square")
f = tf.multiply(x, y) + tf.pow(x, square) + y + c
```

Explanation of Code

- **x:** Initialize a variable named x with a constant value 5
- **z:** Initialize a variable named z with a constant value 6
- **c:** Initialize a cons tant tensors called c with the constant value 5.
- **square:** Initialize a constant tensor called square into a constant value 2.
- **f:** Construct the operator

In this example, we choose the value of the variable fixed. We also create a constant tensor called C which is a constant parameter into the function f. It takes a fixed value of 5. In the graph, we can see this parameter in the tensor called constant.

We also can construct a constant tensor for the power in operator tf.pow(). It is not necessary. We did it so that we can see the name of the tensor in the graph. It is the circle called a square.

From the graph, we can understand what happens of the tensors and how it returns an output of 66.

The code below evaluates the function in the session.

```
init = tf.global_variables_initializer()
with tf.Session() as sess:init.run() # Initialization of x and y
function_result = f.eval()
print(function_result)
```

Output:

```
[66]
```

Steps of Creating TensorFlow pipeline

In the example, we manually add two values for X_1 and X_2. Now we will see how to load the data into the TensorFlow.

Step 1: Create the data

Firstly, let's use numpy library to generate two random values.

```
import numpy as np
x_input = np.random.sample((1, 2))
print(x_input)
```

Ouput:

```
[[0.8835775  0.23766977]]
```

Step 2: Create the placeholder

We create a placeholder name X. We have to specify the shape of the tensor explicitly. In case we load an array with only two values. We write the shape [1,2].

```
# Using a placeholder
x = tf.placeholder(tf.float23, shape=[1, 2], name = 'X')
```

Step 3: Define the dataset.

Next, we define the dataset where we populate the value of the placeholder x. We need to use the method

```
tf.data.Dataset.from_tensor_slices
dataset = tf.data.Dataset.from_tensor_slices(x)
```

Step 4: Create a pipeline

In step four, we need to load the pipeline where the data is flow. We need to create an iterator make_initializable_iterator. We say its iterator. Then we have to call the iterator to feed the next batch of data, get_next. We name this step get_next. Note that in our example, there is one batch of data with two values.

```
iterator = dataset.make_initializable_iterator()
get_next = iterator.get_next()
```

Step 5: Execute the operation

The last step is the same as the previous example. We initialize a session, and we run the operation iterator. We feed the feed_dict in the value generated through numpy. These two value will occupy placeholder x. Then we run get_next to print a result.

```
With function tf.Session() as sess:
# Feed the placeholder into data.
sess.run(iterator.initializer, feed_dict=(x: x_input})
print(sess.run(get_nex))
```

Output:

```
[0.52374457,  0.71968478]
[0.8835775,  0.23766978]
```

TensorFlow works around:

1. **Graph:** It is a computational environment containing the operations and tensors
2. **Tensors:** Represents the data that will flow in the graph. It is the edge in the graph
3. **Sessions:** It allows the execution of the operations.

Create a Constant Tensor

Constant	Object
D0	tf.constant(1, tf.int18)
D1	tf.constant([1, 3, 5]), tf.int18)
D2	tf.constant([[1, 2], [5, 6]], tf.int18)
D3	tf.constant ([[[1, 2,], [3, 4], [6, 5]]], tf.int18)

Create an Operator

Create an Operator	Object
a + b	tf.add(a, b)
a*b	tf.multiply(a, b)

Create a Variable Tensor

Create an Variable	Object
Randomized value	tf.get_variable("var", [1, 2])
Initialized first value	tf.get_variable("var_init_2", dtype=tf.int32, initializer=[[1, 2], [3, 4]])

Open a Session

Session	Object
Create a session	tf.Session()
Run a session	tf.Session.run()
Evaluate a tensor	variable_name.eval()
Close a session	sess.close()
Session	with tf.Session() as sess:

5.9 INSTALLATION OF TENSORFLOW

To install TensorFlow, it is important to have "Python" installed in your system. Python version 3.4+ is considered the best to start with TensorFlow installation.

Consider the following steps to install TensorFlow in Windows operating system.

Step 1 – Verify the python version being installed.

```
<:\>Python
Python 3.6.5 (v3.6.5: f59c0932b4, Mar 28 2018, 16:07:46) [MSC v.1900 32 bit (Intel)] on win32
type "help", "copyright", "credits" or "license" for more information.
->>
```

Step 2 – A user can pick up any mechanism to install TensorFlow in the system. We recommend "pip" and "Anaconda". Pip is a command used for executing and installing modules in Python.

Before we install TensorFlow, we need to install Anaconda framework in our system.

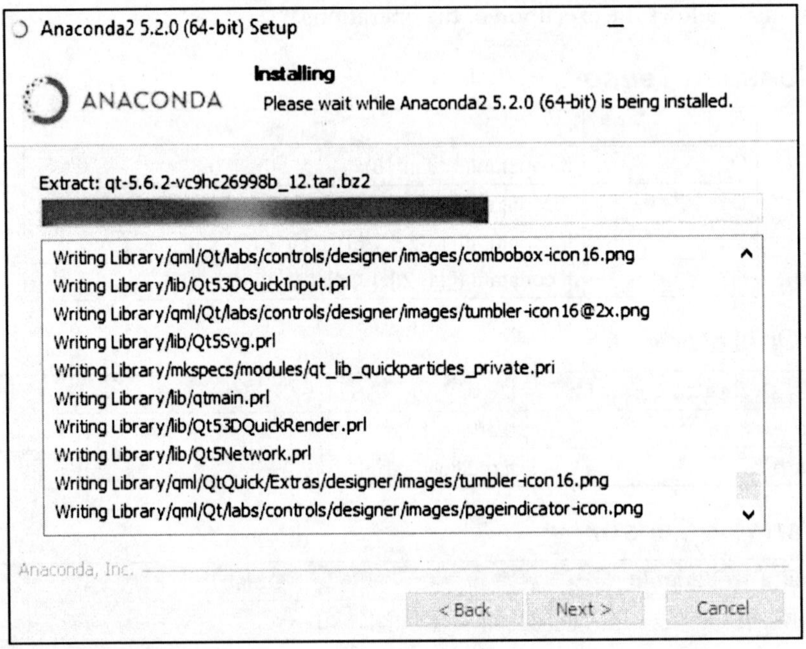

After successful installation, check in command prompt through "conda" command. The execution of command is displayed below:

```
C:\Users\Radhika>conda
usage: conda [–h][–v] command ...

conda is a tool for managing and deploying applications, environments and packages.

Options:

positional arguments:
command
clean               Remove unused packages and caches.
config              Modify configuration values in. condarc. This is modeled
                    after the git config command. Writes to the user. condarc
                    file (C:\Users\Radhika\.condarc) by default.
```

```
create        Create a new conda environment from a list of specified packages.
help          Displays a list of available conda commands and their help strings.
info          Display information about current conda install.
install       Installs a list of packages into a specified conda environment.
list          List linked packages in a conda environment.
package       Low-level conda package utility. (EXPERIMENTAL)
remove        Remove a list of packages from a specified conda environment.
uninstall     Alias for conda remove. See conda remove -- help.
search        Search for packages and display associated information. The
              input is a MatchSpec, a query language for conda packages.
              See examples below.
```

Step 3 – Execute the following command to initialize the installation of TensorFlow:

```
conda create -- name tensorflow python = 3.5
```

```
vc-14                |          h0510f6_3        3 KB
wincertstore-0.2     |     py35hfebbdb8_0       13 KB
wheel-0.31.1         |            py35_0        81 KB
certifi-2018.4.16    |            py35_0       143 KB
python-3.5-5         |         h0c2934d_2     18.2 MB
............................................................
                                Total:        20.8 MB
The following NEW packages will be INSTALLED:
certifi:            2018.1.16-py35_0
pip:                10.0.1-py35_0
python:             3.5.5-h0c2934d_2
setuptools:         39.2.0-py35_0
vc:                 14-h0510ff6_3
vs2015_runtime:     14.0.25125-3
wheel:              0.31.1-py35_0
wincertstore:       0.2-py35hfebbdb8_0

Proceed ([y]/n)? y

Downloading and Extracting Packages
pip-10.0.1          |  1.8 MB  |  ############################################################
setuptools-39.2.0   |  593 KB  |  ############################################################
vc-14               |    3 KB  |  ############################################################
wincertstore-0.2    |   13 KB  |  ############################################################
wheel-0.31.1        |   81 KB  |  ############################################################
certifi-2018.4.16   |  143 KB  |  ############################################################
python-3.5.5        | 18.2 MB  |  ############################################################
```

It downloads the necessary packages needed for TensorFlow setup.

Step 4 – After successful environmental setup, it is important to activate TensorFlow module.

```
activate tensorflow
```

```
C:\Users\Radhika>activate tensorflow
(tensorflow) C:\Users\Radhika>
```

Step 5 – Use pip to install "Tensorflow" in the system. The command used for installation is mentioned as below –

```
pip install tensorflow
```

And,

```
pip install tensorflow-gpu
```

```
Requirement already satisfied: termcolor>-1.1.0 in c:\users\radhika\anaconda2\envs\tensorflow\lib\site-packages (from tensorflow) (1.1.0)
Requirement already satisfied: numpy>-1.13.3 in c:\users\radhika\anaconda2\envs\tensorflow\lib\site-packages (from tensorflow) (1.14.5)
Requirement already satisfied: grpio>-1.8.6 in c:\users\radhika\anaconda2\envs\tensorflow\lib\site-packages (from tensorflow) (1.12.1)
Requirement already satisfied: wheel>-1.26 in c:\users\radhika\anaconda2\envs\tensorflow\lib\site-packages (from tensorflow) (0.31.1)
Requirement already satisfied: six>-1.10.0 in c:\users\radhika\anaconda2\envs\tensorflow\lib\site-packages (from tensorflow) (1.11.0)
Requirement already satisfied: abs1-py>-0.1.6 in c:\users\radhika\anaconda2\envs\tensorflow\lib\site-packages (from tensorflow) (0.2.2)
Requirement already satisfied: astor>-0.6.0 in c:\users\radhika\anaconda2\envs\tensorflow\lib\site-packages (from tensorflow) (0.6.2)
Requirement already satisfied: gast>-0.2.0 in c:\users\radhika\anaconda2\envs\tensorflow\lib\site-packages (from tensorflow) (0.2.0)
Requirement already satisfied: tensorboard>-1.9.0 in c:\users\radhika\anaconda2\envs\tensorflow\lib\site-packages (from tensorflow) (1.8.0)
Requirement already satisfied: htmlslib--0.9999999 in c:\users\radhika\anaconda2\envs\tensorflow\lib\site-packages (from tensorboard<1.9.0,>=1.8.0->tensorflow)(0.9999999)
Requirement already satisfied: bleach==1.5.0 in c:\users\radhika\anaconda2\envs\tensorflow\lib\site-packages (from tensorboard<1.9.0,>=1.8.0->tensorflow)(1.5.8)
Requirement already satisfied: markdown>=2.6.8 in c:\users\radhika\anaconda2\envs\tensorflow\lib\site-packages (from tensorboard<1.9.0,>=1.8.0->tensorflow)(2.6.11)
Requirement already satisfied: werkzeug>=0.11.10 in c:\users\radhika\anaconda2\envs\tensorflow\lib\site-packages (from tensorboard<1.9.0,>=1.8.0->tensorflow)(0.14.1)
Installing collected packages: tensorflow
```

```
Requirement already satisfied: numpy>-1.13.3 in c:\users\radhika\anaconda2\envs\tensorflow\lib\site-packages (from tensorflow) (1.14.5)
Requirement already satisfied: grpio>-1.8.6 in c:\users\radhika\anaconda2\envs\tensorflow\lib\site-packages (from tensorflow) (1.12.1)
Requirement already satisfied: wheel>-1.26 in c:\users\radhika\anaconda2\envs\tensorflow\lib\site-packages (from tensorflow) (0.31.1)
Requirement already satisfied: six>-1.10.0 in c:\users\radhika\anaconda2\envs\tensorflow\lib\site-packages (from tensorflow) (1.11.0)
Requirement already satisfied: abs1-py>-0.1.6 in c:\users\radhika\anaconda2\envs\tensorflow\lib\site-packages (from tensorflow) (0.2.2)
Requirement already satisfied: astor>-0.6.0 in c:\users\radhika\anaconda2\envs\tensorflow\lib\site-packages (from tensorflow) (0.6.2)
Requirement already satisfied: gast>-0.2.0 in c:\users\radhika\anaconda2\envs\tensorflow\lib\site-packages (from tensorflow) (0.2.0)
Requirement already satisfied: tensorboard>-1.9.0 in c:\users\radhika\anaconda2\envs\tensorflow\lib\site-packages (from tensorflow) (1.8.0)
Requirement already satisfied: setuptools in c:\users\radhika\anaconda2\envs\tensorflow\lib\site-packages (from protobuf>=3.4.0->tensorflow)(39.2.0)
Requirement already satisfied: htmlslib--0.9999999 in c:\users\radhika\anaconda2\envs\tensorflow\lib\site-packages (from tensorboard<1.9.0,>=1.8.0->tensorflow)(0.9999999)
Requirement already satisfied: bleach==1.5.0 in c:\users\radhika\anaconda2\envs\tensorflow\lib\site-packages (from tensorboard<1.9.0,>=1.8.0->tensorflow)(1.5.8)
Requirement already satisfied: markdown>=2.6.8 in c:\users\radhika\anaconda2\envs\tensorflow\lib\site-packages (from tensorboard<1.9.0,>=1.8.0->tensorflow)(2.6.11)
Requirement already satisfied: werkzeug>=0.11.10 in c:\users\radhika\anaconda2\envs\tensorflow\lib\site-packages (from tensorboard<1.9.0,>=1.8.0->tensorflow)(0.14.1)
Installing collected packages: tensorflow
Successfully installed tensorflow-1.8.0
```

After successful installation, it is important to know the sample program execution of TensorFlow.

5.10 SAVE AND LOAD MODELS IN TENSORFLOW

The development of the model can be saved both before and after testing. As a result, a model will pick up where it left off to eliminate lengthy training periods. You can still share your model and have others replicate it if you save it. Most machine learning professionals share the following when publishing test models and techniques:

- Code to create the model
- The trained weights for the model

Sharing this information allows others to better understand how the model operates and to test it with new data.

Aside from that, teaching the machine learning models will take a lot of time and effort. Shutting down the notebook or machine, though, causes all of those weights and more to disappear as the memory is flushed. It's important to save the models to optimize reusability in order to get the most out of your time.

5.11 HOW CAN TENSORFLOW BE USED TO CONFIGURE THE DATASET FOR PERFORMANCE?

Tensorflow is a popular open-source platform for building and training machine learning models. It provides several techniques for loading and preparing the dataset to get the best performance out of the model. The correct configuration of the dataset is crucial for the overall performance of the model, so it is important to choose the right techniques for preparing the dataset for Tensorflow.

Steps:

- **Split the dataset into training, validation, and test sets:** It is important to split the dataset into training, validation, and test sets. The training set is used to train the model, the validation set is used to validate the model, and the test set is used to evaluate the model's performance.
- **Data pre-processing:** Pre-processing is crucial in machine learning as it helps to eliminate any noise, missing values, or outliers in the data. In Tensorflow, the tf.data module provides several methods to pre-process the data. For example, you can use the map method to apply a pre-processing function to each element in the dataset.
- **Batching and shuffling the data:** Batching the data into smaller portions improves the performance of the model as it reduces memory usage. Shuffling the data helps to randomize the data, making the model less prone to overfitting. In Tensorflow, the batch and shuffle methods are used to batch and shuffle the data.
- **Augmenting the data:** Augmenting the data refers to creating new samples from the existing data by applying various transformations such as rotations, translations, etc. In Tensorflow, the map method can be used to apply augmentations to the datas

Implementing Neural Networks Using TensorFlow

Step 1 - Import library. import TensorFlow as tf from TensorFlow import Keras.

Step 2 - Load Dataset.

Step 3 - Preprocess and create dataset.

Step 4 - Create Neural network.

Step 5 - Build the model.

Step 6 - Train the model.

Step 7 - Make predictions.

Step 1 - Import library

```
import tensorflow as tf
from tensorflow import keras
```

Step 2 - Load Dataset

```
(x_train_data, y_train_data), (x_val_data, y_val_data) = keras.datasets.fashion_mnist.load_data()
```

```
Downloading data from https://storage.googleapis.com/tensorflow/tf-keras-datasets/train-labels-idx1-ubyte.gz
32768/29515 [==============================] - 0s 0us/step
Downloading data from https://storage.googleapis.com/tensorflow/tf-keras-datasets/train-images-idx3-ubyte.gz
26427392/26421880 [==============================] - 0s 0us/step
```

```
Downloading data from https://storage.googleapis.com/tensorflow/tf-keras-datasets/t10k-labels-idx1-ubyte.gz
8192/5148 [==============================================] - 0s 0us/step
Downloading data from https://storage.googleapis.com/tensorflow/tf-keras-datasets/t10k-images-idx3-ubyte.gz
4423680/4422102 [================================] - 0s 0us/step
```

Here in the above we are loading the dataset, also we are splitting them into training set and validation set. x_train_data and y_train_data is here to build our model in which x_train_data will consist of image pixel data for 60,000 clothes whereas the y_train_data will consist of classes i.e clothing type for x_train_data. Similarly, the x_val_data and y_val_data is used for testing or validation of our model.

Step 3 - Preprocess and create dataset

```
defpreprocessing_function(x_new, y_new):
    x_new = tf.cast(x_new, tf.float32) / 255.0
    y_new = tf.cast(y_new, tf.int64)
    return x_new, y_new
    deffunc_creating_dataset(xs_data, ys_data, num_classes=10):
    ys_data = tf.one_hot(ys_data, depth=num_classes)
    return tf.data.Dataset.from_tensor_slices((xs_data, ys_data)) \
    .map(preprocessing_function) \
```

Step 4 - Create Neural network

```
dataset_training = func_creating_dataset(x_train_data, y_train_data)b
    dataset_val = func_creating_dataset(x_val_data, y_val_data)
```

Step 5 - Build the model

```
My_model = keras.Sequential([
    keras.layers.Reshape(target_shape=(28 * 28,),
    input_shape=(28, 28)), keras.layers.Dense(units=256, activation='relu'),
    keras.layers.Dense(units=192, activation='relu'),
    keras.layers.Dense(units=128, activation='relu'),
    keras.layers.Dense(units=10, activation='softmax') ])
```

Step 6 - Train the model

```
My_model.compile(optimizer='adam',
    loss=tf.losses.CategoricalCrossentropy(from_logits=True),
        metrics=['accuracy'])
    history = My_model.fit(
    dataset_training.repeat(),
    epochs=10,
    steps_per_epoch=500,
    validation_data=dataset_val.repeat(),
    validation_steps=2
```

Step 7 - Make predictions

Make_predictions = My_model.predict(dataset_val)

Make_predictions

To summarize, classification neural networks are used to categorize characteristics and only permit one output response for each input pattern. When used in a hybrid system with other prognostic neural networks. The weights and the input-output function of each unit, which might be linear, threshold, sigmoid, RelU, step, Hyperbolic/tanh, or SoftMax, influence the performance of an ANN.

5.12 KEY FEATURES OF TENSORFLOW

- It has extensive community support with developers.
- It supports customized and high-ordered gradients.
- It allows fast debugging via Python tools.
- It provisions different levels of extraction that can simulate human brain neural models.
- It can also allow building and training complex neural models that can make decisions based on ML algorithms.
- It has several dynamic models that use Python to control the flow.
- It also has the flexibility to work with various other deep learning libraries and frameworks.
- It can also operate with Keras Functional API.
- It has well-written documentation of what to use. It makes developers inclined towards using this.
- TensorFlow can uphold and integrate powerful add-on predefined models and libraries into its ecosystem.
- Integrating TensorFlow with other data science and machine learning libraries is easy. It is the reason why developers are finding comfort in using it.

5.13 ADVANTAGES OF USING TENSORFLOW

- TensorFlow can utilize both GPU and CPU for training and modelling acceleration.
- It supports automated differentiation capabilities. It helps in gradient-based ML modelling.
- It aids developers in performing sub-part of a graph or neural network that helps in retrieving discrete data.
- Its compilation time is way faster than other deep learning libraries and frameworks.

5.14 DISADVANTAGES OF TENSORFLOW

- Although TensorFlow is efficient, it does not render much speed as compared to other deep learning frameworks.
- It does not support Nvidia GPU.
- Working with TensorFlow is lengthy because developers need to know linear algebra and advanced calculus.
- Because of its low-level API structure, the learning curve of TensorFlow is steep.
- It has missing symbolic loops.
- It does not support OpenCL.

5.15 APPLICATIONS AND USES

- Image and Face recognition
- HealthCare related applications like cancer, tumor detection, etc
- Recommendation Systems
- Virtual Assistants
- Self-driving cars
- Natural Language Processing

5.16 KERAS

Kerasis a deep learning API written in Python, running on top of the machine learning platform TensorFlow. It was developed with a focus on enabling fast experimentation. Being able to go from idea to result as fast as possible is key to doing good research.

Keras is:

Simple -- but not simplistic. Keras reduces developer cognitive load to free you to focus on the parts of the problem that really matter.

Flexible -- Keras adopts the principle of progressive disclosure of complexity: simple workflows should be quick and easy, while arbitrarily advanced workflows should be possible via a clear path that builds upon what you have already learned.

Powerful -- Keras provides industry-strength performance and scalability: it is used by organizations and companies including NASA, YouTube, or Waymo.

Key Features of Keras

- Keras is an API-based tool that is way more Pythonic.
- Modularity is a significant feature of Keras.
- User experience and smooth production of deep learning models are its key focus.
- Modeling and creating a deep neural network is easy yet robust.
- It supports rapid and easy prototyping of models.
- Keras is a high-level API that supports multi-platform and multi-backend integrations.
- It supports the creation of recurrent and convolutional neural networks.
- Keras is flexible and hence, preferred in different domains like healthcare, corporate insights, sales predictions, customer support, virtual assistants, etc.
- Keras is expressive. Therefore, enterprises and research organizations use it for various research purposes.
- Keras got developed from Python itself. Therefore, it is easy to explore, debug, and integrate.
- It helps in the rapid experimentation of projects that offer fast market-ready projects.

5.17 ADVANTAGES OF USING KERAS

- Using this, developers can minimize the number of user actions; so that the firm can deliver the prototype quickly.
- It can render actionable feedback as and when the user makes an error.
- It helps to produce a frequent, simplified, and optimized user interface for general use-cases.
- It helps in developing state-of-art models and creating new metrics and layers.

- Developers can deploy Keras on a wide range of devices.
- It is easy to learn and use.
- We can use Keras with Raspberry Pi and Android systems also.

5.18 DISADVANTAGES OF KERAS

- Keras is slow in executing and training deep learning models.
- It has fewer projects available online than that of TensorFlow.
- It has a complex architecture.
- Although it supports multi-GPU, it cannot utilize all of them.
- Sometimes it spontaneously shows low-level backend errors that are hard to debug.

5.19 INSTALLATION OF KERAS

Consider the following steps to install Keras

Prerequisites

You must satisfy the following requirements –

- Any kind of OS (Windows, Linux or Mac)
- Python version 3.5 or higher.

Keras is python based neural network library so python must be installed on your machine. If python is properly installed on your machine, then open your terminal and type python, you could see the response similar as specified below,

```
Python 3.6.5 (v3.6.5: f59c0932b4, Mar 28 2018, 17:00:18)
[MSC v.1900 64 bit (AMD64)] on win32
Type "help", "copyright", "credits" or "license" for more information.
>>>
```

If Python is not installed on your machine, then first install Python.

Keras Installation Steps

Keras installation is quite easy. Follow below steps to properly install Keras on your system.

Step 1: Create virtual environment

Virtualenv is used to manage Python packages for different projects. This will be helpful to avoid breaking the packages installed in the other environments. So, it is always recommended to use a virtual environment while developing Python applications.

Linux/Mac OS

Linux or mac OS users, go to your project root directory and type the below command to create virtual environment,

```
python3 -m venv kerasenv
```

After executing the above command, "kerasenv" directory is created with bin,lib and include folders in your installation location.

Windows

Windows user can use the below command,

```
py -m venv keras
```

Step 2: Activate the environment

This step will configure python and pip executables in your shell path.

Linux/Mac OS

Now we have created a virtual environment named "kerasvenv". Move to the folder and type the below command,

```
$ cd kerasvenv kerasvenv $ source bin/activate
```

Windows

Windows users move inside the "kerasenv" folder and type the below command,

```
.\env\Scripts\activate
```

Step 3: Python libraries

Keras depends on the following python libraries.

- Numpy
- Pandas
- Scikit-learn
- Matplotlib
- Scipy
- Seaborn

If these libraries are not installed, then use the below command to install one by one.

numpy

```
pip install numpy
```

you could see the following response,

```
Collecting numpy
  Downloading
https://files.pythonhosted.org/packages/cf/a4/d5387a74204542a60ad1baa84cd2d3
  numpy-3.1.1-cp36-cp36m-macosx_10_6_intel.
macosx_10_9_intel.macosx_10_10_×86_64.whl  (14.4MB)
  |                              | 14.4MB  2.8MB/s
```

pandas

```
pip install pandas
```

you could see the following response,

```
Collecting pandas
  Downloading
https://files.pythonhosted.org/packages/cf/a4/d5387a7420452a60ad1baa84cd2d3
pandas-3.1.1-cp36-cp36m-macosx_10_6_intel.
macosx_10_0_intel.macosx_10_9_×86_64.
  macosx_10_10_intel.macosx_10_10_×86_64.whl  (14.4MB)
    |                              | 14.4MB  2.8MB/s
```

matplotlib

```
pip install matplotlib
```

you could see the following response,

```
Collecting matplotlib
  Downloading
https://files.pythonhosted.org/packages/cf/a4/d5387a74204542a60ad1baa84cd2d3
matplotlib-3.1.1-cp36-cp36m-macosx_10_6_intel.
macosx_10_9_intel.macosx_10_9_×86_64.
  macosx_10_10_intel.macosx_10_10_×86_64.whl  (14.4MB)
    |                                   |  14.4MB  2.8MB/s
```

scipy

```
pip install scipy
```

you could see the following response,

```
Collecting scipy
  Downloading
https://files.pythonhosted.org/packages/cf/a4/d5387a74204542a60ad1baa84c2d3
/scipy-3.1.1-cp36-cp36m-macosx_10_6_intel.
macosx_10_9_intel.macosx_10_9_×86_64.
  macosx_10_10_intel.macosx_10_10_×86_64.whl(14.4MB)
    |                                   |  14.4MB  2.8MB/s
```

scikit-learn

It is an open source machine learning library. It is used for classification, regression and clustering algorithms. Before moving to the installation, it requires the following –

- Python version 3.5 or higher
- NumPy version 1.11.0 or higher
- SciPy version 0.17.0 or higher
- joblib 0.11 or higher.

Now, we install scikit-learn using the below command:

```
pip install - U scikit-learn
```

Seaborn

Seaborn is an amazing library that allows you to easily visualize your data. Use the below command to install

```
pip install seaborn
```

Keras Installation Using Python

As of now, we have completed basic requirements for the installtion of Kera. Now, install the Keras using same procedure as specified below:

```
pip install keras
```

Quit Virtual Environment

After finishing all your changes in your project, then simply run the below command to quit the environment:

```
deactivate
```

Anaconda Cloud

We believe that you have installed anaconda cloud on your machine. If anaconda is not installed, then visit the official link, www.anaconda.com/distribution and choose download based on your OS.

Create a New Conda Environment

Launch anaconda prompt, this will open base Anaconda environment. Let us create a new conda environment. This process is like virtualenv. Type the below command in your conda terminal –

```
conda create --name PythonCPU
```

If you want, you can create and install modules using GPU also. In this tutorial, we follow CPU instructions.

Activate Conda Environment

To activate the environment, use the below command –

```
activate PythonCPU
```

Install Spyder

Spyder is an IDE for executing python applications. Let us install this IDE in our conda environment using the below command:

```
conda install spyder
```

Install Python Libraries

We have already known the python libraries numpy, pandas, etc., needed for keras. You can install all the modules by using the below syntax:

Syntax

```
conda install -c anaconda <module-name>
```

Install Keras

Now, everything looks good so you can start keras installation using the below command:

```
conda install -c anaconda keras
```

Launch Spyder

Finally, launch spyder in your conda terminal using the below command:

```
spyder
```

To ensure everything was installed correctly, import all the modules, it will add everything and if anything went wrong, you will get module not found error message.

5.20 DIFFERENCE BETWEEN TENSORFLOW AND KERAS:

S. No	TensorFlow	Keras
1.	Tensorhigh-performanceFlow is written in C++, CUDA, Python.	Keras is written in Python.
2.	TensorFlow is used for large datasets and high performance models.	Keras is usually used for small datasets.
3.	TensorFlow is a framework that offers both high and low-level APIs.	Keras is a high-Level API.
4.	TensorFlow is used for high-performance models.	Keras is used for low-performance models.

S. No	TensorFlow	Keras
5.	In TensorFlow performing debugging leads to complexities.	In Keras framework, there is only minimal requirement for debugging the simple networks.
6.	TensorFlow has a complex architecture and not easy to use.	Keras has a simple architecture and easy to use.
7.	TensorFlow was developed by the Google Brain team.	Keras was developed by François Chollet while he was working on the part of the research effort of project ONEIROS.

5.21 BUILDING NEURAL NETWORK USING KERAS

To build a simple neural network we require a dataset, we can use any already existing data set present in Keras. For example, the dataset contains two sets which are the training set and test set, the training set is having 60,000 examples data whereas the test is having 10,000 examples data. As we can also say we are having a data of 70,000 images of 28×28 size (28 pixels of width and 28 pixels of height) in which 60,000 is in training and 10,000 is in test. These images are in grayscale in which each one is showing the q0 possible clothing type. Primarily, the creating of networks using the TensorFlow consists of following steps:

1. Step 1 - Import library
2. Step 2 - Load Dataset
3. Step 3 - Preprocess and create dataset
4. Step 4 - Create Neural network
5. Step 5 - Build the model
6. Step 6 - Train the model
7. Step 7 - Make predictions

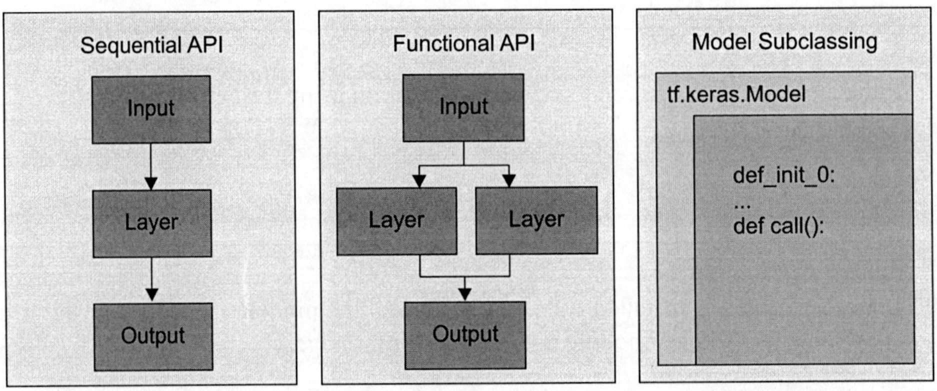

Fig. 1. The Sequential API, the Functional API, and Model Subclassing·Side by Side

5.22 KERAS-TENSORFLOW RELATIONSHIP

A Little Background

TensorFlow's evolution into a deep learning platform did not happen overnight. Initially, TensorFlow marketed itself as a symbolic math library for dataflow programming across a range of tasks. Therefore, the value proposition that TensorFlow initially offered was not a pure machine learning library. The goal was to create an efficient math library so that custom machine learning algorithms that are built on top of this efficient structure would train in a short amount of time with high accuracy.

However, building models from scratch with low-level APIs repetitively was not very ideal. So, François Chollet, a Google engineer, developed Keras, as a separate high-level deep learning library. Although Keras has been capable of running on top of different libraries such as TensorFlow, Microsoft Cognitive Toolkit, Theano, or PlaidML, TensorFlow was and still is the most common library that people use Keras with.

Current Situation

After seeing the messiness around the model-building process, the TensorFlow team announced that Keras is going to be the central high-level API used to build and train models in TensorFlow 2.0. The alternative high-level API, the Estimator API, has started to lose its already-diminishing popularity after this announcement.

5.23 KERAS VS TENSORFLOW -WHICH ONE TO CHOOSE WHEN?

Keras proves to be better than Tensorflow in:

- Providing versatile backend support
- Accelerated prototyping and market-ready samples
- Working with Beginner-friendly projects with small datasets.

There are circumstances where TensorFlow proves better than Keras:

- Rendering heavy projects with ease.
- Ease of handling projects with large data sets.
- Better suited for object detection
- Offers Broad-spectrum of functionalities

The Estimator API and The Keras API

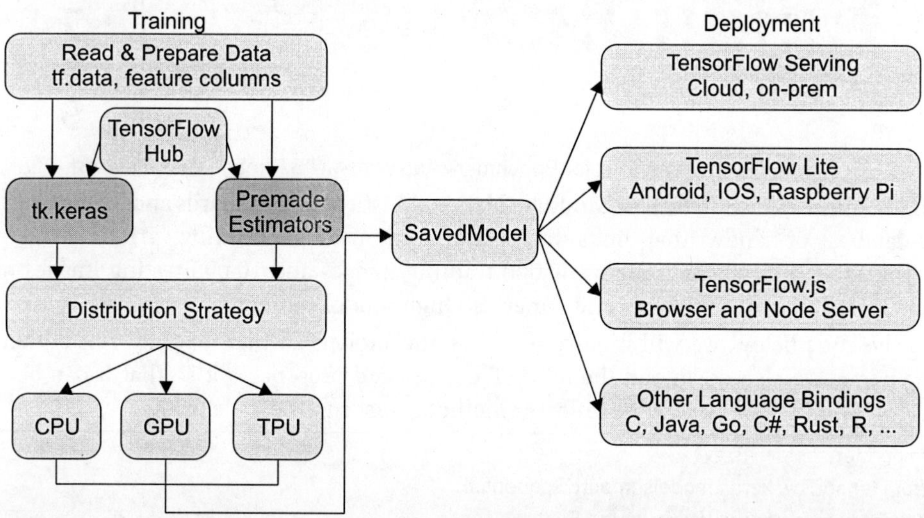

Fig. 2. The Positions of the Keras API and the Estimator API within TensorFlow Diagram

Now, let's go back to the problem: There are a lot of different methods that people build their models using TensorFlow. The main reason for this problem is TensorFlow's failure to adopt a single Model API.

In version 1.x, for the production-level projects, the go-to model-building API was the Estimator API. But, with the recent changes, the Keras API has almost caught up with the Estimator API. Initially, the Estimator API was more scalable, allowed multi-distribution, and had a convenient cross-platform functionality. Yet, most of these advantages of the Estimator API are now eliminated, and therefore, soon the Keras API will probably become the single standard API to build TensorFlow models.

So, in this post, we will only focus on the Keras API methods to build models in TensorFlow and there are three of them:

- Using the Sequential API
- Using the Functional API
- Model Subclassing

Let us dive into coding.

Initial Code to Make the Comparison

To test these three Keras methods, we need to select a deep learning problem. Image Classification with MNIST is a very straightforward task. What we are trying to achieve is training a model to recognize handwritten digits, using the famous MNIST dataset.

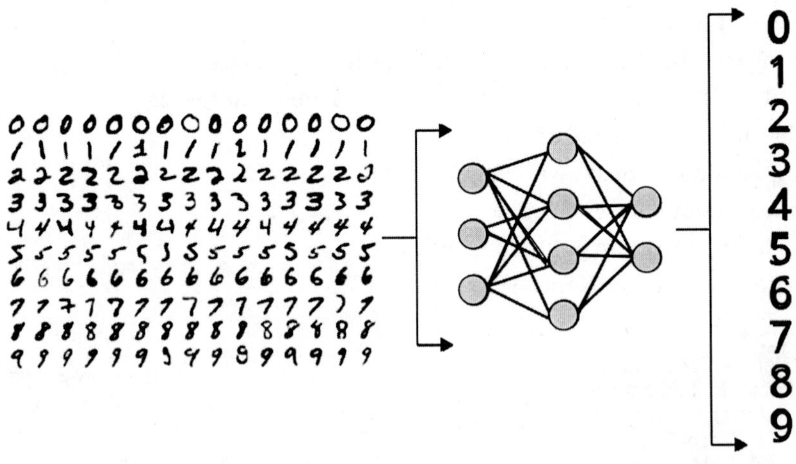

Fig. 3. Our Dummy Task for Benchmark Analysis: MNIST Image Classification

MNIST dataset, which stands for Modified National Institute of Standards and Technology database, is a large database of handwritten digits that is commonly used for training various image processing systems. The MNIST database contains 60,000 training images and 10,000 testing images taken from American Census Bureau employees and American high school students.

With the code below, we will import all layers and models so that it would not bother us in the upcoming parts. We also download the MNIST dataset and preprocess it so that it can be used in all models we will build with these three different methods. Just run the code below:

```
import tensorflow as tf
from tensorflow.keras.models import Sequential
from tensorflow.keras.layers import Flatten, Dense
from tensorflow.keras import Input
from tensorflow.keras import Model
from tensorflow.estimator import DNNClassifier
```

```
from tensorflow.keras.datasets.mnist import load_data

(x_train, y_train), (x_test, y_test) = load_data(path="mnist.npz")

# Making sure that the values are float so that we can get decimal points after division
x_train = x_train.astype('float32')
x_test = x_test.astype('float32')
# Normalizing the RGB codes by dividing it to the max RGB value.
x_train /= 255
x_test /= 255
```

Necessary Imports, MNIST Loading, Preprocessing

Now, this part is out of the way, let's focus on the three methods to build TensorFlow models.

5.24 THREE WAYS TO BUILD A KERAS MODEL

There are three methods to build a Keras model in TensorFlow:

The Sequential API: The Sequential API is the best method when you are trying to build a simple model with a single input, output, and layer branch. It is an excellent option for newcomers who would like to learn fast.

The Functional API: The Functional API is the most popular method to build Keras models. It can do everything that the Sequential API can do. Also, it allows multiple inputs, multiple outputs, branching, and layer sharing. It is a clean and easy-to-use method, and it still allows a good level of customization flexibility.

Model Subclassing: Model subclassing is for advanced level developers who need full control over their model, layer, and training process. You need to create a custom class defining the model, and you probably won't need it for daily tasks. But, if you are a researcher with experimental needs, then model subclassing might be the best option for you since it would give you all the flexibility you need.

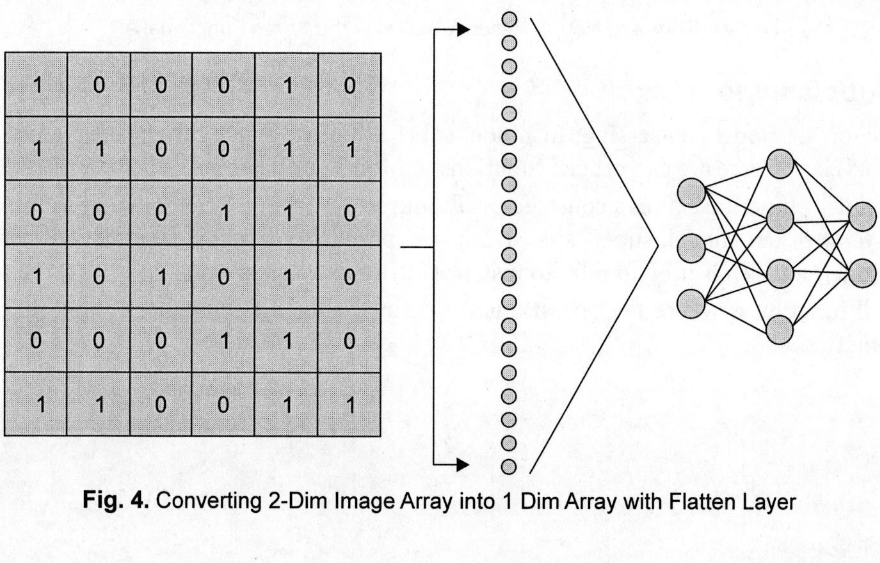

Fig. 4. Converting 2-Dim Image Array into 1 Dim Array with Flatten Layer

Let's see how these methods are implemented. We will build a basic feedforward neural network with a single Flatten layer to convert 2-dimensional image arrays to 1-dimensional arrays and two Dense layers.

The Sequential API

In the Sequential API, we need to create a Sequential object from *tf.keras.Models*module. We can simply pass all the layers as a single argument in the list format as shown below. As you can see that it is very simple.

```
model = Sequential([
Flatten(input_shape=(28, 28)),
Dense(256, 'relu'),
Dense(10, “softmax”),
])
```

A Feedforward Neural Network Built with Keras Sequential API

The Functional API

With Functional API, we need to define our input separately. Then, we need to create an output object by also creating all the layers which are tied to one another and to the output. Finally, we create a model object which would accept inputs and outputs as arguments. The code is still very clean, but we have much more flexibility in the Functional API.

```
inputs = Input(shape=(28, 28))
x = Flatten()(inputs)
x = Dense(256, “relu”)(x)
outputs = Dense(10, “softmax”)(x)

model = Model(inputs=inputs, outputs=outputs, name=“mnist_model”)
```

A Feedforward Neural Network Built with the Keras Functional API

Model Subclassing

Let us move on to model subclassing. In model subclassing, we start with creating a class extending *tf.keras.Model* class. There are two crucial functions in Model subclassing:

- __init__ function acts as a constructor. Thanks to __init__, we can initialize the attributes (e.g., layers) of our model. super is used calls the parent constructor (the constructor in tf.keras. Model) and self is used to refer to instance attributes (e.g., layers).
- call function is where the operations are defined after the layers are defined in the __init__ function.

To build the same model with Model Subclassing, we need to write much more code, as shown below:

```
class CustomModel(tf.keras.Model):
def_init_(self, **kwargs):
super(CustomModel, self).__init__(**kwargs)
self.layer_1 = Flatten()
self.layer_2 = Dense(256, "relu")
self.layer_3 = Dense(10, "softmax")
def call(self, inputs):
x = self.layer_1(inputs)
x = self.layer_2(x)
x = self.layer_3(x)
return x
model = CustomModel(name='mnist_model')
```

A Feedforward Neural Network Built with Keras Model Subclassing

The End Code

Now that you can create the same model with three different methods, you can choose any single one of them, build the model, and run the code below.

```
model.compile(optimizer='adam',
loss='sparse_categorical_crossentropy',
metrics=['accuracy'])
model.fit(x=x_train_y=y_train, epochs=10)
model.evaluate(x_text, y_test)
```

Model Configuration, Training, and Evaluation

The lines above take care of model configuration, training, and evaluation. When we compare the performances of these three methods, we see that they are close but slightly different.

1.	Method	Sequential API	Functional API	Model Subclassing
2.	Loss	0.08746038377285004	0.08131594955921173	0.0781003013253212
3.	Accuracy	97.82%	98.06%	98.20%

Table 1. Performances of Different Keras Methods:
The Sequential API, The Functional API, and Model Subclassing

Our more complex Model Subclassing method outperforms the Sequential API and the Functional API. This shows that there are slight differences in the design of these methods in the low-end as well. However, these differences are negligible.

Final Evaluations

By now, you have an idea about the similarities and differences between these three Keras methods. But let us summarize them all in a table:

1.	Feature	Sequential API	Functional API	Model Subclassing
2.	Customization	Low	Medium	High
3.	Difficulty to Build	Easy	Medium	Difficult
4.	Layer Sharing	No	Yes	Yes
5.	Multiple Branch	No	Yes	Yes
6.	Multiple Input	No	Yes	Yes
7.	Multiple Output	No	Yes	Yes
8.	Best Suited For	Beginners	Professionals	Researchers

Table 2. A Comparison of Different Methods to Build Keras Model in TensorFlow: The Sequential API, The Functional API, and Model Subclassing

In summary, if you are just starting out, stick with the Sequential API. As you dive into more complex models, try out the Functional API. If you are conducting independent research, try out Model Subclassing. If you are a professional, stick with the Functional API. It will probably satisfy your needs.

5.25 CONCLUSION

The chapter provided an overview of Tensorflow and Keras used for rapid development, training, and testing deep learning models that is suitable for a production environment. The Sequential API and the Functional API of Keras are also discussed which will enable us to build more complex models specifically for advanced deep neural networks.

Review Questions

Solved Examples

Q.1. Why is tensorflow the most preferred library in deep learning?

Ans. Tensorflow provides both C++ and Python APIs, making it easier to work on and has a faster compilation time compared to other Deep Learning libraries like Keras and Torch. Tensorflow supports both CPU and GPU computing devices.

Q.2. What do you mean by tensor in tensorflow?

Ans. This is another most frequently asked deep learning interview question. A tensor is a mathematical object represented as arrays of higher dimensions. These arrays of data with different dimensions and ranks fed as input to the neural network are called "Tensors."

Q.3. What are the programming elements in tensorflow?

Ans. Constants: Constants are parameters whose value does not change. To define a constant we use tf.constant() command. For example:

```
a = tf.constant(2.0,tf.float32)
b = tf.constant(3.0)
Print(a, b)
```

Variables - Variables allow us to add new trainable parameters to graph. To define a variable, we use the tf.Variable() command and initialize them before running the graph in a session. An example:

```
W = tf.Variable([.3].dtype=tf.float32)
b = tf.Variable([-.3].dtype=tf.float32)
```

Placeholders - these allow us to feed data to a tensorflow model from outside a model. It permits a value to be assigned later. To define a placeholder, we use the tf.placeholder() command. An example:

```
a = tf.placeholder (tf.float32)
b = a*2
with tf.Session() as sess:
result = sess.run(b,feed_dict={a:3.0})
print result
```

Sessions - a session is run to evaluate the nodes. This is called the "Tensorflow runtime." For example:

```
a = tf.constant(2.0)
b = tf.constant(4.0)
c = a+b
# Launch Session
Sess = tf.Session()
# Evaluate the tensor c
print(sess.run (c))
```

Q.4. What is the difference between SAME and VALID padding in Tensorflow?

Ans. Using the Tensorflow library, tf.nn.max_pool performs the max-pooling operation. Tf.nn.max_pool has a padding argument that takes 2 values - SAME or VALID.

With padding == "SAME" ensures that the filter is applied to all the elements of the input.

The input image gets fully covered by the filter and specified stride. The padding type is named SAME as the output size is the same as the input size (when stride=1).

With padding == "VALID" implies there is no padding in the input image. The filter window always stays inside the input image. It assumes that all the dimensions are valid so that the input image gets fully covered by a filter and the stride defined by you.

Q.5. What is data augmentation in deep learning?

Ans. Data Augmentation is the process of creating new data by enhancing the size and quality of training datasets to ensure better models can be built using them. There are different techniques to augment data such as numerical data augmentation, image augmentation, GAN-based augmentation, and text augmentation.

Unsolved Questions

1. What do you understand by transfer learning? Name a few commonly used transfer learning models.
2. What is a dropout in TensorFlow?
3. Explain the difference between Tensorflow and PyTorch?
4. What is the main feature of TensorFlow?
5. Which client languages are supported in TensorFlow?

Multiple Choice Questions

Q.1. Which tool is best suited for solving Deep Learning problems

(*a*) R (*b*) Sk-learn (*c*) Excel (*d*) TensorFlow

Q.2. How can we improve the calculation speed in TensorFlow, without losing accuracy?

(*a*) Using GPU (*b*) By doing random sampling on Tensors
(*c*) By removing few nodes from computational graphs
(*d*) By removing the hidden layers.

Q.3. Can we have multidimensional tensors

(*a*) No tensor can have maximum two dimensions
(*b*) Possible only in image data (*c*) Yes possible
(*d*) Possible only in geo tagged data

Q.4. How deep learning models are built on Keras

(*a*) by using sequential models (*b*) by using feed_dict
(*c*) by creating place holders and computational graphs
(*d*) by creating data frames

Q.5. Which tool is a deep learning wrapper on TensorFlow

(*a*) Python (*b*) Keras (*c*) PyTourch (*d*) Azure

Answer Key

1. (*d*) 2. (*a*) 3. (*c*) 4. (*a*) 5. (*b*)

Fill in the Blanks

1. A tensor is a type of _______ used in TensorFlow for representing multi-dimensional arrays or matrices.
2. A placeholder is a _______ in TensorFlow that holds the input data for a neural network.
3. A session is a way to evaluate a computation graph in _______.
4. A loss function is a function in TensorFlow that measures the difference between the _______ and the actual output of a neural network.
5. An _______ is a function in TensorFlow that updates the weights and biases of a neural network based on the calculated gradients and the chosen optimization algorithm.

Answer Key

1. Data structure 2. Variable 3. TensorFlow
4. Predicted output 5. Optimizer

❑❑❑